The Evolution of the International Monetary System, 1945–88

Brian Tew has been a professor continuously since 1946 but has always spent a considerable amount of time working with officials and bankers. From 1946 to 1949 he was Professor of Economics at Adelaide, Australia. In 1950 he became Professor of Economics at Nottingham, and in 1968 Professor of Money and Banking at Nottingham. In 1982 he became External Professor at Loughborough University of Technology, the position he currently holds. Brian Tew has published extensively in the field of monetary theory, banking, finance and international monetary arrangements and has since 1982 been a Specialist Advisor to the House of Commons Treasury and Civil Service Committee.

The Evolution of the International Monetary System, 1945–88

Brian Tew

External Professor at Loughborough
University of Technology

Hutchinson
London Melbourne Auckland Johannesburg

Hutchinson & Co. (Publishers) Ltd

An Imprint of the Century Hutchinson Publishing Group

62–65 Chandos Place, London WC2N 4NW

Hutchinson Publishing Group (Australia) Pty Ltd
16–22 Church Street, Hawthorn, Melbourne, Victoria 3122

Hutchinson Group (NZ) Ltd
32–34 View Road, PO Box 40–086, Glenfield, Auckland 10

Hutchinson Group (SA) (Pty) Ltd
PO Box 337, Bergvlei 2012, South Africa

First published 1977
Reprint 1979
Second edition 1982
Reprint 1984
Third edition 1985
Fourth edition 1988

British Library Cataloguing in Publication Data

Tew, Brian
  The evolution of the international
  monetary system: 1945 – 88.——4th ed.
  1. International monetary system — 1945—
  1985
  I. Title
  332.4′5
  ISBN 0 – 09 – 173140 – 2

Contents

6 *Contents*

**Part Four: From pegging to floating,
August 1971 onwards**

Appendices

Tables

Preface to the first edition

This book, like its predecessor *International Monetary Cooperation 1945–70*, treats the international monetary arrangements operated since the war by the central banks and treasuries of the non-communist countries, particularly with respect to the way in which their policies and actions are co-ordinated, whether by market mechanisms, by international negotiation, or through international monetary institutions such as the International Monetary Fund. In taking into my story the turbulent course of events in the 1970s, I came to revise, in the light of hindsight, my perspective on events in the preceding period. Hence it will be found that the new book bears little resemblance to its predecessor. There is less emphasis on co-operation (since, alas, there is less of it in practice), less about sterling and the International Monetary Fund, much more about the dollar and the Group of Ten. In breaking up the old mosaic and reassembling it so differently, some of the old pieces have been sacrificed. In particular, although the system whose evolution I am explaining embraces the whole of the non-communist world, my detailed analysis concentrates mainly on the rich and economically powerful industrialized countries – North America, Japan and Western Europe – which provide the membership of the Group of Ten, the Group of Five, the EEC Monetary Committee, the snake, the various summits and the different groups of central bankers who periodically meet at Basle.

Part One of the book deals with the immediate post-war period, up to the widespread move to convertibility in December 1958. The continuing features of the regime which this event inaugurated, and which have evolved only gradually up to the present time (April 1977), are then treated in Part Two. However, certain aspects of the post-1958 regime were drastically modified in the eventful years 1971–3, and these I have treated separately in Part Three (1959–71) and Part Four (1971 onwards).

I acknowledge my debt of gratitude to the Trustees of the

Houblon-Norman Fund for making possible my fact-finding expedition to Washington and New York. I am no less grateful for all the advice and help I have received from John Kirbyshire of the Bank of England, and from his friends to whom he kindly introduced me – Bruce MacLaury, Samuel Pizer, Jack Polak, Frank Schiff, Robert Solomon, George Willis and Ralph Young in Washington and Jack Bennett, Stephen Clarke and Paul Volcker in New York – all of whom went to great trouble to improve the first draft which I had inflicted on them. In addition to the recipients of my first draft, very many other knowledgeable people, on both sides of the Atlantic, have helped me with information and advice on particular topics, but they are so numerous that I have decided I had best express my deepest gratitude to them all without invidiously mentioning particular names. Though I must leave my reader in no doubt that whatever merit he may find in this book should be very largely attributed to help I have received from others, it is I alone who am responsible for the opinions I have expressed.

Finally I remember with pleasure the assistance and hospitality I enjoyed in Washington from the UK alternate executive director of the IMF and the unfailing helpfulness of his staff, in particular Deirdre Ryan.

April 1977

Preface to the second edition

Once again I have to acknowledge my debt of gratitude to the Trustees of the Houblon-Norman Fund, for making possible a second fact-finding expedition to Washington and New York; to John Kirbyshire and to his American friends who were kind enough to receive me; to the UK alternate executive director of the IMF and his staff; and above all to Deirdre Ryan.

I am also grateful to the editor of the *Midland Bank Review* for permission to draw heavily on the articles on 'benign neglect' and on the European Monetary System, published respectively in the autumn and winter 1979 issues of the *Review*.

August 1981

Preface to the fourth edition

The first nineteen chapters of this edition have been little changed from the second edition, but the rest of the book has been rewritten, to take account of developments in the very eventful period since August 1981.

January 1988

Abbreviations

BIS	Bank for International Settlements
C–20	Committee of Twenty (of the IMF)
ECA	Economic Co-operation Administration
ECE	Economic Commission for Europe
ECU	European Currency Unit
EEC	European Economic Community
EMS	European Monetary System
EPU	European Payments Union
ERM	Exchange Rate Mechanism
FDIP	Foreign Direct Investment Programme
G–5	Group of Five
G–10	Group of Ten
GAB	General Arrangements to Borrow
GATT	General Agreement on Tariffs and Trade
IBRD	International Bank for Reconstruction and Development, *alias* World Bank
IEPA	Intra-European Payments Agreement
IET	Interest Equalization Tax
IMF	International Monetary Fund
OECD	Organization for Economic Co-operation and Development
OEEC	Organization for European Economic Co-operation
OPEC	Organization of Petroleum Exporting Countries
OSA	Overseas Sterling Area
QRs	Quantitative Restrictions (i.e. import quotas)
SDRs	Special Drawing Rights (in the IMF)
VFCRP	Voluntary Foreign Credit Restraint Programme
WP3	Working Party No. 3 (of the OECD)

One billion = 1000 million

Part One

The road to convertibility, 1945–58

1 The bilateral phase, 1945–9

'Par rates' have been fixed for most currencies and at those rates current commercial and other transactions have to be settled, the settlements taking place largely through clearing and other bilateral accounts without any specific transactions in the open exchange markets. Not only capital transfers but current operations, whether commercial or financial, are, in most countries, dependent upon an 'allotment of foreign exchange' by the official Control. This being so, there are normally no fluctuations in the official rates. Any alterations (beyond such minor modifications of a fractional nature as the authorities may decide upon from time to time) are . . . made on the basis of official decisions applicable from certain definite dates . . . any foreign currencies required in excess of what the control authorities obtain from exporters, etc. must be supplied from monetary reserves or from the proceeds of foreign loans or grants.

BIS *Annual Report*, 1949[1]*

The successive post-war annual reports of the Bank for International Settlements make it clear that the concerted move to convertibility in December 1958 (Chapter 3) was the culmination of a progression from a largely bilateral international monetary system to a binary one, with parallel arrangements for 'hard' and 'soft' settlements; and thence in December 1958 from a binary system to a unified one. Very roughly we may look upon the second half of the forties, up to the devaluation of sterling in September 1949, as the bilateral phase, and the fifties up to December 1958 as the binary phase. The broad features of the former are sketched for us in the BIS *Annual Report* no. 19 (1949), in the passage at the beginning of this chapter. A survey of bilateral agreements had been given in the preceding year's BIS report, which tells us that they

were usually concluded between governments, according to a fairly uniform pattern: the central banks, as technical agents, supplied their own currency at a fixed rate of exchange against that of their partner up to a certain limit, which was often referred to as the 'swing', since it was

* Superior figures refer to the Notes and references on pages 260–75.

intended to afford room for minor fluctuations in commercial deliveries between the two countries; beyond the limit thus fixed settlements had generally to be made in gold or convertible currency. . . .

where 'convertible currency' meant in almost all cases US dollars.

Though the bilateral arrangements described by the BIS were widespread in the immediate post-war years, they were not the universal pattern for international payments, since there were two areas, the dollar area and the sterling area, within which two currencies, the US dollar and the pound, respectively circulated without restriction as multilateral means of settlement (see Table 1). A further complication was that bilateral agreements themselves fell into three more or less distinct types, according as to means of settlement prescribed beyond the agreed 'swing':

1   A few agreements, notably those to which Switzerland was party, prescribed 'super-hard' settlement beyond the swing: the Swiss demanded gold, and would not at this time accept anybody else's national currency, not even the US dollar.

Table 1   *Means of payment in early 1947*

Area	Means of payment
Super-hard settlement area Switzerland	Settlement in gold or Swiss francs
Dollar area North and Central America Several countries in northern South America	US dollars
Sterling area British Commonwealth except Canada Some Middle East countries Eire Iceland	Sterling was always accepted in settlement; all settlements within the area were made in sterling; all settlements made outside the area, other than with the dollar area, were through *bilateral accounts* negotiated by the British authorities
Other countries	Bilateral payments agreements (see BIS *Annual Report* 1949, as quoted on page 15)

2   Many agreements prescribed 'hard' settlement, in US dollars, beyond the swing: for example, in the Anglo-Belgian agreement, Belgium agreed to accumulate sterling only up to a very limited swing, beyond which settlement had to be in dollars (with gold as the only acceptable alternative).

3   Yet other agreements provided for 'soft' settlement in sterling. This was in effect true of some of the bilateral agreements negotiated by Britain, in which there was an indefinite swing in Britain's favour which the partner country would finance by accumulating sterling, so that under such agreements Britain did not normally need to settle in dollars or gold.

However, all these bilateral arrangements, operating within an apparently rigid framework of exchange controls, and providing for the 'allotment of foreign exchange' at fixed official par rates for 'approved' transactions, existed side by side with 'tolerated' or 'black' markets in which other transactions were settled at 'free' rates of exchange. In the case of sterling, for instance, there were almost as many 'free' exchange rates as there were bilateral agreements: in the City it was customary to refer to sterling in its 'fifty-seven varieties'. Nor was it only sterling that was exchanged at free as well as at official rates. As the BIS put it in 1949:

The fact that some dealings not within the official range of transactions actually take place accounts for the existence of other quotations, dependent upon the supply and demand in the particular market in which the dealings are carried out. There is a great variety of such outside markets, some being entirely legal, others rather in the nature of black markets even though they may be officially more or less 'tolerated'. At the moment there is not one currency in the world which has only a single quotation. Even for the relations between the dollar and the Swiss franc – two of the strongest currencies nowadays – quotations different from the official 'par' apply to certain transfers, especially of a financial character. A great diversity of rates has come into being: particular rates for notes – and sometimes different rates for different denominations; official rates which are not the same for imports as for exports, and so on. A whole new vocabulary has been formed, rates being variously described as official, free, black-market, parallel, or grey, or classified as security rates, compensation rates, etc. There are rigidly fixed rates – in or out of touch with reality – fluctuating rates, orderly or disorderly cross rates, multiple rates, tourist rates, etc.[2]

These tolerated and black exchange markets of course helped to mitigate the bilateral nature of the early post-war monetary arrangements. So, taking into account also the existence of an extensive dollar area of 'hard' multilateral settlement, the label 'bilateral' may perhaps give a somewhat misleading impression: bilateralism was never complete or unqualified. Moreover, bilateralism also came to be slightly tempered, even before September 1949, by various official initiatives to facilitate greater multilateralism. The intention of some of these early initiatives was indeed far-reaching, but their outcome was by and large disappointing, amounting in one case – the premature dash to sterling convertibility in July 1947 – to complete failure.

Sterling arrangements

This step, taken as early as July 1947 to honour a commitment entered into under the Anglo-American Loan Agreement of 1945, was an attempt by Britain to introduce a regime of non-resident convertibility closely akin to the one eventually adopted in December 1958. Alas, it merely provoked an unprecedented run on the pound, with the result that convertibility had to be abandoned in the following month. Daunted by this setback, Britain none the less retained for some of her trading partners a somewhat circumscribed version of the so-called *transferable accounts* which had been negotiated earlier in 1947 (in replacement of the previous *bilateral accounts*) as a device for operating convertibility.

Let us consider the transferable account arrangements which then would have been made with an imaginary country, Ruritania. First of all, if Ruritania was a country which had, during the war, accumulated a large balance of sterling, there would probably be an arrangement to block part of this balance, or to hypothecate it for some specified purpose. Then there would be an undertaking by Ruritania to accept sterling from all countries in settlement of current (though not capital) transactions. In return Britain would offer Ruritania important concessions. Ruritania would be permitted to draw freely on the sterling 'at the disposal' of her monetary authorities (that is, on the sterling accruing to the new Ruritania transferable accounts from future current transactions or from existing balances which had not been blocked) to make *current* payments to virtually all countries, including payments in convertible sterling to the dollar area. It was this last concession which had to be withdrawn in August 1947.

The dozen or so countries which retained their transferable account status after the suspension of convertibility, and those which acquired it later on, were permitted to transfer their sterling, not only to sterling area countries (which bilateral account countries had always been free to do), but also for making current payments to other transferable account countries, and even, at the administrative discretion of the British authorities, to bilateral account countries.

The transferable account countries in the period after August 1947 were, broadly speaking, those whose monetary authorities could be trusted to keep to the rules of the transferable account game, and whose sterling receipts and payments could be expected to stay reasonably in balance. The British monetary authorities were not inclined to give transferable account status to countries which would have tended to be persistently short of sterling (for example, Greece),[3] since the difficulty which such countries already had in settling their accounts with the sterling area would have been aggravated if they had been free to settle in sterling outside this area. Nor, on the other hand, did the British authorities want to give transferable account status to countries which would have tended to accumulate sterling persistently. This was clearly the case where a country required settlement in dollars or gold beyond a limited swing (as in the case of Belgium, Portugal, Switzerland or Argentina, for example), but even in the absence of such a provision a transferable account arrangement would have caused difficulties. Take, for example, Argentina. Argentina tended in the period after August 1947 to accumulate sterling almost to the point of satiety, so that it had no desire to incur an obligation to accept sterling from countries outside the sterling area, and Britain for its part was also anxious to restrict transfers of sterling to Argentina, for the more Argentina was satiated with sterling the less ready it would be to continue its supplies of meat and other products to the British market. (Of course transfers of sterling *from* Argentina did not give rise to comparable difficulties and were in fact frequently permitted on an administrative basis.)

European arrangements

The attempts of the British authorities to modify their sterling arrangements in the direction of greater multilateralism occurred at about the same time that the European recipients of Marshall Aid were attempting to mitigate in some degree the strictly bilateral nature of their post-war monetary arrangements. The need for this was apparent. By October 1947 it was reported by the Committee on Payments Agreements,[4] which was set up by the recipients of Marshall Aid, that

the margins of credit possible under the payments agreements concluded by some countries are almost exhausted, and this is a quasi-permanent situation. For the expansion of trade to the extent which is possible, increasingly numerous gold payments would be necessary. This situation risks hampering not only the development of trade, but actually its maintenance at the present level. . . . In these circumstances, the Committee considers that greater flexibility in the present payments system is more than ever necessary.

This need for greater flexibility was the motive behind the Agreement on Multilateral Monetary Compensation of November 1947, which came into being largely as the result of the work of the Committee of European Economic Co-operation, which was set up to implement the Marshall Plan and which also brought the OEEC into being in April 1948.[5] Fourteen of the OEEC members were parties to the agreement, but only six (Belgium, Luxembourg, France, Italy, Netherlands and the Bizone of Germany) were 'permanent' members; the other eight were 'occasional' members, with the right to contract out of any operation arising under the agreement.[6] The operations provided for in the agreement were 'first-category compensations' and 'second-category compensations'. In the words of the official agent of the agreement, the Bank for International Settlements,

First-category compensations involve only a reduction of existing balances ('balances' in this context covering both debit and credit accounts). Such operations imply a 'closed circuit' of countries each of which is debtor to its immediately preceding partner, while it is itself a creditor of its succeeding partner, the last country in the chain being the creditor of the first country, thus closing the circuit. These operations are partially automatic (in so far as the 'permanent' countries are concerned) and partially optional (in so far as they apply to 'occasional' members). . . . The simple offsetting . . . of the first category can lead only to reductions of outstanding debts (and credits) and presents no particular difficulties – except that, in some cases, countries may for one reason or another desire to maintain certain balances in one or more particular markets and thus are unwilling to reduce them. . . .

A 'second-category operation' may be defined as a payment made by one country to another by utilising the currency of a third country. A simple example would be the payment of a Norwegian debt to the Netherlands in sterling. It is evident that such a transaction involves a limited transferability of sterling.[7]

Unfortunately, the first-category operations, which were easier to effect, were possible in only a comparatively small number of cases:

The working accounts of the European payments agreements show debts (and credits) entering into the compensations to the equivalent of over 700 million dollars. About 400 million of this total is net debt (or credit) which cannot be offset. Of the 300 million which can be subject to compensation in theory, experience has shown that, at the present time, the maximum possibilities of the first category alone amount to about 30–50 million. From this it follows that the possibilities for the reduction of debts (and credits) by operations of the second category are some ten times as great as those of the first category.

As a result only a very limited amount of first-category compensation was possible. Second-category compensation was in practice also very restricted, for it was optional even in the case of 'permanent' members and almost all the proposals were objected to by the country whose currency was to be transferred. In the event only $5 million of first-category compensations and $46 million of second-category compensations had been effected when the scheme was superseded in October 1948 by the first Intra-European Payments Agreement (IEPA).[8]

The first IEPA, which operated for the nine months October 1948 to June 1949, differed from the preceding arrangement in that it involved all the OEEC countries and also incorporated provisions for *indirect aid*. The provisions for first- and second-category compensations were retained, the former being compulsory,[9] the latter remaining optional, but during the nine months that the scheme was in operation very few compensations were in fact effected.

Indirect aid was so called because the ECA[10] made a portion of the Marshall Aid extended to certain OEEC countries conditional on their undertaking to extend similar aid to other OEEC countries. The motive of the ECA in recommending, and indeed in insisting on, the indirect aid provision of the IEPA was to increase the effectiveness of aid going to needy European countries, for each $1 of aid granted was supposed to benefit the immediate recipient as well as the indirect recipient. The countries through whom indirect aid was granted were those which were expected to run surpluses with other OEEC countries during the period of the scheme. The aid they received took the form of a grant of dollars from the United

States; the aid they granted took the form of bilateral drawing rights in favour of each of the countries with whom a bilateral surplus was expected.[11]

For the purposes of indirect aid, and indeed for all the European payments arrangements described in this chapter and the next, bilateral surpluses were as calculated by the BIS from the reported monthly changes in the balances held by each central bank at each other central bank, prior to any month-end settlement in dollars or gold. Thus Belgium's bilateral surplus with Britain (exactly equal to Britain's bilateral deficit with Belgium) was calculated as the month's change in the Belgian National Bank's sterling balance at the Bank of England minus any change in the latter's holding of Belgian francs.

The intended objective of indirect aid was that each deficit country should have received sufficient means of settlement for covering each of its nine-monthly bilateral deficits with the other OEEC countries. In practice this objective was far from being fully achieved, for the forecasts of bilateral relationships were necessarily rather wild guesses and the rigid bilateralism of the drawing rights prevented them from being utilized where they were actually needed, as distinct from where they were expected to be needed. Even where the estimates did prove reasonably accurate, this may merely have meant that countries simply adjusted their import regulations from time to time so as to make their bilateral deficits run according to plan. Countries certainly had an incentive to act in this way, for the IEPA offered them no inducement to eliminate their deficits.

The total of the drawing rights provided for was initially the equivalent of US $810 million (later revised to $805 million), but in the event only $677 million were used before the termination of the scheme, and of this amount $67 million were used for purposes other than meeting deficits.

The second Intra-European Payments Agreement, for the year July 1949 to June 1950, followed its predecessor closely except that the total of drawing rights was somewhat increased and rather over one-quarter of them was multilateral, that is, capable of being used to settle bilateral deficits with *any* of the participating countries. (In most of the drawing rights granted, 25 per cent, or thereabouts, was multilateral, but the rights granted by Belgium were more than half multilateral.) The multilateral portions of the drawing rights were, however, to be used only after the BIS had performed all possible first-category compensations and had then made the fullest use of bilateral drawing rights.

Conditions for multilateral settlement

Arrangements for international settlements range from the bilateral, like those we have just described as obtaining (with mitigations) immediately after the second world war, to the multilateral, as obtained (with minor qualifications) in the 1960s. As we shall see in Chapter 8, the regime of the sixties was introduced by the widespread introduction of convertibility in December 1958, and the widespread transition from IMF Article XIV status to Article VIII status in February 1961. These two events amounted to the virtual abolition of exchange controls, except to a limited extent on certain capital transactions, and in the absence of such controls the exchange markets automatically provide the facilities needed for multilateral settlement, since the owner of any one currency can obtain any other simply by bidding for it in the market. However, if countries opt for a regime of pegged exchange rates, as under the Bretton Woods Charter of 1944, the absence of exchange controls implies that the monetary authorities of deficit countries must have at their disposal adequate official reserves for supporting their national currencies in the exchange markets at the official par exchange rate. If they do not have sufficient reserves for this purpose – as was undoubtedly the case for most countries outside the dollar area at the par exchange rates obtaining up to September 1949 – then exchange controls are indispensable for pegging at the par rates.

Once exchange controls are introduced, multilateral settlement no longer occurs automatically. What obtains instead will, of course, depend on the nature of the controls imposed. Let us for the sake of argument begin with an extreme case: suppose that the monetary authorities of each pair of countries have a bilateral payments agreement of the kind described in 1948 by the BIS (above, pages 15–16). Under such an exchange control regime, a step towards multilateralism can be achieved if the countries concerned can operate a procedure of circular offsetting of the kind labelled by the BIS 'first-category compensations' (see page 20). Such a procedure is possible and advantageous when the bilateral clearing facilities have been used in a closed circuit – for example, if country A has been running a bilateral deficit with B, B with C, and

C with A – and when in addition the facilities are in each case subject to a risk of eventual exhaustion. In such a case the countries in the circuit will each find it advantageous if they can arrange that each one of them should write down its holding of the 'preceding' country's currency in return for a similar cancellation of its own currency in the hands of the following country in the circuit, the amount of each of the cancellations being equivalent in value to the smallest of the holdings in the circuit.

In the special case of complete international equilibrium (where no country is in *overall* surplus or deficit, each country's bilateral deficits being precisely balanced in total by its bilateral surpluses) it is possible to arrange all countries' bilateral deficits into a series of closed circuits, and to cancel the lot by circular offsetting.[12] Such a state of affairs corresponds perfectly to the ideal of international settlement on a fully multilateral basis, for if all deficits can be offset as they arise, or with only a short delay, no country has any reason to care with whom it runs deficits and with whom it runs surpluses. If, however, our perfect equilibrium gives way to disequilibrium, with some countries developing overall deficits and others overall surpluses, the proportion of deficits which can be arranged in closed circuits and offset undergoes a progressive decline. Disequilibria of the magnitude which occurred in practice in the immediate post-war years reduces the possible amount of circular offsetting to almost negligible proportions.[13]

Another device for facilitating settlements on a multilateral basis is that of transferable currencies. If, for instance, country A has acquired a stock of country X's currency, the monetary authorities of the latter country may refrain from placing any obstacle in the way of A using this currency to make payments to country B. In such a case X's currency qualifies as a 'transferable currency'. It is easy to see that circular transfers of X's currency could serve the same purpose as circular offsetting. For (to adapt our previous example) suppose that X is Britain and that A's deficit with B, B's with C, and C's with A are each the equivalent of £10 million sterling. Then instead of each country using its bilateral settlement facilities against the next country in the circuit, the *status quo* then being restored by circular offsetting, it would be equally satisfactory if the circuit of deficits had been cleared by the payment of £10 million sterling each from A to B, B to C, and C to A. It therefore follows that, provided that each country is in overall equilibrium, circular transfers of one or more unconditionally transferable currencies can, like circular offsetting, provide a completely satisfactory means of achieving international settlement on a fully multilateral basis within a group of countries, but that the scope for such transfers is progressively curtailed to the extent that this condition is unfulfilled.

Now let us consider settlement within a group of countries *not* in equilibrium, that is, where some countries have overall deficits and others overall surpluses. Let us suppose that the various countries have, in respect of a given period, already (by circular offsetting, alias first-category compensations) eliminated all closed circuits of bilateral deficits. What deficits would then remain and how could they be settled? This question can best be tackled as follows. It can be proved that, after all circular bilateral deficits have been eliminated, one country will necessarily emerge as having bilateral surpluses with some or all of the other countries and deficits with none.[14] Let us call this the 'strongest' country.[15] There will also necessarily be a second strongest country with a bilateral deficit with the strongest country but with bilateral surpluses with all the other countries. Similarly a third strongest country will have bilateral deficits with the first and second strongest countries but surpluses with all the remaining countries. These remaining countries can in their turn be arranged in a definite order of 'strength', the weakest country having bilateral deficits with everybody else.

A numerical illustration will help to clarify this point. Suppose that there are only eight countries in the world: Canada, the USA, the UK, Britannica, Europa, Imperia, Latinnia and Miscellannia, and that we have estimated the bilateral balances obtaining between each of the twenty-eight pairs of countries in some particular year. We could then present our estimates in the form of a matrix with each of the twenty-eight bilateral estimates classified according to both the surplus partner and the deficit partner. If we did no more than this our entries would be scattered over the matrix without forming a simple pattern, but if in addition we eliminate all closed circuits of deficits and then arrange our countries in the order of their strength, we shall find, as in Table 2A, that all the entries fall on one side of one of the diagonals, in the form of a compact 'wedge'.[16] The significance of this pattern of entries is that the settlements required to meet all the bilateral deficits represent a uni-directional flow from the weaker to the stronger countries. Thus the weakest country, Europa, has to settle bilateral deficits with the seven countries which are stronger than she is, Britannica with her six superiors in strength, the UK with her five superiors in strength, and so on, until we reach the strongest country, the USA, with no deficits at all.

Table 2 *An illustration of the pattern of bilateral deficits, with all closed circuits of deficits eliminated*

(The figures are expressed to the nearest million of US dollars, and relate to some particular year)

A *The individual bilateral deficits and surpluses*

Countries with their bilateral deficits	Countries with their bilateral surpluses							
	USA	Latin-nia	Canada	Miscel-lannia	Im-peria	UK	Brit-annica	Europa
USA								
Latinnia	1000							
Canada	400	10						
Miscellannia	800	100	80					
Imperia	100	300	10	80				
UK	200	500	500	10	60			
Britannica	400	0	100	200	0	960		
Europa	3300	700	200	30	300	200	500	

B *Summary*

Country	Total bilateral deficits	Total bilateral surpluses	Overall deficits	Overall surpluses
USA	0	6200		6200
Latinnia	1000	1610		610
Canada	410	890		480
Miscellannia	980	320	660	
Imperia	490	360	130	
UK	1270	1160	110	
Britannica	1660	500	1160	
Europa	5230	0	5230	
	11,040	11,040	7290	7290

The summary table tells us that, of eight countries, three have overall surpluses, totalling $7290 million of net credit, while the other five have overall deficits, which total the same amount of net debt.[17] The total of the twenty-eight individual *bilateral* deficits (or surpluses), two of which are so small as to be shown as nil, is of course greater than the total of the *overall* deficits (or surpluses) – the figure being $11,040 million.

The lesson to be learned from Table 2 is that, although bilateral deficits equivalent to $11,040 million have to be settled, means of settlement equivalent to only $7290 million could suffice, provided (1) that a currency could be used which was freely transferable to, and acceptable to, all countries and could therefore flow freely from the weaker to the stronger countries, and (2) that this currency was available to the five deficit countries in amounts sufficient to cover their respective overall deficits. For let us suppose such an international currency to exist. Then Europa, as the weakest country, would have to provide enough of the international currency to settle all her bilateral deficits – a total of $5230 million. Britannica, however, whose bilateral deficits total $1660 million, would have to provide only $1160 million since she would in addition pass on the $500 million received from Europa. Likewise, the UK, Imperia and Miscellannia would need to provide the international currency only to the extent of their respective overall deficits, while Canada and Latinnia (and of course the strongest country, the USA) would not need to provide any of the international currency at all.

The 'saving' of $3750 million of the means of settlement ($11,040 million minus $7290 million) is the measure of the extent to which, in our example, bilateral deficits could be cleared by second-category compensations, as the BIS called them; that is, by 'passing on' currencies, instead of 'passing round' currencies, as in the case of circular transfers. It follows that if overall deficits could be settled in currencies which could be both 'passed on' and 'passed round', so that both first- and second-category compensations could take place without restriction, this would permit international settlement to proceed on a fully multilateral basis, for no country would mind with whom it ran deficits and with whom surpluses, but would be concerned solely with its overall position.

Unfortunately, however, a pattern of bilateral deficits which, as in Table 2, calls for a passing on of means of settlement inevitably leads to difficulties which do not arise where deficits can be arranged in closed circuits. That such is the case can best be seen by considering first the strongest country, the USA in our example. Since the USA does not have to make any settlements, it has no incentive to accept currencies with the idea of passing them on, except possibly in a later period when the pattern of bilateral deficits may have changed. The US authorities are therefore likely to be somewhat cautious in deciding what currencies they will accept in settlement of the US surpluses. Let us suppose that they accept without limit only their own currency (US dollars) and gold, other currencies being accepted only up to the limits of prearranged 'swings'.[18] If the USA be assumed then to continue for a long period as the strongest country, she will steadily drain the five deficit countries of gold and US dollars, until these became scarce or 'hard'. The evil day may be postponed by dollar gifts and credits, but not indefinitely. Thus there will develop an incentive, beginning probably with Europa but spreading to the other relatively weak countries, to try to settle in a softer medium, and to discriminate in favour of countries which will accept it. For example, Europa may try to persuade Britannica to accept settlements in a softer currency (which the USA would not accept) by using the argument: 'We cannot pay you in dollars, because we are running short of them, so if you do not accept a softer currency, we shall perforce have to buy less of your goods.' If Europa's policy succeeds against Britannica and other countries, and if these in turn attempt to follow her example, there will develop a 'soft-currency area' wherein settlements are made in currencies not acceptable to the USA. This development will undermine the multilateral basis of settlement, since countries will have an incentive to attempt to run bilateral surpluses with the hard currency countries rather than with the soft currency countries, and to run bilateral deficits with the soft currency countries rather than with the hard currency countries.

If, as we have imagined, the US authorities will accept certain other countries' currencies up to a limited swing, the hardening of the US dollar may induce the countries enjoying these facilities to restrict the transferability of their currencies. The UK might for instance try to stop other countries from settling with the USA in sterling, since such settlements would use up the limited facility which would otherwise be available to settle in sterling the UK's own bilateral deficit with the USA. In such circumstances countries holding sterling would have an incentive to prefer to run deficits with the UK and with countries to which sterling could be freely transferred, rather than with the USA. Thus here again the multilateral basis of international settlement would be undermined.

In brief, then, the free flow of means of settlement from the weaker to the stronger countries in Table 2 is liable to be inter-rupted in two ways: first, in some parts of the world, certain curren-cies may become too hard for general use in making settlements; and second, the soft currencies used instead may, since they enjoy at best only limited acceptability in the hard currency area, suffer a restriction of their transferability, and in either case the multilateral basis of international settlement will be undermined. Moreover, the process which has just been described can be repeated in respect of some other currency, say the Canadian dollar, which would be unlikely to become harder than the US dollar (since no currency could be more acceptable to Canada than one which, like the US dollar, could be used for settling its deficits with both the USA and Latinnia)[19] but might, however, come to occupy a position some-where between the US dollar and the soft currencies. There might indeed develop almost as many degrees of hardness as there are currencies, which would eventually lead to a reversion to complete bilateralism.

It must not be concluded from this section that prolonged inter-national disequilibria make settlement on a multilateral basis quite impossible, but only that they lead to difficulties whose seriousness depends on the circumstances. It would be possible, for instance, for the currency of a country in a relatively weak position in the league table to remain in widespread use if it was widely believed that the country would improve its position in due course, and this tendency would be strengthened if its currency had long enjoyed the status of a world-wide international currency, as was the case in the 1940s with sterling.

International settlement in practice

The preceding analysis of settlement under conditions of disequilib-rium is only a very oversimplified model of the real world, and must be used with caution for interpreting what was actually happening during the period 1945–9. Our caution must be increased by the fact that statistics are not available to compile a table – let us call it Table X – which would set out for all countries the bilateral balances corresponding to those which we have supposed for an eight-country world in Table 2. All we can do is to try to establish very roughly the order in which the various countries, or groups of countries, might be expected to appear in our imaginary Table X.

Our first task is to settle whether any country was stronger than the United States – the country with the largest overall surplus. Of the countries with overall surpluses, only one – Switzerland – seems to be able to claim a bilateral surplus with the United States: this evidence therefore points to Switzerland as being the strongest country, followed by the United States. Next to the United States, in an order which we cannot satisfactorily guess, would be a group – the 'Intermediate Group', let us call it – comprising the remaining surplus countries and those deficit countries whose appreciable bilateral deficits were solely with the surplus countries.[20] This group would include Canada and most of the Latin American countries. Belgium would also be included, but otherwise it is doubtful whether any other Western European country would fall within this group, taking the period 1945–9 as a whole. After the Intermediate Group of countries in Table X would be countries which ran appreciable bilateral deficits not only with the surplus countries but also with other deficit countries. This 'Weak Group' of countries would be very extensive, and would range from those whose bilateral deficits were solely with Switzerland, the USA and our Intermediate Group of countries to the (unidentifiable) weakest country. The most important members of the Weak Group would be the sterling area and almost all the European countries except Switzerland and Belgium.

The order in which we have placed countries in our imaginary Table X throws a considerable light on the hierarchy of currencies in our period. The strongest country, Switzerland, was prepared to accumulate gold and strictly limited amounts of other countries' currencies, but otherwise it required settlement in its own currency, Swiss francs, of which, however, there were only very limited holdings outside Switzerland after the war. It soon appeared that the total means available to the rest of the world for settling with Switzerland were not sufficient to go round: the Swiss franc became a hard currency – so hard that it was reserved almost exclusively for making bilateral settlements with Switzerland.

In the second strongest country in Table X, the United States, the authorities were prepared to accumulate gold without limit, but otherwise Americans required payment in dollars. However, the rest of the world's official holdings of gold and US dollars at the end of the war were about $20 billion, and in the course of the period 1945–9 there were further immense supplies made available mainly as the result of the output of new gold and official financing by the United States Government. The latter occurred under various guises, including the loan granted to the United Kingdom in 1946, contributions to UNRRA and other relief organizations, credits extended by the Export–Import Bank, and Marshall Aid. Thanks to these supplies of gold and dollars, the United States's vast overall surplus in the 1940s was accommodated with a reduction of only about a third in the rest of the world's official reserves of these assets.

Yet this draining of the rest of the world's means of settlement with the United States, modest though it was in relation to the United States's overall surplus, caused widespread anxiety and led to the adoption of drastic policies to prevent a more rapid depletion of reserves. Countries tried not to waste their gold and dollars in making payments whenever softer currencies, such as sterling, could be substituted. In consequence, dollars went out of use as a regular means of multilateral settlement except in the dollar area, comprising the United States itself and certain of our Intermediate Group of countries. In the remaining Intermediate countries, gold and dollars had to be used for settling with the dollar area, but otherwise were in only occasional use for making settlements.

It will be remembered that countries in our Intermediate Group were either surplus countries with bilateral deficits with the United States and Switzerland or deficit countries whose only appreciable bilateral deficits were with the surplus countries – in practice mainly with the United States. All of the countries in this group had therefore a strong motive for preferring to receive settlements almost exclusively in US dollars. They differed, however, very greatly in their ability to exact dollar settlements from their customers. The ones that were members of the dollar area could all exact dollar settlements by virtue of being exporters predominantly of commodities which were either important United States imports (e.g. wood pulp, sugar, bananas) or which were basic necessities which their customers would otherwise have had to buy from the United States (e.g. oil). The other Intermediate Group countries were exporters either of less essential foodstuffs and raw materials in which the United States was self-sufficient (e.g. meat, cotton) or of manufactured goods. There was little possibility, for example, of Argentina, Brazil or Belgium exacting payment in dollars for all their exports without suffering a very serious contraction in their trade. Most of the Intermediate Group countries outside the dollar area had to accept and accumulate soft currencies from at least some of their customers for at least some of their exports but nevertheless constantly tried to exact gold or dollars wherever possible.

Within our Weak Group of countries, gold and dollars were scarcely used at all except for settling with Switzerland, the dollar area and, much less frequently, with the Intermediate countries outside the dollar area (for example Belgium). In the Weak Group, however, as within the dollar area, there was a widely accepted medium for multilateral settlement, which in this case was sterling. Within this group were the sterling area itself, most of the transferable account countries and many of the bilateral account countries which enjoyed the most liberal facilities for administrative transferability. This is not to say that sterling was the *only* means of settlement in use among the Weak Group of countries: there were, for example, non-sterling payments under bilateral agreements and there were the indirect aid provisions of the two Intra-European Payments Agreements. Nevertheless it is clear that a substantial proportion of settlements was made in sterling.

2 The binary phase, 1950–8

So far as the foreign exchange markets are concerned, the measures taken in December 1958 have brought unification and at the same time greater freedom of movement for rates. Previously each European currency was traded against the US and Canadian dollars in a separate market, while eleven different European currencies were traded against one another on what was one market, under the arbitrage arrangements introduced in May 1953. At the end of December 1958 these two kinds of market were amalgamated and all the principal European currencies are now freely traded against one another and against the US and Canadian dollars in one market.

BIS *Annual Report*, 1959[1]

The evolution of sterling arrangements and of European monetary arrangements proceeded much more quickly in the 1950s than in the 1940s, and in consequence the international monetary system could in due course more correctly be described as binary than as bilateral. The period of accelerated evolution was ushered in by a spate of adjustments to official par exchange rates, touched off by the devaluation of sterling in September 1949. Between then and March 1950 the dollar parity of almost all other currencies had been devalued, though by very unequal percentages, as is apparent from Table 3 (page 34).

The immediate consequences, if any, of these devaluations cannot be disentangled from the consequences of the Korean War and rearmament. The result of the 1950 rearmament and stockpiling programmes in the United States was to increase the volume of its imports and reduce the availability of goods for export. Moreover (and more importantly), the increased demand for primary commodities, not only in the United States but also in all the rearming countries, very greatly bid up their prices, and this affected the value of US imports considerably more than that of US exports.[2]

Thanks to these factors the dollar shortage seemed, in late 1950

Table 3   *Devaluations, 15 September 1949 to March 1950*

	Devaluation in relation to the US dollar (per cent)
The sterling area except Pakistan	30
European countries	
Greece	33
Denmark	
Finland	
Netherlands	30
Norway	
Sweden	
France	22
Germany	20
Belgium	13
Portugal	13
Italy	8
Switzerland	0
Other countries	
Egypt	30
Canada	9
Japan	0

Source: BIS *Annual Report* no. 20 (1950), p. 154.

and the early part of 1951, to be in the course of disappearing altogether[3] – which raised the issue of whether the devaluations may not have been excessive. However, none of the devaluing countries retreated from the decisions taken in September 1949 with the exception of Canada, where in October 1950 the official par value which had been in force for twelve months was cancelled and the value of the currency left to 'be determined by conditions of supply and demand'.[4]

In the event the widespread reluctance to reverse the devaluations of September 1949 turned out to be justified, for with the subsiding of the Korean crisis the dollar gap began to reopen.

In 1951 the factors tending to reduce the deficit of the rest of the world with the United States in 1950 were reversed. A fall in United States consumption in relation to disposable income after the first quarter of the year was accompanied by an involuntary accumulation of inventories as a result of which [US] private imports for consumption declined. At the same time there was a fall in new governmental commitments for strategic stockpiling owing to the abnormally high prices for some of the stockpiled commodities in the previous period. [US] exports, however, rose sharply from the second half of 1950 to the first half of 1951, and still further in the second half of 1951, reflecting the rise in dollar earnings by the rest of the world during earlier periods, and notwithstanding the marked fall in the supply of dollars by the United States between the first and second halves of 1951. The gap resulting from these opposite movements in exports and imports was magnified by speculative capital movements. . . . Owing to the fact that foreign economic aid from the United States declined much more slowly after 1949 than the surplus on goods, services and private capital accounts, the rest of the world as a whole was not required to draw upon its gold and dollar reserves for the financing of dollar deficits until the second half of 1951.[5]

It was also in the second half of 1951 that the fall in the prices of primary commodities showed itself in the balance of payments of the sterling area with the rest of the world. Drastic action had to be taken to curb these developments, and the Commonwealth Prime Ministers' Conference in January 1952 ushered in a period of tightening restrictions on imports into most sterling area countries from sources outside the sterling area.

1952 and 1953 were both years of movement towards equilibrium:

There was a partial recovery in United States imports of goods and services. In addition, the net outflow of United States private capital for direct investment abroad . . . rose sharply in the first half of 1952. . . . The partial recovery of imports, together with the increased outflow of private capital, more than offset the continuing decline in economic aid to foreign countries, so that the total supply of dollars by the United States in the first half of 1952 considerably exceeded the level to which it had fallen in the previous half-year and nearly regained the high level of the first half of 1951. [US] exports, on the other hand, began to decline, reflecting a fall in the rate of inventory accumulation in other countries and the reimposition of more severe restrictions on purchases of dollar goods by countries which had encountered difficulties in their dollar balances during 1951.[6]

The effect of these restrictions was undoubtedly supplemented by the effect of the devaluations of September 1949, which were by this time beginning to have an appreciable (if not readily calculable) influence on the pattern of world trade. Moreover there was also a considerable easing of the pressure of demand in the rest of the world. 1952 will be remembered as the year of the 'textiles slump' (which in fact spread to other industries producing durable consumption goods) in Britain and many other Western European countries,[7] while in the overseas sterling area the collapse in the preceding year of the boom in primary commodities was beginning to exert a strong deflationary effect. Several countries, notably Denmark and the Netherlands, introduced generally restrictive fiscal and credit measures, and even pushed them to excess.[8] Thus while in the United States 1952 was a year of both low and declining unemployment, this was not the case in important parts of the rest of the world.

United States prosperity continued at a high level throughout 1953, and though there was a modest revival of demand in the rest of the world the dollar gap did not reopen. It did, however, reopen somewhat in 1954, as the result of an American recession, but for a variety of reasons the impact on the rest of the world was unusually slight,[9] and in any case full prosperity returned to the United States in the course of 1955.

The next US recession, that of 1958, also had little impact on the rest of the world; indeed that year saw the recognition of what came to be called the *negative* dollar gap – a development which from that year onwards assured a steady outflow of gold and dollars from the United States to the rest of the world (see page 103) and which both facilitated and justified the concerted move to convertibility in December 1958.

Sterling arrangements

Though sterling was under severe pressure early in 1952, the position (as we have seen) afterwards became easier in 1953, and in March 1954 the first post-devaluation move was made to extend the area within which sterling served to provide a means of multilateral settlement. In that month bilateral account status was abolished and transferable account status extended to virtually all countries outside the sterling and dollar areas. Combined with this extension of the transferable account area there was a liberalization of the transferable account system as such. First, Britain no longer insisted on the *quid pro quo* which had previously been exacted from any country wishing to qualify for transferable account status, namely that it should undertake to accept in sterling any current payments made to it by another transferable account country or from the sterling area. Second, the whole distinction between current and capital transactions was swept away, transferability being made automatic in both cases. (The previous arrangements governing the sterling area, the dollar area and blocked sterling were not affected by these changes.)

The motive of the British authorities in abolishing bilateral account status and liberalizing the transferable account system seems to have been that the need for restrictions was diminishing – in that the bilateral account countries which had originally been either chronically short of sterling, or chronically satiated with it, had gradually achieved a more balanced position.[10] The relevant restrictions had indeed been increasingly inoperative for some considerable time and by March 1954 were being honoured more in the breach than in the observance.[11]

Another change made about the same time by the British authorities was the reopening of the London foreign exchange market. Before May 1953 the market in foreign currencies was wholly bilateral, except for freedom of arbitrage between US and Canadian dollars. Thus authorized dealers,[12] when dealing with Brussels, could do so only in sterling against Belgian francs. But in the course of 1953 they were permitted to undertake spot arbitrage transactions as between any of the following countries: France, Switzerland, Belgium, Netherlands, Western Germany and the Scandinavian countries (and subsequently Italy in 1955 and Austria in 1957). These arrangements were later extended to include forward operations for periods up to three months ahead, but otherwise remained virtually unchanged until December 1958.

The reopening of the London foreign exchange market fundamentally changed the *modus operandi* of the foreign exchange transactions of the British monetary authorities. Instead of being a party to every exchange transaction, as they had been since the introduction of the wartime exchange control, they were able to revert to their traditional practice of simply dealing in the market, to ensure that the spot value of the pound always stayed close to its parity.

Sterling's return to convertibility

By according transferable account status to all countries which previously had had bilateral status, the varieties of 'free' sterling ceased to be very numerous in respect of current account transactions[13] since there were henceforth only two kinds of sterling outside the sterling area: convertible sterling, the medium in which sterling area residents settled their approved transactions with dollar area residents, and which exchanged against the US dollar at very close to the official parity of £1 = \$2.80; and transferable account sterling, which was officially inconvertible but which was in fact exchanged against the dollar, in free markets in Zurich and other foreign financial centres, at a rate below parity, and which served to finance transactions which (though contrary to the intentions of the sterling area exchange controls) could not conveniently be suppressed.[14]

Towards the end of 1954 the free market price for transferable account sterling declined from only slightly below the then official parity of \$2.80 to a level of little more than \$2.70 to the pound, and the daily amount of transferable account sterling sold against dollars increased considerably. On 24 February 1955 the Chancellor of the Exchequer, concerned with these 'markets through which sterling is traded at a discount to the detriment both of our traders and of our reserves', announced that (among other measures) he had authorized the UK monetary authorities 'to use wider discretion in operating in these markets, so that they may be in a better position to carry out our general exchange policy and make the most prudent use of our reserves'.[15]

After the date of this announcement, the free rate for transferable account sterling was hardly ever at a discount of more than 1 per cent, which may be taken to imply that the Bank of England was almost always prepared to buy such sterling for dollars, whenever its price would otherwise have fallen to a larger discount. In other words, transferable account sterling became as from February 1954 *de facto* convertible, at a modest discount as compared with the official rate.

The European Payments Union

When the second Intra-European Payments Agreement came to an end at mid 1950, it was succeeded by a much more ambitious arrangement, the European Payments Union.[16] The *modus operandi* of the EPU was basically as follows:

1   Each month the union took over all bilateral surpluses and deficits of each of the members. If, for example, during July 1950 Belgium ran a bilateral surplus with Britain, this would be treated as a surplus with the union in the case of Belgium and as

a deficit with the union in the case of Britain, and Britain would not be called upon to make any settlement direct with Belgium. The sum of all Belgium's bilateral surpluses with other members in July 1950, minus all bilateral deficits, would be recorded by the BIS, in its capacity as the union's agent, as Belgium's 'net position' for the month and similarly for the other members. (The BIS calculated Belgium's bilateral surplus with Britain as the month's increase in its official holding of sterling minus any change in the British official holding of Belgian francs.)

2 The monthly net positions of each member since mid 1950 were recorded by the BIS, with the appropriate sign, and cumulated, so that at the end of each month each member had a 'cumulative net position' with the union. Since in the calculation of each member country's cumulative net position all its monthly bilateral deficits to date were set off against all its monthly bilateral surpluses, all compensable deficits (and surpluses) between members were simply cancelled out, without the need to undertake first- or second-category operations needed under the IEPA.

3 At the end of each month the change in a member's cumulative net position, as compared with a month ago, had to be settled as between the member and the union. Either the member had to settle with the union (in the case of a cumulative net deficit which had increased or a cumulative net surplus which had diminished) or the union had to settle with the member (in the case of a cumulative net surplus which had increased or a cumulative net deficit which had diminished).

4 The means prescribed for settling any change in a member's cumulative net position did not depend on why that change occurred. It did not, for instance, make the least difference to the British monetary authorities whether British tourists chose to visit Switzerland rather than Norway, whether British importers bought in Germany or in Greece, or whether British exports went to Turkey or to Belgium – although prior to the EPU there was a strong incentive for preferring the latter alternative in each of the three examples (as being much less likely to cause an outflow of dollars or gold). The EPU thus provided machinery for fully multilateral settlement between its members.

5 The principal means of settlement (whether from a member to the union or from the union to a member) were US dollars (or gold) and so-called 'credits'. The latter were expressed in terms of the union's 'unit of account'. The value of claims on the union

(recorded as so many 'units of account') to a member holding them was solely as a means of settling with the union in future months and as a claim on the union's assets when the union was disbanded.

6   The union's 'unit of account' also served as the accounting unit in which members' cumulative net positions were recorded. The translation of amounts expressed in units of a member's own currency (sterling in Britain's case) into so many of the union's units of account was achieved by the provision that for this purpose the union's unit of account should have a par value equal to one US dollar. (There was provision for revaluation of the unit in certain unlikely circumstances which did not ever arise in practice.)

7   The formula for settling the proportion between dollars (or gold) and credit in any particular monthly settlement depended prior to July 1954 on the *quota* allocated to each member (see Table 4) and a formula which related the dollar–credit proportion to the member country's cumulative deficit or surplus expressed as a percentage of its quota. However, as from mid 1954 to August 1955 the dollar–credit ratio became invariably 50:50 and thereafter 75:25 until the demise of the union at the end of 1958.

8   To provide for the contingency that the union's receipts of dollars might fall short of its payments, the USA contributed an initial 'kitty' of US $350 million.

Table 4   *Members of the EPU, with their respective quotas in June 1954 (US $ million)*

Country	Quotas	Country	Quotas
Austria	70	Norway	200
Belgium	360	Portugal	70
Denmark	195	Sweden	260
France	520	Switzerland	250
Germany	500	Turkey	50
Greece	45	UK	1060
Iceland	15		——
Italy	205	*Total*	4155
Netherlands	355		

The wider area of multilateral settlement

Owing to the way in which the BIS calculated surpluses and deficits, the effective area of multilateral settlement under the EPU was very much greater than that comprised by its European members, due to the fact that several members' currencies were the usual, or even the sole, media for making international settlements in other large areas of the world. Of the Western European currencies thus used for making international settlements, sterling was much the most important, but the Belgian, Dutch, French and Portuguese currencies were also used extensively within their respective empires. As an example of the wider area of multilateral settlement facilitated by the EPU, we may note that France (or any other continental member of the union) had no monetary incentive to prefer making payments to (or getting receipts from) Australia rather than Britain, since French sterling holdings (and therefore the French cumulative net position in the EPU) were affected in precisely the same way in the two cases.

In broad terms, we may conclude that the establishment of the EPU in 1950 and the evolution of sterling arrangements had by 1955 provided the non-communist world outside the dollar area with facilities for more or less multilateral settlement between the countries concerned. On this basis we can reasonably speak of a 'binary system' of two multilateral settlement areas, kept apart until December 1958 by exchange controls: the dollar area, within which settlement was in US dollars; and the soft settlement area, in which settlement was mainly in sterling or through the machinery of the EPU.

But just as the pre-1950 phase was bilateral only with certain qualifications, so the subsequent phase cannot without some qualification be described as binary. This is so because there were three different media of settlement in use in the soft settlement area, offering differing access to US dollars:

1   Settlement through the EPU, which after August 1955 was three-quarters in dollars (or gold) and one-quarter in credit.
2   Convertible sterling, which was convertible at very close to parity into US dollars, but which was not freely available outside the dollar area.
3   Transferable account sterling, which after February 1955 was *de facto* convertible into US dollars at a modest discount.

The existence of these different media of settlement was not relevant to the trading of most countries, since they were not free to make their own choice of media, but it was undoubtedly relevant to Britain, a member of the EPU whose national currency was itself in use as another medium for soft international settlements. For example, the British authorities probably had some incentive to prefer a bilateral deficit with Australia to one with France, although they could not be sure unless they could judge whether and where Australia would spend her sterling earnings.

Thus the existence up to December 1958 of several different means of soft settlement did offer some incentive to discriminate in trade and payments even within the soft settlement area, and to some extent such discrimination did indeed persist until then, although to a progressively diminishing extent in the course of the 1950s. As we have seen, in January 1952 the Commonwealth Prime Ministers' Conference actually tightened up the restrictions on imports into the sterling area from all outside sources, in order to conserve the exiguous stock of gold and dollars held by the British authorities as the central reserve of the whole area. However, by the mid 1950s discriminatory quotas on imports into the sterling area from non-dollar sources other than Japan had been virtually abolished. So far as Britain herself was concerned, she participated in the trade liberalization programme organized by the members of the OEEC. Under this programme, member countries undertook to liberalize (in the sense of freeing from quantitative restrictions) an agreed minimum percentage of their private imports from other member countries. By mid June 1955, Britain had liberalized only 84 per cent of such imports – a laggard's performance, inferior to that of all other major European trading nations except France. Within a year, however, the British percentage had been increased to 94 per cent, which put it at about the top of the league.

By and large, from about 1956 onwards, the commercial policies pursued by most countries of the soft settlement area show very little discrimination as between their trading partners in that area, except for a continuing discrimination against Japan, where the motive was political rather than monetary. Thus the continued existence of several different means of settlement within the area seems to have lost most of its significance by 1956. So this area may reasonably be regarded in 1956–8 as a multilateral payment area, in more or less the same way as the dollar area, the two areas together embracing virtually the whole of the non-communist world.

The end of the binary phase

As will already have been clear from the quotation at the beginning of this chapter, the binary arrangements we have been considering were brought to an end in December 1958. The EPU was in that month wound up[17] and non-resident sterling became officially convertible into dollars: thereby the hard and soft currency areas coalesced into what may as a first approximation be regarded as a unified, and greatly expanded, dollar area.

Part Two

Convertibility, liquidity and adjustment, 1959–88

3 Convertibility, December 1958

The outstanding development in the foreign exchange field ... was the simultaneous introduction at the end of December 1958 by [thirteen Western European countries] of current-account convertibility for non-residents ... Two of them – Germany and the United Kingdom – have now put their current payments with all other countries on a basis of convertibility and they now have only one kind of current account for non-residents, freely convertible into any foreign currency and freely transferable between all non-residents. The other eleven countries – Austria, Belgium, Denmark, Finland, France, Italy, the Netherlands, Norway, Portugal, Sweden and Switzerland ... now distinguish only between countries with which transactions take place on the basis of convertibility and those with which payments are still strictly bilateral. The number of bilateral payments agreements still maintained is different in each of the eleven countries, but in none do they comprise more than a small fraction of the foreign trade and payments of the country concerned.

BIS *Annual Report*, 1959[1]

The US Council of Economic Advisers' *Annual Report* of January 1973 emphasized two criteria for a satisfactory international monetary system. First it should be *market-oriented*, with a minimum of official interference with individual market transactions. Second, it should be *multilateral*, such that receipts from any one country may be used to make payments in any other. These criteria are highly relevant to the 'convertibility' introduced in December 1958 and described by the BIS in the above quotation, since it served to inaugurate a regime of convertibility-in-the-market which largely satisfied them and which has proved resilient enough to survive to this day (January 1988), although with considerable adaptations to changing circumstances.

The changes made in December 1958 amounted to a drastic dismantling of exchange controls by thirteen countries, which had the effect of merging the hard and soft settlement areas of the preceding period, such that the major currencies of the world became convertible *in the market*: henceforth the holder of any one of these currencies enjoyed considerable freedom to convert it into any other by buying the one for the other in any foreign exchange market. Admittedly the dismantling of exchange controls, even on current payments, was still not complete, as is clear from the quotation from the BIS report, but the process was carried an important stage further in February 1961 (see Chapter 8). Restrictions which survived in the major countries after February 1961 were almost exclusively on international capital flows, which have indeed never been wholly free of exchange controls and regulations with equivalent effect, so that convertibility in the market has never obtained in a wholly unalloyed form: nevertheless after December 1958 ready access to the market was the norm and restrictions on access the exception. For ease of exposition we shall consider here the implications of the norm, and defer the exceptions to later chapters.

Official transactions in foreign exchange

The widespread commitment in December 1958 to a free market regime did not in itself settle the issue of how much (if any) official *management* there should be, in the sense of official market transactions undertaken to determine, or at any rate to influence, the level of exchange rates brought about by the play of market supply and demand. In practice the issue was not an open one in 1958, thanks to decisions which had already been taken at the Bretton Woods conference in July 1944 and which were not decisively called into question until the 1970s, but it is none the less instructive to see what options were theoretically available, other than the one actually adopted. At one extreme there was the possibility of free floating, with no official transactions at all. At the other extreme was official pegging, at immutable officially determined target rates of exchange, such as was later envisaged for the EEC member countries in the abortive Werner plan for a stage-by-stage approach to eventual European monetary union. In between these extremes there were the possibilities, first, of managed floating, with official transactions in foreign exchange but no official target exchange rates ('parities'), such as has been practised by a number of major powers since 1973; and second, of official pegging but with adjustable (instead of inflexible) parities.

The Bretton Woods prescription, based on the original Articles of Agreement of the International Monetary Fund, was for official transactions conducted so as to keep market rates very close to official parities, plus a procedure, which in the 1960s most countries proved most reluctant to invoke except *in extremis*, for adjusting these parities in circumstances of 'fundamental disequilibrium'. The Bretton Woods system came to an end in August 1971 and was succeeded by a rather different pegged-rate regime, which we shall refer to as the dollar standard, with much more readily adjustable target rates ('central values'). This in turn gave way in 1972–3 to a floating regime. Thus the post-1958 period divides into three phases, each with its own distinctive characteristics, as will be apparent from Parts Three and Four of this book.

What, however, needs to be noted here, in respect of the period 1959–88 as a whole, is that the exchange markets have always been managed, continuously or intermittently, by official transactions. These transactions are almost always conducted by central banks – the Bank of England, the Federal Reserve Bank of New York, the German Bundesbank and their equivalents in other countries. Sometimes these banks deal exclusively on their own account, as with the Bundesbank, sometimes on behalf of their country's treasury or finance ministry; to cover these various possibilities we can refer to transactions on behalf of a country's 'monetary authorities'.

To facilitate their market operations in foreign exchange, monetary authorities also undertake transactions with each other – in particular, credits, swaps (see page 111), and gold sales – and with international institutions such as the Bank for International Settlements (BIS), the International Monetary Fund (IMF) or the European Economic Community (EEC). The portmanteau label for all transactions of monetary authorities, whether between themselves, with international institutions, or in the foreign exchange markets, is 'official reserve transactions'.

A very widespread feature of central banks' *market* transactions is that the intervention currency they use, when buying or selling their own currency in the market, is the US dollar. If the Bank of England wants to support sterling in the market it uses US dollars to purchase pounds. If the Bundesbank wants to prevent, or moderate, a rise in the market value of its currency, it sells marks against US dollars. Up to the birth of the European 'snake' in April 1972 (see page 158), the only exceptions to the use of the dollar as intervention currency have been the use of sterling by the central banks of the overseas sterling area,[2] and (less important) the use of the French, Dutch and Belgian currencies by the countries formerly comprising the respective colonial empires; and even in these cases the dollar came to be increasingly preferred. Moreover in the pegging regimes operated from December 1958 to March 1973, the pegged rates (except in the sterling area) were rates on the dollar. One may thus regard the events of December 1958 as having produced a great expansion of the previous dollar area – the characteristic features of that area (ready access to exchange markets, multilateral settlement, pegging on the dollar by market intervention in dollars) henceforth obtaining throughout much the greater part of the non-communist world.

The expanded dollar area of post-1958 also retained the asymmetric feature of its earlier pegging arrangements, namely that (of n participants) $n-1$ undertook market transactions to peg on the dollar, while the nth participant, the United States, had no say in determining the official par values at which the $n-1$ exchange rates should be pegged, nor any compelling need to participate in the official market transactions needed to hold the $n-1$ market rates (the dollar prices of the $n-1$ other currencies) close to the corresponding official parities. (Indeed the US monetary authorities undertook very few market transactions before the 1970s, though in the course of the 1960s they came to do substantial reserve transactions with other countries' central banks, and with the BIS and IMF.)

What applied in the extended dollar area of the 1960s also applied, on a much smaller scale, in the sterling area, with, however, the vital difference that the UK herself was one of the $n-1$ members of the dollar area that pegged on the dollar. Each country of the overseas sterling area settled a parity between its own currency and sterling and pegged at this parity by buying and selling sterling at prices within 1 per cent of parity: in this way its own currency was pegged on sterling. Sterling in turn was pegged on the dollar (at a parity of £1 = \$2.80 up to November 1967; thereafter at £1 = \$2.40) by the Bank of England buying and selling dollars freely in the market so as to keep the market rate within the narrow limits of two cents each side of parity.

The pegging practices of the 1960s resulted in the use of the word 'convertible' in two different senses. A currency may be convertible *in the market*, which means, as we have seen, that the individual's access to exchange markets anywhere in the world is not seriously impeded by exchange controls. A currency may also be *officially* convertible, in the sense that in 1960 the pound was convertible through the Bank of England being always prepared to supply the market with dollars against pounds at £1 = $2.78 and pounds against dollars at £1 = $2.82. The events of December 1958 inaugurated a period of convertibility in both senses of the word: however the subsequent transition in the 1970s to floating retained convertibility in the former sense but abandoned it in the latter.

Bretton Woods convertibility

What in this book is called 'Bretton Woods convertibility', as it obtained from December 1958 to August 1971, also incorporated yet another kind of convertibility: the official convertibility of the US dollar into gold. This feature of the system was achieved by the readiness of the US authorities to deal in gold with other central banks at buying and selling prices very close to $35 an ounce. Thus Bretton Woods convertibility involved not only convertibility in the market but also several levels of official convertibility. The US operated official convertibility as between the US dollar and gold; the majority of other countries (including the UK) each operated official convertibility as between its own currency and dollars; countries of the overseas sterling area (and other subsidiary monetary areas) each operated official convertibility as between the local currency and sterling (or the French or Belgian franc or the florin, as the case might be).

Official reserves

All the countries comprising the post-1958 Bretton Woods system (that is, virtually the whole of the non-communist world) accepted that operating official convertibility required them to hold *reserves* of the asset into which they undertook to convert their national currency (see Table 5). The USA had an official reserve of gold, the UK one of US dollars, Australia one of sterling. These, however, were only the first-line reserves: most countries chose to hold a mixed bag of reserve assets, not just a reserve of the asset required to operate official conversion. Thus not only the USA, but also the UK and many other countries, including those of the overseas sterling area, held gold as well as foreign exchange, and some OSA countries held dollars as well as sterling. Even the USA intermittently held amounts of other countries' currencies. Moreover, most of the countries concerned were members of the IMF and as such had 'reserve positions' in the IMF General Account (see note 7 to Chapter 8, on page 265) and as from January 1970 reserve holdings of IMF Special Drawing Rights (see page 136).

Table 5   *Total international reserves, end of years 1958, 1969 and 1975*

| | $ billion | | |
	1958	1969	1975
Gold: US holdings	20.6	11.9	13.6
Other countries' holdings	17.0	27.0	27.9
Sub-total, gold	37.6	38.9	41.5
Official claims on the US, in dollars	9.6	14.2	78.3
Official claims on the US, in other currencies*	—	1.8	1.6
Sterling claims on the UK	5.9	5.2	7.5
Identified Eurodollars	—	4.9	47.5
Other foreign exchange, including Eurocurrencies	3.0	6.9	26.1
Sub-total, foreign exchange	18.5	33.0	161.0
Reserve position in IMF General Account	2.6	6.7	14.7
IMF Special Drawing Rights	—	—	10.3
Total reserves	58.7	78.7	227.6

* See Table 8 below (page 114), last column.

Source: IMF, mainly *Annual Report* (1976), tables 11 and 15 (where the end-1975 figures are shown in SDRs but are expressed here in US dollars). Gold is valued at 35 SDRs an ounce.

The reason for the diversification of official reserves was in the early 1960s largely historical[3] and need not detain us here, but the fact that they were so diversified is one of the reasons why official reserve transactions in currencies were not all market transactions, but also occurred as between two central banks or between a central bank and the IMF: central banks might have to undertake such transactions in order to mobilize their second-line reserves. Non-market transactions also occurred in connection with the rescue operations which were mounted from time to time to restore the depleted official reserves of a country in persistent deficit.

In the course of the 1960s, the central bankers of the major countries, and particularly of the so-called Group of Ten,[4] became increasingly adept at mounting such rescue operations, so that a country suffering a run on its currency (as for example the UK did from time to time) was enabled to honour its official conversion obligations on a scale in excess of its owned reserves at the beginning of the run. Hence the resources at the disposal of a central bank, to maintain the official convertibility of its currency, comprised not only its owned reserves but also the substantial rescue facilities on which it might reasonably hope to draw – the combination of the two being subsumed in the jargon-term 'international liquidity'.

The official convertibility provisions of the Bretton Woods system came to an end in August 1971 in respect of convertibility as between US dollars and gold and subsequently in respect of convertibility as between the US dollar and the other major currencies. Thus in the 1970s the era of official convertibility came to an end, though convertibility in the market remained. The demise of official convertibility has not, however, meant the end of official reserve transactions in the foreign exchange markets on a scale at least as great as was ever required under the Bretton Woods system, so that important features of the old regime have been retained in the new. In the new arrangements the United States's partners, at any rate those in the Group of Ten, no longer peg on the dollar, but they still deal in the foreign exchange markets and, except in snake intervention,[5] they still use the dollar as the intervention currency. They still hold reserves, still with a large dollar component. They still enjoy much the same kind of rescue facilities, by which they can supplement their owned reserves of dollars should these become unduly depleted, and in addition have now learned how to draw dollars from the Eurocurrency markets (see Chapter 13). Thus liquidity facilities are as important under the floating regime as under Bretton Woods.

The effect on reserves of official reserve transactions under Bretton Woods

To clarify the way official transactions affect reserves, let us in this chapter imagine an over-simplified version of the Bretton Woods system. Let us suppose it to comprise the United States and $n-1$ other countries, all of which peg on the dollar by trading their own currency against the dollar in the foreign exchange market but otherwise do no official market transactions of any kind (though they may undertake transactions with the Federal Reserve authorities, with each other and with the IMF).[6] How in such a system do official market transactions affect dollar reserves? Let us for simplicity consider a period in which the $n-1$ official parities remain unchanged, so that variations in exchange rates do not play any part in the adjustment of supply to demand. If, at the prevailing pattern of exchange rates, there is any imbalance between demand and supply from sources other than $n-1$ central banks, it is simply made good by the official market transactions which these banks undertake.

Now any such imbalance must be a surplus in respect of one currency and a deficit in respect of another, since two currencies are involved in each one of the countless flood of transactions concluded all day long in the foreign exchange markets: hence a disequilibrium in any month's total trading in the world's exchange markets taken as a whole may be represented either as a list of the surpluses of the countries whose currencies are in excess demand[7] or as a list of the deficits of the countries whose currencies are in excess supply, since the two lists must necessarily tot up to the same total. Let us provisionally suppose that in some month or other period the USA, whose currency has been adopted as the intervention currency, is neither in surplus nor in deficit: then what happens to countries' reserves in the period in question is that the official market transactions of the surplus countries result in an inflow of so many million dollars to their reserves, while the official market transactions of the deficit countries result in a precisely equal outflow. Thus such a disequilibrium produces a redistribution of dollar reserves from the deficit to the surplus countries.

If now we suppose the United States to be in either surplus or deficit, the outcome will be different, since the official market transactions of other countries will then not simply effect a redistribution of dollar reserves, they will also effect a change in the total amount of such reserves, which will increase by the amount of a US deficit or decrease by the amount of a US surplus. When the USA is in deficit, in the sense we are now using the term, dollar bank deposits recently acquired from US residents by (say) exporters to the United States are bought in the market by other countries' central banks in exchange for bank deposits denominated in the local currency. Dollars thus purchased have not come out of any other country's reserves: if, as could well be the case, they were until very recently in American ownership, the American owner would have been (say) an American importer, or an American investor investing overseas.

Although when the United States is in deficit (in the sense we have been using the term) the corresponding official market transactions of the other countries necessarily cause a like increase in total dollar reserves, this is by no means the only way by which total dollar reserves may be changed. This is because monetary authorities conduct official reserve transactions not only in the foreign exchange market but also with each other and with the IMF. Thus the $n-1$ countries in the system may add to their total dollar reserves by selling gold to the US authorities, or by borrowing dollars from them, or by drawing dollars from the IMF; or again they may undertake swap transactions with the Federal Reserve Bank of New York (see Chapter 9). Moreover any of these transactions may be conducted in the opposite sense; that is, to reduce dollar reserves. Thus there is no necessary correspondence between the US deficit and the growth of other countries' official dollar reserves. For example, in the decade of the 1960s, official native dollar reserves (that is, excluding Eurodollars, which require a separate explanation, given in Chapter 13) increased by $5½ billion, or only half the US deficit.

This provides an illustration of the general proposition that surpluses and deficits on our definition (which is such that total surpluses and total deficits are necessarily equal) cannot be measured statistically simply by noting (in the case of the USA) the change in any period in the United States's dollar liabilities to the central banks of the $n-1$ other countries and (for each of these other countries) the change in its official dollar reserves. We have to adjust all these amounts for non-market transactions undertaken by the n countries' monetary authorities. This is in effect what statisticians seek to do when they produce a figure for a country's 'official reserve transactions balance' in any year or other period. In the case of the United States's deficit in the 1960s as a whole, we know this to be $11 billion because such was the amount of the United States's official reserve transactions balance, the components of which were, in billions of dollars, as follows:[8]

Increase in other countries' reserves of US dollar liabilities	5½
Depletion of US gold reserve	7½
Increase of US official holdings of foreign currencies	−2½
Increase in US official non-dollar liabilities } *less* net repayments to IMF General Account }	½
Deficit financed by official reserve transactions (ten-year period)	11

What are the motives which lead the monetary authorities of the United States and of the other $n-1$ countries operating a system of 'pegging on the dollar' to undertake non-market official reserve transactions? In the case of such of the $n-1$ countries as are in deficit, their reason, we have already seen, is to get their hands on more dollars with which to continue to support their own currencies in the market. What then about the other countries? Here the main motive is to avoid the risk of capital loss on holding dollars when revaluations of parities (or a transition from pegging to floating) may be imminent. Greater immunity from such capital loss may be sought by buying gold for dollars from the US authorities, by buying non-dollar securities from them, or by undertaking swap transactions, of a kind described in Chapter 9, with the Federal Reserve Bank of New York.

The United States's own motive for undertaking non-market official reserve transactions, during the Bretton Woods regime, was to offer other countries, worried about a possible exchange loss on holding dollars, an acceptable alternative apart from gold. The USA was losing gold from its reserves almost continuously during the 1960s (see Table 6, page 104) and it became US policy to seek to moderate the outflow, among other things by swap transactions with other countries' central banks and by the sale to them of securities denominated in non-dollar currencies.

I have in this section dealt with the effect on reserves of official reserve transactions *under the Bretton Woods regime* simply because it is convenient to postpone until later chapters (especially 13, 17 and 19) our consideration of the additional complications (alluded to already in note 6, page 262) which arose during the 1970s from the increasing readiness of monetary authorities to borrow and lend foreign currencies in the credit markets, especially the Eurocurrency markets, as well as continuing their earlier practice of buying and selling them in the foreign exchange markets.

Liquidity and adjustment

Under the Bretton Woods system of the 1960s, the immediate need for dollar liquidity (in the sense of dollar reserves and facilities for supplementing them) arose in any period only for such of the $n-1$ countries pegging on the dollar as were in that period in deficit. If the USA were in deficit too (as was the case throughout most of the 1960s) its preoccupation would be different: its persistent concern lest officially held dollars might be presented for conversion into gold would be that much greater when other countries' central banks were having to buy yet more dollars in the market to hold their currencies down to their dollar parities.

But whether a deficit was being run by the United States or by one or more of the $n-1$ other countries, there would be a financing or 'liquidity' problem if it persisted long enough. If deficits tended to be persistent, as proved to be the case in the 1960s, the difficulty could be diagnosed in either or both of two ways: as an inadequacy of 'liquidity' facilities for the financing of disequilibria or as an inadequacy in the 'mechanism of adjustment' for the correction of disequilibria. The corresponding remedy was in the one case an improvement in financial facilities and in the other an improvement in the mechanism of adjustment, to make it operate more reliably and expeditiously.

The 1960s saw an immense and continuous effort, especially by officials of the Group of Ten, to explore, and in some cases to try out, remedies of both kinds, but with very unequal success. On the one hand the 1960s saw a remarkable development of financial facilities by the central banks of the Group of Ten and by the IMF, as we shall see in Part Three. On the other hand there were only minor changes to the adjustment mechanism until the eventual reluctant acceptance in the 1970s (as we shall see in Part Four) of the case for greater variation in exchange rates: however, the lack of action in previous years did not imply lack of constructive thought, for much intellectual effort was devoted to the problem of adjustment, notably by Working Party No. 3 of the OECD, whose report, *The Balance of Payments Adjustment Process*, was published in August 1966. To this report we shall return in Chapter 5, after having attempted to clarify some at least of the basic mechanisms involved in the adjustment process, including variations in exchange rates, in Chapter 4.

4 Adjustment in theory

With a low rate of exchange we can sell more of our goods abroad and so should be able to earn more dollars in total.

Sir Stafford Cripps,
Chancellor of the Exchequer,
18 September 1949

Monetary effect and income effect

The so-called 'adjustment problem' is so important in the case of a national economy like the UK, with its own national currency, that we are inclined to wonder why it does not seem to arise, at any rate in an acute form, in the case of a subdivision of a national economy, for example Nottinghamshire. Let us therefore consider what would happen if the residents of this county, whom we may call Nottspeople, persistently made more payments in the rest of Britain than the inhabitants of the rest of Britain made in Nottinghamshire. Clearly Nottspeople would eventually run out of money; their holdings of notes and bank deposits would be depleted and ultimately exhausted. In practice such a depletion of money holdings has never occurred on a scale sufficient to attract attention to the problem, but if a considerable depletion did occur the consequences would be serious, since if Nottspeople ran short of money they would have little to spend and in consequence there would be local depression and unemployment. Such would be, in technical jargon, the 'monetary effect of external disequilibrium'.

In practice, there are corrective forces which would come into play long before this monetary effect progressed very far. One such corrective force is the so-called 'income effect'. If Nottinghamshire has developed a deficit in her payments with the rest of Britain because of a falling-off in her exports across the county boundary, or because of a switch of Nottspeople's purchases from Nottinghamshire products to goods produced in Leicestershire or Yorkshire, then the consequences for Nottinghamshire will be not only a payments deficit but also business depression and unemployment in the industries immediately concerned, which will rapidly spread to other industries; and even a mild local depression is an appreciable corrective to any outflow of money from the county. For unemployed workers and impoverished businessmen are poor customers, and in particular poor customers for goods produced over the county boundary, so that any diminution in the prosperity of Nottinghamshire, compared with that of other counties, would produce a contraction in Nottinghamshire's imports from, and payments to, other counties. Here then is a powerful corrective to any outflow of money, though it involves a local depression unless and until Nottinghamshire's prices can be made more competitive.

Apart from this unpleasant income effect, there are other forces at work to correct the shortage of money. In the first place, Notts-people own a large amount of securities which can be sold at any time on the stock exchanges. If the purchaser of the securities is not a Nottsperson – as is likely if Nottspeople are getting short of money – the sale of any of these securities represents a transfer of money to Nottinghamshire from the rest of the country. In much the same way, Nottspeople may remedy a shortage of money by borrowing from Nottinghamshire branches of the nation-wide joint-stock banks. Many Nottspeople are sufficiently creditworthy to qualify for overdrafts at their bank, and an overdraft granted represents so much more money at the disposal of Nottspeople. Moreover, Nottinghamshire businesses in need of money may issue new securities to the British public at large, including that part of the British public which lives outside Nottinghamshire, and Nottinghamshire local authorities may likewise borrow from the British public at large.

The ability of Nottspeople to borrow or sell securities – whether old ones or new ones – over the county boundary, is facilitated by two factors: first, the existence of a common currency – sterling – throughout Britain is a great help, for all loans and securities are promises of money in the future, and investors commonly prefer promises of the type of money with which they are familiar; and second, neither Nottinghamshire nor any other British county imposes restrictions on capital transactions (whether in loans or securities) between one county and another or on the payment of interest or dividends over a county boundary.

Now let us give rein to our imagination and suppose Nottinghamshire to be not just a county but an independent country, with its own national currency, the 'Nottspound', pegged on sterling by the market transactions of the Nottinghamshire central bank. In these imaginary circumstances, what would now happen if Nottspeople persistently spent more in the rest of Britain than the inhabitants of the rest of Britain spent in Nottinghamshire is that the Nottinghamshire central bank would be persistently buying Nottspounds for sterling. Thus there would still be a 'monetary effect', since the Nottspounds available to Nottspeople would be steadily depleted. Indeed this effect would now be accentuated by a contraction of bank credit, since losses of sterling from the central bank's reserves would reduce not only the deposits held by Nottspeople at the commercial banks, but likewise the balances held by the latter at the Nottinghamshire central bank.

Let us further assume that although Nottinghamshire has achieved monetary independence, neither it nor the rest of the UK has yet imposed any restrictions on trade, on capital transactions, or on payments, between the two economies. In these hypothetical circumstances it is clear that despite the absence of any such restrictions, Nottspeople's capital transactions with the rest of Britain would be much less helpful, from the point of view of correcting external disequilibria, than at present. The existence of the two currencies, the Nottspound and the pound sterling, would be a deterrent to investors, whose future profits would be more uncertain if there was a risk that the official exchange rate might eventually be changed or that exchange restrictions might be imposed. Moreover, such borrowing and lending as remained would be considerably distorted by factors which are at present largely absent. Political and social changes affecting only one of the two economies, such as changes in taxation or in official regulations, a change of government, a deterioration of industrial relations, or an increase in social unrest, might greatly upset the balance of borrowing and lending between the two economies. Even the fear that such changes might occur would act in the same way. In addition there might be speculative capital movements, in anticipation of imminent changes in the exchange rate, or panic capital outflows due to fears that exchange controls might be imposed. It is easy to imagine that capital movements between independent economies, far from being an equilibrating factor, might well be the reverse.

The Nottinghamshire central bank need not passively acquiesce in disequilibrating capital movements since it could take measures to counter them, particularly by bringing about changes in interest rates: however, in practice remedial measures are unlikely to work successfully in circumstances of a speculative 'run' unless they are confidently expected to influence the flow of *trade*, and not just the flow of capital.

So we need to pursue the question of whether, and in what circumstances, an independent Nottinghamshire's external trade would be equilibrating. Let us first consider how the 'income effect' would operate. An external deficit due to a falling-off in an independent Nottinghamshire's exports to the rest of Britain would be to some extent self-correcting if no steps were taken to offset the depression (and the consequential reduction in imports) due to the decline in exports and also to the resulting decline in Nottspeople's demand for goods and services. And if the automatic decline in imports proved to be inadequate, the Nottinghamshire government could always take steps to intensify the depression, for example by adopting deflationary fiscal or monetary policies.

But curing an external deficit by deflation is an unpleasant treatment if it leads to an unacceptable level of unemployment, so we need to consider the other available remedies. One such remedy might arise merely with the passage of time and the pressure of circumstances: the depression might well in due course become unnecessary (as a means of dealing with the external deficit) if the effect of the unemployment in Nottinghamshire was to act on the level of wages, and thus to cheapen the prices of Nottinghamshire's goods in relation to goods produced elsewhere. In this respect the outcome would be similar to that of a depreciation of the Nottspound in relation to the pound sterling, which (it will now be shown) would in favourable circumstances reduce Nottinghamshire's deficit.

Devaluation in favourable circumstances

If the Nottspound were reduced in value from £1 sterling to (say) 90p, this would increase the prices in Nottspounds which Nottspeople would have to pay for goods imported from the rest of Britain. When such goods became dearer, Nottspeople would buy less of them and consequently would need less sterling to pay for them. If goods previously bought outside the county include a goodly proportion for which passable substitutes can be made locally, and if in addition the prices (in Nottspounds) of locally produced goods do not appreciably rise (whether through being bid up by the diversion of demand from imported goods or through the operation of the so-called 'wage–price spiral'),[1] the reduction in sterling expenditure on imports would be considerable. In technical language we can say that a devaluation of the Nottspound would be particularly efficacious because of Nottinghamshire's high price-elasticity of demand for imports, that is, because her imports would be choked off rapidly by a rise in their local currency prices.

Let us turn now from Nottinghamshire's imports to her exports. The demand for Nottinghamshire's exports would also be highly price-elastic if Nottinghamshire's customers (counties importing Nottinghamshire's exports) had, like Nottinghamshire herself, a high price-elasticity of demand for imports. Moreover a reduction in the sterling prices of Nottinghamshire's exports would enable her to underbid her competitors and thus to supply a higher proportion of her customers' import requirements. Hence, provided that the competitive advantage afforded to Nottinghamshire's exports is not offset by a rise in their prices (in Nottspounds), the effect of Nottinghamshire's devaluation would be to increase the volume of her exports in a much greater proportion than the reduction in their sterling prices,[2] so that her total sterling earnings from her exports would considerably increase.

Devaluation in unfavourable circumstances

On the assumptions we have made as to the conditions governing Nottinghamshire's demand for imports and supply of exports and those governing the demand for her exports[3] we can conclude that devaluation would be a highly efficient way of improving Nottinghamshire's balance of external trade and thereby correcting her external deficit. Let us now consider how much less efficient devaluation would be if the relevant conditions were otherwise. To start with, let us reverse our previous assumptions as to Nottinghamshire's demand for imports and supply of exports by supposing Nottinghamshire to be (1) liable to suffer excess demand, (2) highly inflexible in her economy, and (3) subject to the wage–price spiral – wage-rates being in some degree geared to the workers' cost of living. Then, when we have followed through the implications of these possibilities, we can complete the story by reversing our previous assumptions about the demand for Nottinghamshire's exports.

1   If the level of demand for Nottinghamshire's goods were already so high that output was nearly at its maximum, both the diversion of demand from imported to locally produced goods and

the increase in the demand for exports would probably result in the bidding up of home prices, thereby offsetting the effect of the devaluation. It would then be up to the Nottinghamshire authorities, if they wished the devaluation to be successful in its objective, to eliminate the excess demand by adopting deflationary fiscal or monetary policies. (It would be useless to keep prices down by official controls if excess demand prevented the volume of exports from increasing: such a policy would merely make Nottinghamshire's sterling earnings lower than ever.)

2 Unfortunately the avoidance of an excess of *overall* demand for locally produced goods is not a sufficient condition for the avoidance of a serious rise in home prices. Devaluation stimulates the demand for specific types of goods, namely those which are the closest substitutes for imported goods and those which are suitable for export. If the output of these particular types of goods can be increased only with difficulty, and if the home demand for them cannot be much reduced, then a relatively large devaluation will be required to effect a given improvement in the balance of external trade. An increase in the output of the relevant types of goods may well be difficult to achieve if the industries producing them are already operating to the limit of their existing resources of manpower, land, or equipment, since the expansion of output would then require that additional resources of a suitable type should be attracted from other industries – which would be impossible if such resources simply did not exist or if they were located in the wrong place and immobile. A reduction in the home demand for the relevant types of goods would be difficult to achieve if these goods happened to be necessities or, in the case of exportable goods, if the proportion of output sold on the home market was in any case very small.

3 In so far as wage-rates are geared to the wage earner's cost of living, a devaluation (by raising the prices of imported goods consumed by wage earners) is liable to provoke a wage–price spiral, thereby reducing the competitive advantage afforded by the devaluation.

Let us now reverse our previous assumption of a highly elastic demand for Nottinghamshire's exports. The lower the elasticity of demand for Nottinghamshire's exports, the larger the devaluation needed to achieve a given increase in the county's sterling earnings from her exports. Indeed, below a certain critical elasticity, technically known as the point of 'unit elasticity', Nottinghamshire's sterling earnings would actually fall, the increase in the volume of exports being insufficient to compensate for the reduction in their sterling prices. The outcome would be better, but only slightly so, if the demand for Nottinghamshire's exports were of more than unit elasticity, but not much more, that is if devaluation would have increased Nottinghamshire's sterling earnings but not by very much. For if (to give a hypothetical example) the conditions of export demand were such that a 10 per cent reduction in the sterling prices of Nottinghamshire's exports would cause an increase of only 12 per cent in the quantity bought, and therefore an increase of less than 1 per cent in the total sterling value of Nottinghamshire's exports,[4] the extra sterling earned by an increase in export production would represent a poor return for the extra effort involved. In other words, Nottinghamshire would obtain a mere 1 per cent increase in her sterling export earnings at the cost of a 10 per cent change in her *terms of trade* (an economy's terms of trade being the ratio of its export prices to its import prices).

Thus with an elasticity of export demand of little more than unity, a devaluation turns the terms of trade against the devaluer without significantly improving foreign currency earnings: the contribution made by devaluation to the adjustment process is then almost solely by choking off imports. If the elasticity of import demand is very high the required fall in imports can be achieved by a very small devaluation, and hence with a negligible deterioration in the terms of trade. If, however, imports are less readily choked off, a substantial devaluation will be required, so the devaluing economy then suffers not only by the imports forgone, but also by a substantial deterioration in its terms of trade.

In the even less satisfactory case where the elasticity of export demand is appreciably *below* unity, devaluation could even aggravate the external deficit, in that imports may be choked off insufficiently to offset the *fall* in foreign currency earnings.

Factors affecting the elasticity of demand for exports

Let us now abandon our imaginary independent Nottinghamshire and consider as realistically as possible the conditions which determine the elasticity of demand for an economy's exports. The elasticity of demand for our country's exports depends on (1) the elasticity of demand for imports by the various foreign countries which buy our exports; (2) the importance of the home country as an exporter, compared with rival countries exporting the same kind of goods as we do; (3) the extent to which our rivals retaliate against a cut in our export prices by cutting theirs too, for instance by following our example and devaluing their currencies.

The importance of (1) is diminished if, as regards (2), our country contributes only a small proportion of the world total of exports of each of the commodities she exports. If, for example, our country is an exporter of (let us say) coal, but in small quantities compared with the total coal exports of all countries, a small cut in our export price will probably be sufficient to enable us to undercut our rival exporters to an extent which will represent a large proportionate increase in our export tonnage. We might perhaps double our export tonnage by a (say) 5 per cent reduction in our export price, even if the coal-importing countries did not increase their tonnage imported at all. If on the other hand our country were the *only* coal exporter, we should have no rival exporters to undercut and a 5 per cent price reduction would decrease our foreign currency earnings unless there followed an increase in tonnage imported by over 5 per cent. In general, therefore, countries whose exports are small in amount and widely diversified are likely to experience a much more elastic demand for their exports than are countries whose exports are large in amount and confined to a narrow range of products.

As regards (3), even when our country would enjoy a highly elastic demand for its exports if we alone reduced our prices (measured in the importing countries' currencies), we may nevertheless effect little or no increase in our export earnings if the action we take to reduce our prices – in this case currency devaluation – is also taken by our rival exporters.

Another consideration which is relevant to the elasticity of the demand for our country's exports is the period which is allowed for the adjustment of demand to occur. For example, a 5 per cent cut in our export prices, taking effect as from (say) January, would almost certainly be less effective in increasing the volume of our exports in the following month than in increasing it in the following January, simply because it would take time for the purchasers of our goods in the importing countries to change their trading arrangements so as to take advantage of our lower prices. This delay in the reaction on the part of our customers would be longest if we specialized in the export of finished goods, particularly manufactured articles, rather than of primary commodities. The purchaser of almost any kind of manufactured article tends to be loyal to the brand, or the design, or the producing firm, with which he is already familiar, and in consequence he is not readily induced to transfer quickly his allegiance to another source of supply merely by the quotation of a lower price. For this reason the countries specializing in the export of manufactured articles (Britain, for example) are almost certainly faced with a low short-term elasticity of demand for their exports, quite possibly one of less than one-half. With such a low short-term elasticity of demand for our country's exports, combined with initial bottlenecks in supply, it is quite conceivable that devaluation might cause a short-term reduction in its foreign-currency earnings greater than the short-term reduction in its foreign-currency expenditure on imports (induced by the rise in the sterling prices of imports). In this case the short-term effect of devaluation would be not to cure an external deficit but to aggravate it. Admittedly, as we saw in Chapter 2, the argument is not supported by the course of events immediately after the British devaluation in September 1949, when British export earnings quickly increased, but this outcome can reasonably be attributed to the consequences of US rearmament and the outbreak of war in Korea. The second devaluation of sterling, from \$2.80 to \$2.40 in November 1967, was, however, followed by a worsening of the UK external deficit – the eventual improvement following only after a delay of more than a year. This phenomenon, which was watched very anxiously at the time, was given the label 'J-curve', since the course of the graph of the UK monthly trade balance was initially downwards, followed by a satisfactory, if belated, recovery.

An annex to a report dated July 1973, published by the US Committee for Economic Development,[5] leads us to suppose that the J-curve is not a uniquely British phenomenon:

The short term effects of a devaluation are likely to work in reverse to the long term expected results . . . In the mid term, exports of the devaluing country must increase by more than the devaluation before the desired impact begins to be felt. This means, for example, that sales organizations must be redirected to take advantage of their new competitive price advantages and companies must develop and produce new or modified products for foreign sale. This takes time. Only after decisions on the location of new plants to serve international markets begin to be made in light of changed cost structures, and these new plants are built and in production, will the full impact of the changes in exchange rates be felt.

5 Adjustment in practice

From an international viewpoint, one country's deficit is the reverse side of surpluses elsewhere; and in general, prolonged imbalance in either direction is undesirable.

The Balance of Payments Adjustment Process, a report by WP3[1] of the OECD, August 1966, paragraph 10

As the above quotation emphasizes, it is misleading to suppose that adjustment means simply adjustment of deficits; it means adjustment of *disequilibria* which necessarily manifest themselves in both surpluses and deficits. What the quotation condemns as undesirable is that a particular pattern of international disequilibria should freeze over a long period, with many of the same countries remaining either in deficit or in surplus, without changing places or (better still) getting into balance. If therefore we are looking for a mechanism of adjustment, we must look for processes which operate in both deficit and surplus countries to bring them both back into balance or, failing that, to reverse at intervals their respective roles. Such processes may be discretionary (that is, may require deliberate official action) or alternatively automatic, but it is clear from the Working Party No. 3 (WP3) report quoted above that in a regime of pegged rates, the latter are not very reliable, among other things because 'they may run counter to other objectives of economic policy' and hence be 'offset by countervailing action'.

Automatic adjustment

'The initial effects of these automatic mechanisms are of two sorts: a payments imbalance has an effect on incomes' (and hence triggers off an income effect) 'and also an effect on monetary liquidity in the country concerned' (and hence triggers off a monetary effect).[2] The report then goes on in paragraphs 22 to 25 to comment on these two effects as follows:

22   The direct impact of changes in imports and exports on domestic *incomes* probably plays an important part in the maintenance or restoration of balance of payments equilibrium, particularly in the case of the smaller industrialized countries, which are heavily dependent on international trade. For example, in a country which develops a payments surplus because of a rise in export demand, higher earnings from exports will set off an expansion of both consumers' demand and investment. This in time will lead to a rise in imports and a retarding effect on exports, so reducing the surplus.

23   Second, an excess or deficiency in the private sector's external receipts and payments will normally be settled by the conversion of foreign currency into domestic currency, or vice versa; and if no countervailing action is taken will lead directly to an increase or decrease in the private non-bank sector's holdings of domestic currency or other liquid assets. A balance of payments surplus or deficit (suitably defined) thus has a primary effect on domestic *liquidity*.[3] The further monetary effects which follow from this depend on how a country's monetary institutions operate. In most countries, a change in domestic liquidity arising from an external surplus or deficit will improve or impair the liquidity position of the commercial banking system. Depending on the circumstances, this may lead to a change in the cost and availability of bank credit and to a further increase or decrease in the supply of liquid assets.

24   Thus a strengthening of the current external account increases incomes and demand in the country concerned; and this impact on internal demand may be enhanced by the liquidity effects of a balance of payments surplus. The increase in demand thus generated will tend to reverse the initial movement in the current account, and the liquidity effects may tend to produce equilibrating capital movements. Furthermore, in the case of persistent tendencies towards surpluses or deficits, the impact on demand (unless offset by domestic demand management policies) is likely, in time, to cause prices in the surplus countries to rise relative to those in deficit countries; and thus produce further equilibrating movements in current balance.

25   For many countries these automatic mechanisms tending to restore external equilibrium are an important reason why surpluses and deficits have not been larger relative to total external transactions and to GNP. They do not, however, generally dispense with the need for a deliberate economic policy. Left to themselves, they might seriously interfere with internal policy objectives. Even in terms of the balance of payments objective as such, their effect may be too slow and too small, or in some cases too quick and too large. And, since their impact varies considerably from country to country, there is little reason to suppose that the burden of adjustment will be equitably shared.

Discretionary adjustment

Paragraphs 13, 14 and 15 of the report deal with discretionary adjustment thus:

13 In its discussions the Working Party has found it useful to make a broad distinction between cases where an imbalance is due to an inappropriate level of internal demand in the country concerned, to excessive or deficient competitive strength in world markets, or to excessive capital movements. This does not mean that all imbalances can be neatly classified in this way; indeed, in most cases, two or more of the above factors and perhaps others are present at the same time. Moreover, an analysis of the nature of a payments imbalance is not in itself sufficient to determine the appropriate choice of policies.

14 In some cases, nevertheless, the origin, and the cure, of a payments imbalance are comparatively straightforward. Thus, if conditions of excess demand develop, the balance of payments of the country concerned will usually deteriorate. Elimination of the conditions of excess demand may in such a case suffice to restore payments equilibrium. In this case there would be no conflict between the internal and external requirements of economic policy; correction of the level of internal demand will be desirable, both to promote external balance and to restore internal demand to a more normal level and maintain internal price stability.

15 In practice, payments imbalances are usually far more complex. Even if demand pressures are one factor, they will rarely be alone and external balance will not be restored merely by appropriate demand management. In extreme cases, there may be an external deficit despite low levels of demand, or an external surplus despite clearly excessive demand, so that a demand management policy that would restore external balance would further worsen the internal balance of the economy, or vice versa. Other measures have then to be adopted; measures to affect the external current or capital account directly; or action to adjust the country's competitive position.

Where the imbalance may be attributed to 'deficient competitive strength in world markets', it may be possible to introduce policies

to influence prices and the rise of money incomes. Improved prospects for reasonable price stability obtained through these policies or in other ways, are highly desirable, and should give greater freedom to the authorities to direct the use of other instruments towards the maintenance of internal and external equilibrium and rapid and balanced growth. Though the effects of such policies on the balance of payments will often only make themselves progressively felt over a number of years, success in this direction would clearly lead to a basic improvement in the adjustment process.

Where the imbalances may be attributed to excessive, or per-verse, capital movements, for example when countries with large export surpluses have at the same time experienced substantial net inflows of capital, the Working Party (paragraph 35) laid the blame, in part, on the 'wide disparities among countries in the degree of liberalization of international capital movements, and particularly, in the freedom of international access to national capital markets'. To this issue we shall be returning in Chapters 6 and 7; it should, however, be made clear right away that both deficit and surplus countries have in practice sought to restore external balance no less frequently by imposing new restrictions, respectively on capital outflows and capital inflows, than by dismantling existing ones.

The incentive to adjust

Throughout the 1960s the major countries, and particularly the Group of Ten, were prepared to change their pegged exchange rates only *in extremis*, as Britain did in 1967, when other adjustment mechanisms had shown themselves to be wholly inadequate or to be in unacceptable conflict with the internal aims of economic policy: likewise in the 1970s the widespread adoption of more flexible exchange-rate arrangements occurred under duress, when other adjustment mechanisms were manifestly unable to cope.

Why did these other adjustment mechanisms perform so badly that in the end there had to be recourse to exchange-rate variation? Their various shortcomings, as seen by the WP3 in its report, have been noted above, but in addition they allegedly share the weakness that many countries had little incentive to make them work – and consequently showed little enthusiasm for operating any of the available discretionary mechanisms, unless they also contributed to achieving internal objectives; nor did they have much hesitation in offsetting the effects of automatic mechanisms, unless they too were compatible with internal objectives.

Which countries have been supposed to lack adequate incentives to make the adjustment mechanism work? In the first place, it has been argued that the surplus countries were in this category, since all they suffered in circumstances of disequilibrium was an increase in their reserves, which was not in any sense a severe penalty and might well be quite acceptable. In the second place it has been argued, especially by the French,[4] that one of the countries in persistent deficit, the United States, fell into the same category,[5] since her deficits put no strain on her reserves, being financed by an increase in other countries' official dollar holdings.

Neither of these propositions, and especially the latter, can be allowed to go unchallenged. Let us first consider the United States's position. As we saw on page 56, the US deficit in the 1960s was on a modest scale, averaging $1.1 billion per annum, and the US authorities were not conspicuously less ready than those of other deficit countries to adopt measures to prevent it getting any worse. When after all it did get worse, as happened in the 1970s, the US authorities undoubtedly became very concerned to force through what seemed to them the appropriate remedial action. And last but not least: the US did not in fact finance its deficit in the 1960s without depleting its official reserves, which (as we also saw on page 56) were drawn upon to finance about half the US deficit in the period.

The other proposition, that the surplus countries lacked adequate incentives to undertake adjustment, was widely accepted among the deficit countries, especially by the USA and the UK, but some surplus countries, and in particular Germany, vehemently disowned it, arguing that given the structure of their banking systems the monetary effect of a disequilibrium was very severe, and was indeed asymmetrical in the opposite way to that supposed by the USA and UK. In the words of Dr Otmar Emminger, of the German Bundesbank,

any country taking in foreign exchange in order to keep its exchange rate stable, creates in this process additional high-powered money ('central bank money') while the country losing foreign exchange is under no real constraint to reduce its money stock correspondingly (and even less so if it happens to be a reserve currency country like the United States). In the years of the immense dollar outflows from the US, i.e. from 1970 to 1973, this monetary asymmetry was largely responsible for the huge increases in the money stock of the industrial countries outside the United States (about 73 per cent for the Group of Ten countries, including Switzerland but excluding the US).[6]

Be it said straight away that Germany and similarly placed countries consistently adopted monetary policies designed to offset the monetary effects of their surpluses, and so were clearly not prepared to allow free play to this particular bit of automatic adjustment mechanism;[7] nevertheless they could argue that their distaste for its consequences induced them to search for alternative discretionary remedies for their surpluses at least as earnestly as the deficit countries sought remedies for their deficits. In particular the Germans could instance their acceptance (albeit reluctant) of the need to re-peg the dollar value of their currency twice in the 1960s (from 23.81 cents to 25.00 cents in March 1961, and to 27.32 cents in October 1969) and to unpeg altogether from May 1971 to December 1971.

Exchange rates and adjustment

Given that without recourse to exchange-rate variations the adjustment mechanism was seen to be performing unsatisfactorily in the 1960s, why were statesmen and officials so reluctant to experiment with more flexible pegging or with floating? One answer that has been given to this question is that too many countries had little incentive to adjust, and hence showed little enthusiasm for trying out adjustment mechanisms of any kind. However, as we have seen, this argument cannot be accepted without reservations: all countries seemed to have some sort of motive for adjustment, but it was typically not very strong and hence was frequently outweighed by other, conflicting, policy objectives.

More to the point is the argument that the one-at-a-time procedure for adjusting parities under the Bretton Woods system was a deterrent to adjustment in that any one country was reluctant to take the initiative of repegging its currency, since it could never be sure how much the burden of adjustment might be shared by other countries changing their pegs soon afterwards. (This procedural weakness was remedied in December 1971, when at the Smithsonian conference a multilateral renegotiation of parities[8] was successfully achieved.) The extreme case of this procedural weakness was the seeming inability of the United States to take any initiative at all. The $n-1$ par rates in the system were settled by the $n-1$ countries which pegged on the dollar: this left no scope for US initiative except for a change in the dollar price of gold, which it was widely believed, prior to the reformed procedure adopted at the Smithsonian conference, would not lead other countries to change their pegged rates on the dollar.[9]

In addition to this procedural obstacle to changing pegged rates there is a political obstacle attributed by Dr Conrad J. Oort to 'the political asymmetry between positive action and non-action':

Why are countries reluctant to change their parities promptly? It is my conviction that this is basically due to the political asymmetry between positive action and non-action on parities. Governments are rarely criticized for not changing the par value, and when they are, it is easy to silence such criticism by appealing to the national interest that forbids open debate on such sensitive issues. A change of the par value, on the other hand, is a conscious, overt policy action that is unavoidably accompanied by all the trappings of a major public decision: comments in the press, complaints from groups that are injured, windfall profits and losses by 'speculators' and traders, book gains or losses for the Central Bank or the Treasury, parliamentary debates, international repercussions, etc., etc. Behind all this commotion are the very real facts that a parity change does hurt certain sectoral interests, particularly in the case of revaluation, and that a devaluation adds to cost-push inflation at home . . . Left to themselves, governments will continue to take delayed, discontinuous action on parities.[10]

A more specifically *economic* reason for the unpopularity of exchange-rate changes lies in the long time interval we have noted between administering the medicine and the recovery of the patient – a time interval which may include an initial period in which (due to the J-curve phenomenon) the patient's condition deteriorates even further, before it begins to improve. As the US Council of Economic Advisers put it:

. . . the response to any devaluation is generally delayed. First, it takes some time before a devaluation is reflected in the relative prices obtained by exporters and paid by importers. In the short run, to protect their market shares, foreign exporters frequently do not increase their list price in the US market by the full amount of devaluation. Conversely, foreign importers frequently do not reduce their list price of US goods in the foreign market by the full amount of the devaluation.

Second, when the change in relative prices does occur, its initial impact is likely to be perverse . . . before the volume of exports and imports responds to the changes in relative prices. In time, the effect of devaluation on real trade flows is expected to outweigh the change in prices. It is because of this sequence of events that one expects the trade balance of a devaluing country to improve in real or volume terms before it improves in value terms, which is what happened in 1972.[11]

An equally important consideration in accounting for the reluctance of statesmen and officials to permit changes in exchange rates was the belief that completely invariable pegged rates were the only effective device for preventing speculative short-term capital flows. In a regime of pegged rates, as prescribed by the Bretton Woods charter, any change in parities leads to the expectation that further changes can occur in the future, and since there is never much doubt

about the *direction* of a possible parity change, speculation is virtually risk-free. Hence the official dealers in the central banks of the
major powers always feared the speculative consequences of any
change in parities. They also feared that the abandonment of the
pegged-rate system in favour of floating rates would likewise provoke disastrous speculative capital movements:[12] 'corrections of
temporary balance of payments disequilibria by exchange-rate
appreciations or depreciations invite and stimulate speculation
which could easily amplify the initial rate disturbance'.[13]

International co-operation

As has been noted, the Smithsonian conference of December
1971 tried out for the first time a multilateral renegotiation of
exchange rates, thereby successfully achieving a realignment of
currency values which had not been possible with the previous
one-at-a-time procedure. Would not all official action to promote
adjustment, by whatever means, be more successfully accomplished
if co-ordinated in an appropriate international forum? The WP3
report thought it would: 'Most countries have aims regarding the
composition of their external balance, i.e. as to the size of their
surplus or deficit on current and capital account respectively':[14] if
these aims of the separate countries could be reconciled, so that *ex
ante* surpluses matched *ex ante* deficits, the countries concerned
could then proceed to discuss what action each should take to
achieve the common objective. Something of this sort was indeed
attempted at the Smithsonian conference, but not on any earlier
occasion. What accounts for the delay? Mainly it was that the WP3
report appeared at an unfortunate time, August 1966. The UK was
then at the very edge of the devaluation precipice: it was indeed
forced into devaluation in November 1967. In these circumstances
the UK was in no mood to co-operate in the proposed procedure.
To table a dispassionately realistic balance of payments projection,
which would probably have been leaked to the press, would have
precipitated an immediate devaluation, which the British government wanted at all costs to avoid.

Devaluation in November 1967 removed this particular obstacle
to the procedure proposed in the WP3 report, but similar situations
in relation to other major currencies occurred in such frequent
succession that no suitable occasion ever presented itself prior to
the meetings which led to the Smithsonian agreement of December

1971 (see page 154). Nor has the procedure ever been given a second trial. The enthusiasts for the Grand Design of 1972–3 (below, Chapter 16) would undoubtedly have wished to institutionalize the co-ordinating procedure commended in the WP3 report had their Design not been side-tracked by the pressure of circumstances in the course of 1973 and the associated recourse (page 164) to floating exchange rates. What happened instead, once floating came to be accepted as a viable regime, was a swing of opinion, and especially of American opinion, towards *laissez-faire* and away from any form of co-ordination based on statistical projections of no matter what kind: co-ordination was, on this view, best left to the mechanism of the free market. To this controversial issue we return in Chapter 20.

Post-1973 controversies

There was indeed, as we shall see in Chapters 20 to 22, a great deal of controversy as to how adjustment was to operate, once pegging had given way to floating. The extreme *laissez-faire* school of thought maintained that if only exchange rates were allowed to float cleanly, without any official transactions in the market, the adjustment problem would simply disappear. To this it was objected that clean floating would lead to unacceptable fluctuations in exchange rates, so official market transactions would be as necessary under floating as under pegging; that changes in exchange rates still presented political difficulties, in the 1970s no less than in the 1960s; and that such changes were still liable to provoke destabilizing capital flows. Moreover the efficacy of flexible exchange rates in restoring equilibrium came increasingly to be called into question, not only because of the J-curve effect but also because (with national economies becoming ever more closely integrated one with another) changes in costs arising from exchange rate movements appeared to feed through into an economy more and more quickly and completely: hence exchange rate adjustment was becoming progressively less efficacious as a means of changing international competitiveness (see page 201).

6 Adjustment: long-term capital

The high level of long-term capital outflows from the United States that developed under the Bretton Woods system was to a large extent attributable to the long-maintained disequilibrium in exchange rates which prevailed under that system.

John H. Makin[1]

The exchange rate

Although the exchange rate affects a country's surplus or deficit by affecting the balance between its imports and exports of goods and services, the United States' deficit in the 1960s may to some extent also be attributed to the effect on long-term investment of the overvaluation of the dollar. John H. Makin argued this in an essay (published in 1974) from which the above quotation is taken. Without attempting here to summarize his argument, one may say that it applies mainly to direct investment abroad by US companies (that is, the setting up or buying up of branches or subsidiaries abroad) and to direct investment by foreign companies in the US. In the former case, it is reasonable to suppose that US companies would attempt to preserve their markets, despite their relatively high costs of production in the US, by investing in manufacturing facilities abroad. In the latter case it is reasonable to suppose that foreign companies may have been deterred from setting up production facilities in the US until the dollar devaluations of 1971–3. As was noted in 1973:

To the extent that the recent dollar devaluations have rendered US products more competitive, both in export markets and in relation to imports, it should become more attractive for foreigners to establish manufacturing and other operations in the United States. This will be particularly true in cases where US operations constitute an alternative to direct exports from abroad.[2]

By all accounts the allegedly harmful effects on direct investment of the overvaluation of the dollar were being strongly urged on the US President from 1968 onwards.

Apart from direct investment, the other main kind of long-term international investment, portfolio investment (that is, purchases of securities for income and capital gain, but not to obtain management control), seems much less likely to be sensitive to the level of the exchange rate, though the *expectation* of a fall in the exchange rate, with its implication of a capital gain, would act as a stimulus to outward portfolio investment, as indeed to all kinds of foreign investment.

Taxation and exchange control

Apart from the exchange rate, the main instruments of economic policy which have been used to influence long-term capital flows have been tax provisions and exchange control (or other regulations having equivalent effect). Interest-rate policy might possibly be added to this list, but in practice the main use of the interest-rate instrument has been to influence *short-term* capital flows, by the manipulation of short-term interest rates.

The tax provisions mainly relevant to long-term capital flows are on the one hand the nature of the tax rebates enjoyed by resident recipients of overseas profits, interest or dividends which have already been taxed by a foreign government, and on the other hand the incidence of withholding and other taxes levied on profits, interest and dividends paid from the home country to overseas recipients. Most countries accept the desirability of avoiding double taxation of the same income, and have concluded international double taxation agreements to that end, but the precise definition of double taxation in this context still leaves room for manoeuvre to a finance minister who wants to discourage capital outflows and encourage inflows (as Mr Callaghan did in 1965) or to do the opposite.

As regards exchange controls on long-term capital flows, Article VIII of the Bretton Woods charter, under which most developed countries have been operating since February 1961 (see page 97), is intended to prevent recourse (save by special exemption) only to restrictions on *current* account. According to the IMF:

Members of the Fund are specifically authorized to exercise such controls as are necessary to regulate international capital movements, provided these do not unduly delay or otherwise restrict payments for current transactions; in addition, the Articles limit the ability of members to use the Fund's resources to meet a large or sustained outflow of capital, and the Fund may request a member to exercise controls on capital movements to prevent such use of the Fund's resources.

In practice, the intended distinction in the treatment of payments for current transactions and for capital transactions has been only partially observed. This has reflected a recognition that international capital flows of a number of kinds have an important positive role to play in the development of the world's productive resources. Perhaps equally important, the form in which major countries have established convertibility of their currencies – through the mechanism of exchange markets – has not been susceptible to a close distinction between current and capital transactions in exchange regulations. In a number of these countries, to be sure, such a distinction has been made in exchange regulations applying to domestic residents. In some countries, access to foreign exchange on the official market has been reserved for payments in connection with current transactions; as a result, parallel markets have usually emerged in foreign exchange available to domestic residents for foreign investment. In some other cases, access to the official foreign exchange market has not been available for settlements of capital transactions (and certain current transactions) by non-residents as well as residents, resulting in a separate exchange rate for capital transactions. But in general, the countries that have attained formal convertibility have taken the view that the increasing integration between the major economies imposes practical limits on the extent to which restrictions can be placed on capital flows without risking restriction or distortion of trade and other current payments.

Admitted, controls on certain capital flows (principally outflows of domestic funds) have not only been retained in a number of countries, but in some countries have been newly imposed, or reimposed. For the most part, however, such newly imposed controls have been intended as temporary in duration . . .[3]

and have been predominantly on short-term capital flows, which we shall be turning to in the next chapter.

The British exchange control

The UK, beset by balance of payments difficulties throughout much of the post-war period, provided up to 1979 an extreme example of recourse to exchange control on long-term capital flows. As regards investment by foreigners in the UK, this was little impeded by controls: the only problem was to decide how severely to control the repatriation of existing investments. Up to April 1967 foreign holders of sterling securities were allowed to sell them only on condition that the sterling proceeds went into a 'security sterling' account from which payments could be made only for the purpose of buying other sterling securities (other than short-term ones) to be held by the same, or some other, foreigner. Hence there was a market for security sterling, in which the rate of exchange usually stood at a discount in relation to the rate on convertible sterling. However, as from April 1967 the proceeds of foreigners' sales of sterling securities were given the status of convertible sterling, and security sterling disappeared from the scene.

As regards investment by UK residents in foreign countries, the UK control was until its abolition in 1979 continuously restrictive, so much so that both portfolio investment and direct investment were financed almost exclusively by foreign currency borrowing.[4] However, UK residents could deal among themselves in foreign currency securities, which were traded on the London stock exchange at a premium in relation to their price on their domestic exchanges (for example on Wall Street). This premium, called the security dollar premium, was settled competitively by the London jobbers at a level which roughly equated their purchases from, and sales to, UK residents, of foreign-currency securities as a whole.

The dissolution of the sterling area

A notable feature of the UK exchange control was the meaning it attached to 'resident' and 'foreign'. Up to the time that sterling was floated in June 1972, the aim of official regulations was broadly to erect a ring fence around the sterling area as a whole, within which the UK control permitted freedom of capital movement. Thus, up to that date, 'resident' meant resident anywhere in the sterling area and 'foreign' meant resident outside the sterling area. In June 1972, however, the ring fence was drastically contracted, and 'resident' henceforth meant resident in the UK or the Irish Republic (or, as from January 1973, in Gibraltar), and the exchange control status previously reserved for foreigners resident outside the sterling area was extended to apply to residents outside the British Isles.

This step, though announced as a temporary one, was never reversed, and in retrospect must be regarded as marking the beginning of the dissolution of the sterling area. For its effect, in combination with the floating of sterling, was to provoke most overseas sterling area countries to abandon their practice of pegging their currencies on the pound, and to diversify their reserves out of sterling into other currencies, especially the US dollar (see below, page 123).

Other restrictions on capital outflows

Apart from exchange controls as such, there is a variety of possible restrictions having roughly equivalent effect on long-term capital outflows. In the period 1964–73 the US had recourse to such devices, including a tax on foreign issues on the US stock exchanges and a number of formal and informal restraints on the method of financing US direct investment in many foreign countries. These various devices will be explained in Chapter 9.

7 Adjustment: short-term capital

Volatile short-term capital movements brought about serious difficulties in the world economy over the last fifteen years. Such capital flows were the immediate cause of the end of the Bretton Woods system and of the excessive swings in major exchange rates since. The original Bretton Woods concept foresaw a problem in this area and solved it on paper by not providing for freedom of capital movements, and in fact assuming that short-term capital movements would be strictly controlled. Reality turned out to be different: controls on outward capital movements in the major countries were essentially removed, and the rapid growth of the industrial countries together with the internationalization of financial markets set the stage for huge flows of funds across national borders. As confidence in major currencies waxed and waned, speculative movements, including leads and lags, gathered force.

Alfred Hayes,
lecture in August 1975[1]

In the course of the 1960s, and even more in the 1970s, international short-term capital movements have emerged as a major problem. In the IMF's view:

The rapid growth in the size of international markets in short-term funds in the late 1960s, mainly in the form of 'Euro' markets in bank deposits denominated in foreign currency, induced a number of major countries to impose or extend regulatory measures. . . . [However] comprehensive and effectively restrictive controls on international capital movements were widely considered neither feasible nor, at least in their entirety, desirable. . . . At the same time, partly in association with the increasing integration of the world economy, the actual and potential movements have become very large – far larger than expected in 1958 on the eve of the general move by European countries to external convertibility. As a result . . . international capital movements have played a larger role in exchange markets and in the working of the international monetary system than was originally envisaged. The emergence of large and effectively integrated capital markets in conditions of currency convertibility has created a huge and progressively increasing pool of liquid funds which may be switched between currencies for precautionary or speculative reasons at times of particular uncertainty. This has contributed to the strains to which the system has been subjected.[2]

The 'speculation' referred to in this passage has, in the context of the 1960s and 1970s, to be interpreted increasingly in terms of the operations of international trading companies and banks, especially of large multinational ones, rather than as private speculation, whose effects have by comparison come to be only marginal.[3] The short-term switching between one currency and another by bankers and corporate treasurers may be 'speculative' only in the technical sense of placing surplus funds so as to increase the chance of capital gain and reduce that of capital loss: however, in the 1970s such operators became increasingly prepared to take uncovered positions or make use of borrowed funds. Moreover, in the case of companies engaged in international trade, speculation may take the form not of a redeployment of liquid funds but simply of a variation in the leads and lags in ordinary commercial payments. For example, a British importer can speculate against sterling by paying his foreign suppliers more promptly, a British exporter by giving his customers extended credit, and such practices are virtually immune to restraint by exchange control. A very substantial component in short-term capital flows comprises variations in leads and lags.

Short-term capital outflows and inflows, predominantly speculative in one way or another, have both presented problems. Outflows have threatened the exhaustion of countries' reserves: the UK is an example of a country which has frequently had anxiety on this account. Inflows have also been unwelcome, most commonly for their expansionary effect on the domestic banking system, by increasing at the same time the liquid assets and the deposit liabilities of the commercial banks. Until 1977 the UK was not often worried by short-term capital inflows, partly because her reserves were frequently so exiguous that additions to them were welcome, partly because the UK authorities have better techniques than most other countries for insulating her banking system and security markets from external capital movements.[4] Yet the flight from the dollar in the last quarter of 1971 reached such proportions that even Britain had to take steps to ward off the capital inflow; and later on, as from 1977, an inconveniently persistent capital inflow developed as overseas investors took into account the vast potential of the North Sea oil fields. Britain's troubles in this regard were broadly similar to those experienced, in the early 1970s and on subsequent occasions, by many countries of continental Europe and by Japan.

Interest rates and capital flows

Short-term capital movements are motivated both by interest-rate differentials between short-term debts denominated in different currencies and by the expectation of capital gains or losses arising from prospective changes in exchange rates. Interest differentials have tended to become more serious in the course of the post-war period, because the monetary policies of different countries have come to be pursued more vigorously, without necessarily being in phase. As Alfred Hayes put it:

with the increasing reliance on monetary policies in one major country after another, interest-rate differentials between the main financial centres periodically widened and set off flows of interest-sensitive funds. Such flows in turn often triggered speculative flows. . . .

Interest-sensitive movements of funds, for their part, can be minimized by closer coordination of monetary policies among the major countries. . . . It seems to me, however, that it will not be easy to advance such coordination much beyond adjustments in the *timing* of policy moves.[5]

The forward market

If a country, say the UK, wants to attract an inflow of short-term capital, or to prevent an outflow, it may be reluctant for reasons of internal monetary policy to jack up sterling interest rates high enough to compensate for the risk of a possible future depreciation of the pound. Indeed if sterling is thought to involve a serious exchange risk, many capital owners will refuse to hold sterling at *any* practicable interest rate unless they can enter into a forward contract which assures them the right to dispose of their sterling at a known exchange rate at a future specified date (say a month, three months or a year hence).

Hence to keep a short-term investor loyal to sterling it may not be sufficient to rely on interest-rate policy alone. It may also be necessary to provide him with an opportunity to sell sterling forward at a price which is not too low to offset the advantageous sterling interest rate. By way of illustration, suppose that an investor can get 10 per cent per annum interest on a three-month sterling asset and 6 per cent per annum on an equivalent dollar asset, so that covered sterling investment is attractive only provided that the discount on three-month forward sterling, as compared with the spot rate, is less than 1 per cent for the three months: then if in the absence of official support the forward rate would be at a greater discount, a possible way to make sterling investment attractive is for the central bank to deal in the forward market to bid up three-month forward sterling to a discount of somewhat less than 1 per cent. We know that the Bank of England did indeed follow such a policy during the prolonged sterling crisis which began in the last quarter of 1964. Thereafter, until the devaluation of sterling on 18 November 1967, the Bank intervened so as to prevent the forward rate falling to a serious discount, and the intervention was eventually on a massive scale. Unfortunately a policy originally adopted mainly with the object of retaining a loyal clientele of foreign investors ended up, in the weeks immediately preceding devaluation, by affording almost unlimited opportunities for bear speculation, with the Bank not daring to withdraw its support in the forward market lest this be taken to imply that the British authorities had taken the decision to devalue. So when devaluation was finally forced on the authorities, and the spot rate re-pegged at $2.40, instead of $2.80, they found themselves committed by outstanding forward contracts to the purchase of large amounts of sterling at a price near to the old parity of $2.80 per pound. After devaluation the Bank apparently reverted to its earlier policy of severely limiting its intervention in the forward market.[6]

Other countries, including the United States, have also on occasions in the post-war period intervened in the forward exchange market with the object of reducing the forward discount on their currencies, and of thereby retaining internationally mobile capital which might otherwise have moved to other centres.

Yet other countries, for example Germany and Italy, have on occasions intervened in the forward market in the opposite sense, that is, to prevent a forward premium on their national currencies in relation to the dollar. The motives for such interventions have been various, but usually have been related to the objective of limiting the effect of capital inflows on the domestic banking system.[7]

Exchange-rate regimes

Unless exchange rates can be pegged and unless it is also credible (which is rarely the case) that the pegs will be kept unchanged, there is always an incentive to undertake 'speculation' in the technical sense of the word: that is, to seek to make a capital gain or avoid a capital loss. *Adjustable* pegs are for obvious reasons the speculator's paradise: he can confidently guess which way a peg will be changed, if it is changed at all, so it is almost impossible for him to make appreciable losses, and may be possible to make large capital gains. He is therefore most unlikely to be dissuaded from speculating by any practicable official manipulation of interest rates. He may, as we shall see, be somewhat hampered by exchange controls on short-term capital movements, but such controls are always very far from watertight in practice and seem wholly incapable of preventing variations in leads and lags.

Hence in due course a number of major powers, having failed to achieve invariable pegs, and having found speculation intolerable with adjustable pegs, opted to unpeg and float, which they did in 1972–3, as we shall see in Chapter 15. As Dr Emminger of the Bundesbank put it in 1976:

It has become obvious that capital movements, originating from a variety of causes, are one of the determining factors for the relation between the dollar and the main European currencies.

In a world where there are hundreds of billions of liquid dollar funds (including those in the United States), which can be converted at short notice into other currencies (and vice versa), it is difficult for these other currencies to protect themselves from such disturbances to their stability, except by recourse to more flexible exchange rates.[8]

Alas, the protection which (according to Dr Emminger) more flexible exchange rates afforded against volatile capital movements was at best only relative: such capital movements remained a major cause for official concern after the transition to floating in 1973 and differences of view as to how best to deal with them underlie controversies about the appropriate role of official market transactions in a floating-rate regime. To this we shall return in Chapter 20.

Controls on inflows

In the period since the widespread move to convertibility in December 1958, although this has witnessed the dismantling of exchange controls on current transactions, almost every major industrial country has felt it necessary to impose at some time or other exchange controls on capital movements, in most cases on short-term rather than long-term capital.

In a paper by Rodney H. Mills Jr, dated October 1972[9] and covering developments since the late 1950s in Belgium, France, Germany, Italy, Japan, the Netherlands, Sweden, Switzerland and the United Kingdom, the author tells us:

The new regulations instituted to prevent or moderate short-term net *inflows* (a category that encompasses measures to encourage outflows as well) by and large have been imposed on banks rather than nonbanks. Capital movements that take place through operations of banks are less complex than those occurring at the direct instigation of corporations and other nonbanks, and they involve a far smaller number of individual participants. Consequently, it is easier in the case of banks to design regulations that are relatively simple and that can be put in place quickly, while at the same time being readily enforceable and fairly equitable to all those directly involved. It appears that the regulations on banks have been quite effective in achieving their purpose. But they have not, of course, eliminated speculative capital inflows. For one thing, regulations on banks do nothing about speculative flows outside the banking system, such as shifts in leads and lags in payments for trade and services. Moreover, monetary authorities have not wanted to keep banks under permanent tight control, and so have generally taken action on speculative inflows only after these have already been set in motion.

Mr Mills continues:

Measures to limit inflows were adopted on an increasingly widespread scale in the period from 1958 to mid 1966. That period was, generally speaking, one of strong economic expansion in the industrial countries as a whole, and most of the time monetary authorities were concerned about actual or potential inflation. To reinforce policies of monetary restraint, Germany, Italy, France, Switzerland, the Netherlands, Sweden and Japan instituted new regulations on banks, and the Netherlands and Sweden also used exchange controls on nonbanks, to limit net capital inflows or to encourage funds to flow out. . . .

After mid 1966 the temporary abatement of inflationary pressures in Europe led to the abolition or deactivation of many of these regulations [as did afterwards] the very restrictive monetary policy in the United States that pulled funds from Europe, *via* the Eurodollar market, in 1968–9. However, Germany retained or revived (sometimes with modifications) all the regulations employed earlier, partly to discourage speculative inflows generated by expectations of the revaluation of the mark that eventually materialized in the autumn of 1969. . . .

There was a spate of new measures to limit short-term capital inflows in the early 1970s, in an attempt to check the speculative flight out of the dollar into other currencies, and the same phenomenon obtained when the dollar weakened again in 1977–8. We shall return to this in Part Four.

Controls on outflows

With regard to techniques to limit short-term net capital *outflows*, some measures of this kind have been placed on banks. All of these regulations have dealt either with limits on banks' net foreign assets (used in five countries) or limits on banks' net foreign-currency position . . . The United Kingdom, France (since 1968), Italy and Sweden have used exchange controls on nonbanks to limit short-term outflows for balance of payments reasons.[10]

In addition to the European cases covered in Mr Mills's survey, the US authorities imposed in the 1960s regulations (repealed in January 1974) on short-term lending abroad, as will be described in Chapter 9.

Mr Mills summarizes the history of controls on short-term capital outflows thus:

New regulations since the 1950s to prevent short-term capital outflows, or intensifications of existing controls on outflows, have made their appearance in three situations. First, the events of May–June 1968 in France led to extraordinarily large wage increases, seriously impaired France's international competitiveness, and caused the reimposition of exchange controls on all outflows of resident nonbank funds as well as new regulations affecting French banks. . . . The second situation was in 1969 when US banks were borrowing heavily in the Eurodollar market [see below, Chapter 14] and European banks and nonbanks stepped up their lending in that market to meet part of the increased demand. At various times in 1969 Italy, Belgium, the Netherlands and Sweden moved to prevent further net lending abroad by their commercial banks, or to force a reflow of funds, in order to protect their official reserves. In the Italian case, an additional objective was to prevent net foreign lending by banks from tightening domestic monetary conditions.[11]

Finally, it must be added that throughout the post-war period until the abolition of the British exchange control in 1979, the UK imposed regulations to prevent outflows of short-term funds owned by residents (with the exception, prior to June 1972, of outflows to the rest of the sterling area).

Part Three

Bretton Woods convertibility, December 1958–August 1971

8 The Bretton Woods charter

The Articles of Agreement which established the International Monetary Fund ... permitted changes in a country's parity when its balance of payments was in fundamental disequilibrium. In practice the parities were changed only infrequently, generally after a prolonged period of disequilibrium in external payments. There was also a widespread belief that, because of the importance of the United States in world trade and the central role of the dollar in the international monetary system, the United States could not change its exchange rate. In any case, since most countries were pegging their rates to the dollar in the foreign exchange market, the United States could not be certain that a change in the price of gold would actually result in a change in the value of the dollar in terms of foreign currencies.

Report of the US Council of Economic Advisers, January 1973[1]

The Bretton Woods charter is the name popularly applied to the original IMF Articles of Agreement,[2] negotiated at Bretton Woods in July 1944, along with those of the Fund's sister institution, the International Bank for Reconstruction and Development. The Fund agreement had already been foreshadowed by the publication in 1943 of the British Keynes plan[3] and the American White plan.[4] In the event its provisions followed much more closely the latter plan, but the Keynes plan made certain proposals, concerning the provision of additional liquidity, which went much beyond the provisions of the 1944 agreement and which in many ways foreshadowed the first amendment, adopted in 1969, providing for the Special Drawing Rights scheme (see Chapter 12).

The second amendment to the Fund's Articles, drafted at the Jamaica conference of January 1976 (below, page 186) and operative as from 1 April 1978, made such substantial changes that we should not refer to the present Fund Articles as the 'Bretton Woods charter'; instead we shall in this book refer to them as the 'Jamaica charter', whose provisions will be considered in Chapter 18. The

Fund commenced operations in March 1947, a few months later than the IBRD. The membership by end-1987 was 151. The main non-members are Switzerland and all the communist countries except China, Hungary, Poland, Romania, Vietnam and Yugoslavia.

The Fund is required by its charter to appear in two roles. First, it has to provide its members with a code of international behaviour, and to ensure, so far as possible, that it is respected. The two subjects with which this code is mainly concerned are international payments restrictions and exchange rates. The second role allotted to the Fund by its charter is that of an international financial institution for the provision of additional liquidity to its members, for use in official transactions in the foreign exchange market. This financial role of the Fund was until 1969 solely the concern of the General Account, as provided for in the original charter.[5] Later, in 1969, there was added the Special Drawing Account as provided for by additional Articles in the first amendment to the charter. In addition to playing the roles specifically assigned to it by its charter, the Fund has also developed as a forum for consultation between members and a source of counsel and technical assistance to the developing countries.

The Fund is run by a Board of Governors, on which all member countries are represented, a much smaller Executive Board, and an international staff. Since 1974, there has been yet another organ of the Fund, the Interim Committee, but we shall defer reference to this until later. The Board of Governors, which in practice meets only once a year, in a joint annual meeting of the Fund and Bank, is the supreme authority in the Fund, but with the exception of several reserved subjects, for example the admission of members, quota increases and amendments to the Articles, it has delegated most of its power to the Executive Board. The Executive Board, whose membership was originally twelve but has now risen to twenty-two, consists of six appointed directors appointed by France, Germany, Japan, the UK, the USA and Saudi Arabia; and sixteen elected directors each elected by a constituency comprising a group of countries. The managing director, who is appointed by the executive directors, is chairman of the Executive Board and chief of the Fund staff.

An important feature of the Fund is that it has to be staffed for the efficient transaction of large and complex financial deals, as well as for reporting on the performance of member countries in the observance of the various rules laid down in the Articles of Agreement and for drafting memoranda on general policy. Another feature which distinguishes the Fund from most other international organizations is the system of weighted voting. The voting strength wielded by each governor or executive director is based primarily on the quotas of the country or countries which appointed or elected him, the quotas of the member countries corresponding roughly to their respective economic importance.

The procedures laid down in the Fund's Articles for making decisions provide for a large number of actions to be taken by a member country on its own initiative without the requirement of a decision by the Fund. Moreover, on two issues the Fund's decision is made to depend, among other things, on the view of the individual member – the fixing of individual currency parities and of quotas requiring the approval of (and in some cases a proposal from) the members concerned. Otherwise, decisions are to be taken by voting and, except on certain reserved subjects, voting is by majority of votes cast. The most important of these reserved subjects, where more than a simple majority is required, are as follows:

1 Special provisions, invoked for the first time in 1969, govern the procedure for the amendment of the Fund's Articles.
2 Quota changes, which need to be supported by 80 per cent of the voting power (amended to 85 per cent in 1969) as well as the approval of the member.

'Tranche' drawings under the IMF General Account

The IMF's General Account, unlike the Special Drawing Account established in 1969 by the first amendment, had its origins in the Bretton Woods charter, which provided that each member country shall have a *quota*, and must make a subscription to the Fund, normally 25 per cent in gold and 75 per cent in its national currency, equal in value to its quota. (The Jamaica charter replaced the gold subscription by an SDR subscription.) The total of all quotas was initially about $9 billion, but subsequent increases in quotas and the accession of new members had by the end of the 1960s brought the total to about $21 billion and by the end of 1975, on the eve of the Jamaica conference, to about $34 billion.

These resources enable the Fund to honour the 'tranche' drawing rights which its members enjoy. In the words of the IMF's publication *Survey* of 5 January 1976:

When a member draws on the Fund, it purchases the currencies of other member countries with its own currency; thus, a drawing results in an increase in the Fund's holdings of the member's currency and a decrease in the holdings of the currencies that are purchased. Starting from a position where Fund holdings of a member's currency are equivalent to 75 per cent of the member's quota (as is usual when the member has subscribed 75 per cent of its quota in its own currency and 25 per cent in gold), the member is said to have utilized the gold tranche[6] if Fund holdings of the member's currency rise to 100 per cent of quota as a result of purchases.[7] Each succeeding tranche is a credit tranche and is equal to 25 per cent of quota; normally, under tranche policies, a member may draw four credit tranches – that is, it may draw until Fund holdings of the member's currency are at 200 per cent of quota.

For any drawing, a member is required to represent to the Fund that the desired purchase of the currency of another member (or members) is needed for making payments in that currency (or currencies) that are consistent with the provisions of the Articles of Agreement. Since July 1969 when the Articles of Agreement were amended, gold tranche drawing by a member has been legally automatic because the Fund cannot challenge the representation of a member requesting a gold tranche purchase.

All requests for the use of the Fund's resources other than use of the gold tranche are examined by the Fund to determine whether the proposed use would be consistent with the provisions of the Articles and with Fund policies. Under the policies on the use of the Fund's resources in the credit tranches, such use must be in support of the member's economic measures designed to overcome its balance of payments difficulties. Members discuss their program with the Fund staff prior to its submission to the Fund, describing their fiscal, monetary, exchange rate, trade, and payments policies for at least the following year. The criteria used by the Fund in determining whether assistance should then be given are more liberal when the request is in the first credit tranche (Fund holdings of a member's currency rising above 100 per cent but not above 125 per cent of the member's quota) than when it is in the higher credit tranches (i.e. when the Fund's holding resulting from the drawings would increase to a level of between 125 and 200 per cent of quota).

In the case of a first credit tranche request, the member's program is expected to show that it is making reasonable efforts to overcome its difficulties. In practice, this standard has often meant that, where differences of judgement might arise, the member is given the benefit of the doubt. . . . Requests for purchases in the higher credit tranches require substantial justification. . . . The program presented in connection with a request for assistance in an upper tranche is usually comprehensive and in a quantified form. . . . The policies described in a program depend, of course, on the factors causing the balance of payments difficulties and their expected duration, as well as on institutional circumstances in the economy.

Under the Bretton Woods charter, a member country's indebtedness to the Fund (i.e., its obligation to repurchase) began when the Fund holding of its currency exceeded 75 per cent of the member's quota.[8] (Under the Jamaica charter the percentage has been increased to 100.) A member country is expected normally to repay its indebtedness as its balance of payments and reserve position improve; and in any case the Fund usually requires repayment within three to five years, though a decision in 1974 may permit a rather longer term.

The provisions for 'tranche' drawings under the General Account, which date back to the original Bretton Woods charter, have subsequently been supplemented by other (and in some cases rather more liberal) provisions. These are described in Appendix A, page 245.

The choice of national currencies which a member may draw rests with the Fund, which observes rules laid down in the Articles or introduced subsequently by the decision of the Executive Board. The choice of currencies for repayment also rests with the Fund, again subject to various rules, one of which is that it will not accept in repayment any currencies of which its stock is already more than a prescribed percentage of the quota of the country whose currency it is (75 per cent under the Bretton Woods charter, increased to 100 per cent, and rather more in certain circumstances, under the Jamaica charter). The effect of these rules was that until about 1962 almost all drawings and repayments were in US dollars. Thereafter, as explained in Chapter 10, a much wider choice of currencies was used in Fund transactions.

Restrictions on payments and trade

The ground rules operative since the early 1960s for recourse to official restrictions on international payments and trade are those in the IMF Articles of Agreement (in respect of payments) and in the General Agreement on Tariffs and Trade (in respect of trade). These two charters negotiated in the 1940s commit the signatories (which by the end of the 1950s embraced most of the non-communist world) to guidelines which may be summarized as follows:

Tariffs are to be reduced and bound by a process of multilateral bargaining, organized by GATT in a series of 'rounds'.

Quantitative trade restrictions (QRs) and exchange controls on current account transactions are condemned outright, subject, however, to a loophole in case of balance of payments difficulties.

Exchange controls on capital account transactions are *not* subject to such a condemnation (above, pages 77–8).

All restrictions are to be non-discriminatory, though in the case of tariffs with loopholes for such arrangements as the EEC and EFTA, for agricultural products, and for developing countries. (In addition there is the IMF 'scarce currency clause', to which we return on page 97.)

These guidelines conform to the prescription of certain kinds of remedies, outlined below, for problems which beset member countries.

Protection

Uncompetitive industries may continue to be afforded protection by non-discriminatory tariffs, but such protection should if possible be progressively dismantled by multilateral bargaining.

Excessive or inadequate demand

It would seem to be implied that governments should seek to influence the demand for goods and services in the domestic market by monetary and fiscal policy; at all events they are not supposed to pursue this objective by imposing restrictions on trade or payments, nor by manipulating the value of their national currency in the foreign exchange market (see page 100). In particular, restrictions on trade and payments are *not* to be used to combat unemployment arising from a general deficiency of effective demand. Such action, which could relieve unemployment in one country only at the cost of aggravating it elsewhere, is an inadmissible beggar-my-neighbour remedy.

Balance of payments difficulties

A deficit country faced with difficulties in financing its deficit may unilaterally impose exchange controls on external capital transactions. It may not, however, under the IMF charter impose restrictions on current payments, nor under the GATT charter on the import of goods and services, unless the Executive Board of the IMF confirms that the balance of payments difficulties are genuine. If the IMF's confirmation is obtained then exchange controls on current payments or quantitative restrictions on imports may be used.

The above IMF and GATT rules appropriate to a country in balance of payments difficulties were in the immediate post-war years honoured more in the breach than in the observance, since restrictions already in force at the time of joining these organizations might under the 'transitional provisions' of Article XIV of the IMF charter, and corresponding provisions in the GATT, be maintained and adapted to changing circumstances. However, the United States and Canada never made use of Article XIV, and the other major powers, in particular the members of the Organization for European Economic Co-operation (established in 1948 by the recipients of Marshall Aid), progressed steadily in the course of the 1950s towards the liberalization of their trade and payments. The crucial milestone along this road was the concerted move to convertibility in December 1958. Then in February 1961 ten countries which had hitherto availed themselves of Article XIV (Belgium, France, Germany, Eire, Italy, Luxembourg, Holland, Peru, Sweden and the United Kingdom) all agreed to emerge from the shelter of this Article. Japan followed suit in April 1964 and Australia in July 1965.

Once a member country abandons Article XIV status, it assumes the obligation under Article VIII to avoid restrictions on current payments – an obligation which is more far-reaching than the *non-resident* current account convertibility introduced by thirteen countries in December 1958 (see the quotation on page 47). Moreover, the step once taken is an irreversible one, since once a member country ceases to appeal to Article XIV it has no right to invoke it again. However, a member can still seek a special dispensation from the Fund under Article VIII, and there is also in principle the possibility of invoking the 'scarce currency clause' of Article VII, though this has so far been a dead letter in practice. The main provisions of this Article are as follows:

(a) If it becomes evident to the Fund that the demand for a member's currency seriously threatens the Fund's ability to supply that currency, the Fund ... shall formally declare such currency scarce and shall thenceforth apportion its existing and accruing supply of the scarce

currency with due regard to the relative needs of members, the general international economic situation, and any other pertinent considerations. The Fund shall also issue a report concerning its action.
(b)   A formal declaration under (a) above shall operate as an authorization to any member, after consultation with the Fund, temporarily to impose limitations on the freedom of exchange operations in the scarce currency. . . .

Thus the formal declaration by the Fund that a member's currency is scarce would allow all other members to introduce restrictions directed solely against that member, this discrimination being wisely conceived to prevent the deficit countries from having, quite pointlessly, to impose restrictions against each other.

The scarce currency clause had been included in the Bretton Woods charter on British initiative. Britain was at the time a deficit country and the US the main surplus country; Britain 'complained of the United States' attitude as a creditor', and sought 'some formula which would pin them down to a share of responsibility'.[9] In other words the UK, as a deficit country, like other deficit countries on later occasions (including the US in the 1970s), wanted to ensure that surplus countries shouldered their fair share of responsibility for operating the adjustment mechanism, and favoured the scarce currency clause as the best device for applying sanctions against a recalcitrant surplus country. In the event the clause has never been invoked or even threatened, among other things because it could be triggered only when a currency became scarce *in the Fund*.

Let us now turn from the Fund to the GATT. The GATT contains important provisions which permit the temporary use of *trade* restrictions by a country in balance of payments difficulties. Trade restrictions of a *non*-discriminatory nature may be imposed by such a country even when it has emerged from the transitional period provided for in Article XIV of the Fund charter, provided that such measures are necessary:

1   to forestall the imminent threat of, or to stop, a serious decline in its monetary reserves, or
2   in the case of a [country] with very low monetary reserves, to achieve a reasonable rate of increase in its reserves,

where the interpretation of the key words 'serious', 'very low' and 'reasonable' rests with the Fund. The GATT charter is, however, much stricter about discriminatory trade restrictions than about non-discriminatory ones. The former would be permissible for balance of payments reasons only for a country able to claim the privileges of the transitional provisions or the scarce currency clause of the Fund agreement, or in rare cases which could arise only through the unwillingness of a trading partner to adopt any form of multilateral settlement. Otherwise the GATT condemns discrimination in trade restrictions imposed for balance of payments reasons.

Among the major developed countries, very little use has been made since February 1961 of the exceptional provisions in the IMF and GATT charters for countries in surplus or deficit. The only such provision relevant to surplus countries, the scarce currency clause, has never been invoked. In the case of deficit countries, non-discriminatory exchange controls on current transactions have occasionally been authorized under IMF Article VIII and non-discriminatory QRs have also been somewhat more frequently authorized under the relevant GATT Articles. On several occasions devices equivalent to tariffs (for example the UK's 'import surcharge' of 1964–6) have been imposed for balance of payments reasons, contrary to the intention of the GATT. But, by and large, developed countries' disequilibria have not in practice since 1961 been treated to any significant extent by exchange controls on current transactions or by restrictions on imports. The avoidance of restrictions on current transactions is clearly in accord with the intentions of the founding fathers of the IMF and GATT at Bretton Woods and Havana, though they had to wait until December 1958 for a decisive indication that their intentions were being carried into effect.

The founding fathers' intentions with regard to the progressive reduction of import restrictions imposed for the protection of uncompetitive industries also largely came to be realized, except in the case of foodstuffs, thanks mainly to the successive rounds of tariff negotiations conducted under GATT auspices, though the business depression of the 1980s brought a reversion to protection. Finally (and most importantly, in the eyes of the founding fathers) their intention that there should not in the post-war period be a reversion to the pre-war beggar-my-neighbour remedies for unemployment was not disappointed prior to the depression of the 1980s (when there was, unfortunately, some renewed recourse to pre-war 'remedies').

Exchange rates

We have seen that the monetary regime inaugurated in December 1958 owed to the original IMF and GATT charters its rules for recourse to restrictions on payments and trade, and subsequent changes in these charters have left the rules substantially intact. It also in great measure owed to the original IMF charter its two basic rules on exchange rates. The first of these (drastically changed in 1978 by the second amendment) stipulated that each IMF member country should agree with the IMF an official par value for its currency, and should take steps (unspecified in the charter) to keep the actual market value of its currency within a narrow margin (no more than 1 per cent) each side of its par value. Parities were by the original Article IV of the Fund charter to be denominated in terms of gold, but it is more realistic to think of them being set in terms of the US dollar, since in the 1960s it was generally believed that most countries would continue to peg on the dollar at an unchanged rate in the face of a change in the official dollar price of gold, then $35 an ounce. This widespread belief was never put to the test in the 1960s, since the dollar price of gold was never changed: when it *was* changed, at the Smithsonian conference in December 1971, the outcome admittedly suggests that the participating countries were adhering to parities in terms of gold, rather than dollars, but the Smithsonian agreement is not really relevant to the 1960s, since it introduced a completely new procedure for negotiating parities multilaterally at an international conference, instead of unilaterally (subject to the consent of the IMF). The available testimony about the 1960s, as reported for instance in the quotation at the beginning of this chapter, supports the view that countries using the dollar as their intervention currency would then have continued to peg at the same dollar value irrespective of changes in the gold value of the dollar.

These pegged values were in principle adjustable, in the words of the Fund charter, 'to correct a fundamental disequilibrium', though they might *not* be changed *simply as a cure for unemployment*. In the event, however, member countries throughout the 1960s showed little inclination to change their pegs at all, except *in extremis*.

The second basic rule post-1958 on exchange rates – that the market value of each currency should be held within the permitted margin, not by recourse to exchange controls, but by official trans-actions in the exchange markets – also owes much to the IMF charter, in that Article VIII (which has been operative in the case of the developed industrial countries ever since they emerged from the shelter of the transitional provisions of Article XIV) condemns regular recourse to exchange controls on current transactions.

Hence Article IV in its original Bretton Woods version clearly implies pegging by some kind of official reserve transactions. But the form that such transactions actually took post-1958, particularly the crucial role of transactions in the market using the US dollar as the intervention currency, were *not* spelt out in the Bretton Woods charter, and may indeed not have been intended by some of the founding fathers.

The part played by gold in the Bretton Woods system from December 1958 until August 1971 (when President Nixon declared the US dollar to be no longer officially convertible into gold) is likewise not spelt out at all precisely in the Bretton Woods charter, but once again the dollar's special role during this period enabled the provisions of the charter to be put into effect. Article IV in its Bretton Woods version required members to settle parities in terms of gold or (what amounts to the same thing) parities 'in terms of the United States dollar of the weight and fineness in effect on July 1, 1944', and this could be reconciled with the *de facto* practice of pegging on dollar parities so long as the US authorities afforded other countries' central banks the right of official convertibility between dollars and gold at an unchanged 'official price'; namely at the price ($35 an ounce) implied by the par value of the dollar initially agreed by the US with the IMF.

9 The dollar in the 1960s

The gold outflow of the past three years has dramatically focused world attention on a fundamental change that has been occurring in the economic position of the United States. Our balance of payments . . . has become one of the key factors in our national economic life. Mainly because that balance of payments has been in deficit we have lost gold.

President Kennedy's message to Congress, 6 February 1961

Prior to the move to convertibility in December 1958 the US dollar shared with gold the role of providing the non-communist world with media for *hard* settlement. Dollars enjoyed central-bank convertibility into gold and gold into dollars at a fixed rate of $35 an ounce, the price at which the Federal Reserve Bank of New York, acting as agent for the US Treasury, would deal in gold with other central banks.

During this part of the post-war period, the division of the world into separate monetary regions called for extensive exchange controls, but all the devices adopted to regulate settlements as between the different regions were applied to the various media for soft settlement, such as sterling and the EPU, and not to the dollar, which was not subject to any exchange control by the American authorities (and was incidentally one of the few currencies which never needed to take advantage of the transitional provisions of Article XIV of the IMF charter).

The international position of the dollar at this time has been explained in an essay, published in May 1957, by F. H. Klopstock, then head of the balance of payments division of the Federal Reserve Bank of New York, who summarized the then recent history of the dollar in the following terms:

With the sudden termination of Lend Lease after the war, and as a result of heavy dollar requirements of foreign countries, dollar balances of foreign monetary authorities in 1946 and 1947 had to be drawn down considerably. . . . The year 1947 saw foreign short-term dollar holdings reaching their post-war low of $4.8 billion; since then there has occurred an unprecedentedly large rise, carrying these assets to $8.9 billion by the end of 1952 and to more than $13 billion at the end of 1956.[1]

Of this total, about $8 billion were officially held, predominantly in the reserves of other central banks. The United States official gold reserve at the end of 1956 was $22 billion, more than sufficient, in Mr Klopstock's view, to silence 'any alarmist concern over the adequacy of the United States gold stock'[2] as a guarantee of the central-bank convertibility of dollars into gold. Indeed he thought it 'difficult to visualize a deterioration of faith in the soundness of the dollar sufficient to make foreigners wish to withdraw their dollar balances'.[3] Nor was he alone in this opinion. Outside the United States, 'the world dollar problem', as Sir Donald MacDougall called it in his book published in 1957,[4] was a problem of a dollar shortage, not a dollar glut. Yet, as Sir Donald subsequently reported in an essay written in the summer of 1960,[5] there began in 1958 a 'great debate' about whether the position of the dollar had undergone a dramatic reversal:

While the book was going through the press, in the autumn of 1956 and the first half of 1957, the dollar did well. . . . Then towards the end of 1957 there was an equally dramatic reversal . . . in 1958 . . . no less than $2¼ billion was taken out in gold – the heaviest annual loss in American history. It was this, more than anything else, that started the great debate on the balance of payments.

The gold drain slackened somewhat in 1959 but towards the end of the year the US balance of payments again deteriorated, and this ushered in a decade in which (contrary to Mr Klopstock's prediction) the dollar problem arose from the possibility of excess supply, though not on an unmanageable scale until the early 1970s, when it became acute.

The course of the dollar's fortunes is slightly difficult to chart statistically since prior to 1960 there are no official figures of the US surplus or deficit measured on the official reserve transactions basis. Nevertheless the events which Sir Donald describes are well enough illustrated by the course of the US annual export surplus on goods and services (the excess of exports over imports, as shown in Table 6) which fell substantially in the years 1958 and 1959, but thereafter recovered to a more satisfactory level until 1967, after which it again gave ground for anxiety. The same table also shows that in the 1960s up to 1967 the US export surplus on goods and services must have been more than counterbalanced by other overseas payments net of receipts, since official reserve transactions (second column) were in every year but one needed to support the dollar at the prevailing pegged exchange rates. These other payments and receipts were mainly capital outflows and inflows; the details for the eight years 1960–7 are given in Table 7.

Table 6   *US balance of payments and gold loss, annually, 1956–73 ($ billion)*

	Export surplus on goods and services	Deficit (−) financed by official reserve transactions	Change in gold reserve
1956	5.2		+0.3
1957	7.1		+0.8
1958	3.1		−2.3
1959	1.2		−1.1
1960	5.1	− 3.4	−1.7
1961	6.3	− 1.3	−0.9
1962	6.0	− 2.6	−0.9
1963	7.2	− 1.9	−0.5
1964	9.6	− 1.5	−0.1
1965	8.3	− 1.3	−1.7
1966	6.0	+ 0.2	−0.6
1967	5.7	− 3.4	−1.2
1968	3.6	+ 1.6	−1.2
1969	3.4	+ 2.7	+1.0
1970	5.6	−10.7	−0.8
1971	2.3	−30.5	−0.9
1972	− 1.9	−11.0	−0.5
1973	11.0	− 5.2	——

Source: *Report* of the US Council of Economic Advisers (January 1980), pp. 316–17; US Dept. of Commerce, *Survey of Current Business* (June 1970, June 1975 and June 1979).

The final column of Table 6 shows the annual change in the US gold reserve, and here too we note an annual outflow every year 1958–68 inclusive. United States anxiety about the depletion of the official gold reserve resulted in remedial action in a variety of forms. In the first place, the US authorities took steps to contain the growth of the US deficit by restrictions on outward capital movements, with equivalent effect to an exchange control on capital outflows. Such restrictions were imposed as from 1964. Second, the US joined with other central banks in arrangements designed to mitigate the attrac-

Table 7 *US balance of payments, 1960–7*

	$ billion, annual average
Export surplus on goods and services	6.8
Remittances, pensions and other transfers	−2.7
Government capital net outflow (excluding official reserve transactions)	−1.5
Private US investment abroad	−6.0
Private foreign investment in US	1.9
Errors and omissions	−0.4
Deficit (−) financed by official reserve transactions	−1.9

Source: *Report* of the US Council of Economic Advisers (January 1980), pp. 316–17.

tiveness of gold as a monetary asset by preventing, or moderating, the rise in the price of gold in the free market, and more particularly in the London market. The initial form of these arrangements was the gold pool, which began operations in 1961. Third, the US authorities introduced new devices, the Federal Reserve swap network and Roosa bonds, both of which enabled them to relieve other countries' central banks of the exchange risk of holding dollars, thereby reconciling them to holding US debts which otherwise they might have presented for conversion into gold at the Federal Reserve Bank of New York.[6]

US restrictions on capital outflows

Beginning in 1964 the US imposed a variety of restrictions on capital outflows, all of which were eventually repealed in January 1974. They were the interest equalization tax (IET), the Voluntary Foreign Credit Restraint Program (VFCRP) and the Foreign Direct Investment Program (FDIP).

The IET

After receiving a special balance of payments message from President Kennedy, the US Congress enacted in 1964 the so-called interest equalization tax. This was a tax on purchases by Americans from foreigners of new or outstanding securities issued on behalf of a borrower resident in any advanced industrial nation. The principal object of the legislation was to reduce foreign securities issued in New York by increasing costs to foreigners of long-term financing in the United States by the equivalent of approximately 1 per cent per annum on annual interest costs. Subsequently an understanding was reached with the Canadian government to exempt new Canadian issues needed to maintain an unimpeded flow of trade and payments between the two countries; the Canadian authorities simultaneously agreed not to increase Canada's official reserves through the proceeds of borrowings in the United States.

The interest equalization tax, originally imposed on a temporary basis, was renewed from time to time and under the Democratic administration was in various ways made more onerous. Thus in 1965 (as the result of evidence that bank credit was being used to avoid the tax) bank loans with maturities of one year or more were brought within its scope, and later its rate was increased. However, the Nixon adminstration reduced the rate to the equivalent of about 0.8 per cent on annual interest costs.

The VFCRP

In February 1965, at the same time as the inclusion of certain bank loans within the scope of the interest equalization tax, the US government also introduced a programme of voluntary restraint on lending abroad. This programme had three facets.

1   The US monetary authorities issued guidelines to the *commercial banks* requesting them to limit the increase in their foreign claims during 1965 to no more than 5 per cent of the amount outstanding at year-end 1964. Within this ceiling, banks were to give priority to the financing of United States exports and to loans to less developed countries and were to avoid placing an undue burden on the balance of payments of Canada, Japan and the United Kingdom. In December 1965 the ceiling on foreign credits applicable in 1966 was increased from 105 to 109 per cent of their 1964 base, but banks were asked to space out the use of the leeway 'to a rate not exceeding 20 per cent thereof per quarter beginning with the fourth quarter of 1966'.[7] In January 1968 the ceiling was reduced from 109 to 103 per cent and in addition the banks were asked to reduce outstanding term loans

to the developed countries of continental Western Europe and also to cut outstanding short-term credits to these countries by 40 per cent during the course of 1968, with each bank's general ceiling lowered by the amount of such reductions over the course of the year. On the other hand all claims on Canadian residents were shortly afterwards (March 1968) exempted from the banks' ceiling. The banks were offered a minor easement in April 1969, in that they were permitted to opt for an alternative ceiling equivalent to 1½ per cent of their total assets as at the end of 1968. This easement chiefly benefited smaller banks. In December 1969 the guidelines for US banks were changed

to give greater and more explicit recognition to the established priority for export financing. . . . Under the revised program, each bank is to have a ceiling exclusively for loans of one year or longer that finance US goods exported on or after 1 December. This Export Term-Loan Ceiling is to be separate from a General Ceiling that will be available for loans of any type and of any maturity. Under the new program, the aggregate General Ceiling of banks currently reporting to the Federal Reserve Board will be $10.1 billion, and the Export Term-Loan Ceiling for these banks will be about $1.3 billion, for a total ceiling of $11.4 billion. Aggregate ceilings under the previous guidelines were $10.1 billion.[8]

Subsequently the Export Expansion Act (1971) wholly exempted export credit from the lending restraints.

2   Guidelines were issued early in 1965 to *nonbank financial institutions* (such as insurance companies and pension funds) on broadly similar lines to those for banks. The 1965 increase in foreign credits maturing in ten years or less was to be kept within 5 per cent of the amount outstanding at year-end 1964, and short-term investments in foreign money markets were to be reduced to the year-end level of either 1963 or 1964, whichever was lower. In 1966 these guidelines were simplified: institutions were requested to limit the increase in certain types of loans and investments in selected foreign countries until the end of 1967 to no more than 5 per cent of the level on 30 September 1966. In January 1968 the guidelines became stricter, in line with the stricter ones imposed on the banks: nonbank financial institutions were requested to reduce their holdings of certain foreign assets by 5 per cent during 1968 and also to repatriate all liquid assets not essential for the conduct of their foreign business. However (as in the case of the commercial banks) the

guidelines for nonbank financial institutions were amended in March 1968 to exclude Canadian claims from restriction, and in April 1969 the 5 per cent reduction in specified foreign assets imposed by the 1968 guidelines was rescinded. The principle of a separate ceiling for *export* term loans introduced in December 1969 into the guidelines for banks was not extended to nonbank financial institutions, which continued to operate under a single ceiling. 'However, an institution may exceed its ceiling moderately if the excess reflects new export credits which could not be accommodated under its ceiling. In addition, an institution that has had either a low ceiling, or none at all, may now hold certain covered foreign assets up to a total of $500 000.'[9]

3   The guidelines of early 1965 also covered the overseas financial business of *industrial companies*. The US Department of Commerce asked US firms with substantial business abroad to improve by 15 to 20 per cent the aggregate of selected components of their individual balance of payments. The choice of means to achieve this target was left to the co-operating companies, which could increase their exports, accelerate repatriation of income from their direct investments abroad,[10] or decrease their direct investments financed from the US by postponing or cancelling marginal direct investment in developed countries and by relying more on foreign financing. In addition, the firms concerned were requested to reduce their short-term investments held abroad to a level no higher than the amount outstanding at the end of 1963. The guidelines were in December 1965 extended to a larger number of industrial companies and reinforced by setting a specific target for cuts in direct investments for each company. Further guidelines issued for 1967 were stricter still: as part of the overall target, the total of direct investment outflows and retained earnings in selected countries, minus borrowings abroad, was limited under a formula designed to hold the net total of such flows close to the 1966 experience.

The FDIP

In January 1968 the tightening up of the guidelines for financial intermediaries was accompanied by measures imposing *mandatory* restrictions on direct investment abroad.[11] Net transfers of capital by US investors for direct investment in all advanced continental European countries and South Africa were subject to a moratorium. For certain developed countries, such as Canada, Japan, the

United Kingdom and Australia, in which a high level of capital inflow was considered essential either for the maintenance of economic growth or for financial stability, the total of new capital transfers plus reinvested earnings might not exceed 65 per cent of the average of direct investment in these countries during 1965–6. The ceiling for the less developed countries as a group was, however, 110 per cent of the average in 1965–6. These regulations were relaxed, but only very slightly, by the Nixon administration in April 1969, and again as from the beginning of 1970. They were repealed, along with all the other regulations described in this section, in January 1974.

The gold market

Holders or would-be holders of gold, other than central banks, have in the post-war period enjoyed no rights of official conversion of national currencies into gold: at the best they have been able (legally or illegally) to buy gold (at its free market price) in one of the free gold markets, of which the most important in the 1960s was the London market.

The gold market in London was closed altogether in the post-war period until March 1954, when it was reopened to non-residents able to pay in dollars or in other currencies convertible into dollars. By March 1954 the immediate post-war demand for gold for private hoarding purposes had for the time being considerably declined, and with it the premiums which had on earlier occasions obtained in other gold markets.[12] However, the deterioration in the US balance of payments in the late 1950s and the consequential accumulation of dollars in the official reserves of many countries, especially those of continental Europe, led to a rise in their demand for gold. To this was added from time to time a speculative demand on the part of private operators fearful of a devaluation of the dollar and other currencies in relation to gold. During the third quarter of 1960,

with a more or less continuous demand for gold against dollars, mainly by continental central banks, the price rose from the equivalent of $35.09 per fine ounce to $35.26 at the end of September . . . [and] at one time on the 20th October touched the equivalent of $40 per fine ounce. On the following day, after a denial by the US Treasury of any intention to change the gold parity of the dollar, the price fell to the equivalent of $37. By the end of October it had declined to $36.[13]

The dangers of a widespread scramble to exchange dollars for gold were, however, now plain to all, and measures were concerted among the major central banks to preserve a semblance of order in the gold market.

Following the upheaval in world gold markets in October 1960, agreement for joint action to stabilize the price of gold was reached between the Federal Reserve Bank of New York, acting on behalf of the US Treasury, and the central banks of Belgium, France, the Federal Republic of Germany, Italy, the Netherlands, Switzerland, and the United Kingdom. Representatives of these central banks from time to time consider methods by which effective monetary control, with particular reference to the price of gold, may be maintained. The Bank of England acts as agent for this group and, within certain limits, both sells and buys gold for account of the members of the pool.[14]

As a result of these measures, the speculative demand for gold during the Berlin crisis in September 1961 and the Cuban crisis in October 1962 did not result in any appreciable rise in the price of gold in the London market. The next test occurred when, immediately after the sterling crisis at the end of 1964, the French government disclosed its intention to convert into gold a part of its reserves then held in dollars, but even then the gold pool was so well able to meet the resulting speculative demand for gold that the London price never rose above $35.35.

The final crisis in the history of the gold pool began with a surge of speculative gold buying in the final quarter of 1967:

January [1968] and much of February were quieter. . . . Early in March buying accelerated rapidly, in the belief that the official price of gold could not be held. The run on gold quickly became very serious and a conference of the active members of the gold pool[15] was convened in Washington for 16th and 17th March. Those taking part expressed their resolve that all gold in their hands should be used for monetary purposes only. Consequently they would no longer sell gold in the market, nor did they feel it necessary to buy it; nor would they sell to monetary authorities to replace gold sold in the market. They invited the co-operation of other monetary authorities in making these policies effective. The conference effectively brought to an end the gold pool arrangements which had been in existence since 1961 and re-established a system of free gold markets in which central banks would not deal.[16]

The March 1968 communiqué only precluded *market* transactions by central banks, not sales from one central bank to another – indeed such sales continued to take place up to the time that the official convertibility of the dollar into gold was suspended in August 1971. In particular central banks were in principle free to buy US Treasury gold for dollars, though some were restrained from so doing by a reluctance to rock the boat: moreover, Germany undertook, as part of an agreement with the US in 1967 about the occupation costs of the US military presence in Europe, not to exercise her right to convert.

The intention behind the discontinuance of official market trans-actions in gold was twofold. The absence of official *purchases* meant that central banks would not contribute to the demand for gold and thereby bid up its market price. (Such official purchases at more than the official price, at that time $35 an ounce, were in any case forbidden by the IMF charter, but it was apparently feared that South Africa might sell some new gold directly to central banks at $35 so as to divert supplies from the free market and thereby jack up the market price.)[17] The absence of official *sales* meant that the United States would not be called upon to sell gold at $35 an ounce to other central banks for them to re-sell in the free market at a higher price.

In the course of 1969 the trend of the gold price in the London market was downwards, so much so that by December it became a live issue whether the agreement reached at the Washington con-ference meant, or alternatively did not mean, that central banks would not buy gold in the market even if the market price should fall as low as the official price of $35 an ounce. However, the issue ceased to be a serious one as from the following year, since when the free market price remained above the official price.

The Federal Reserve swap network

The dollar was in 1961 subject to the speculative pressure gener-ated by the German and Dutch revaluations of March that year. To combat this pressure the US authorities departed for the first time from their previous practice of dealing in only one international reserve asset – gold.

The United States Treasury, operating through the New York Reserve Bank . . . began dealing in foreign exchange, in close consultation with foreign monetary authorities. These consultations were aided by Federal Reserve participation, on a regular basis, in the monthly meetings of central bankers in Basle.[18]

In February 1962 the Federal Reserve System took over from the US Treasury the conduct of operations in other national currencies. In that month, the chairman of the Federal Reserve Board stated that the System was entering into cooperative arrangements with foreign central banks to help to steady the rate for the United States dollar, and on 1 March an agreement was announced by which the Federal Reserve Bank of New York provided $50 million for the dollar account of the Bank of France, in exchange for a corresponding transfer of NF 245 million for the account of the Federal Reserve Bank with the Bank of France. It was explained that the funds were provided to facilitate official intervention in markets for foreign currency to support the dollar–franc rate. . . .

Since then, further reciprocal arrangements on similar lines between the Federal Reserve Bank of New York and central banks of other countries have been made.[19]

Under these reciprocal arrangements, or 'swap lines' as they were called, the Federal Reserve Bank of New York would offer (say) the Bank of England a standby facility which either country could activate on demand, this being effected by the New York bank crediting the Bank of England with, say, $50 million and the Bank of England crediting the New York bank with its sterling equivalent. Both parties would then by agreement reverse the transaction on a specified date, three months later, at the same rate of exchange, so that for practical purposes the partner activating the swap facility would obtain a loan from the other partner denominated in the latter's currency.

The foreign currency thus obtained by the drawing partner could be used for official market transactions, and this is how it has in fact been used when the United States' partners have activated the swap network. For instance, one contribution to most of the operations for the rescue of sterling has been a drawing of dollars by the Bank of England under its swap line with the Federal Reserve Bank of New York; dollars obtained in this way have then been available for supporting sterling in the market.

When, however, the US has itself activated one of the swap lines, the foreign currency thereby obtained by the Federal Reserve Bank of New York, say guilders, was not usually in the 1960s sold against dollars in a market transaction; instead it was used to buy dollars spot from the partner's central bank, the Netherlands Bank in this case. What, then, has been achieved by such transactions? This question is answered by a hypothetical illustration provided by Gerald H. Anderson:

Assume that a flow of capital into the Netherlands, believed to be temporary, had threatened to push up the dollar price of the Netherlands guilder, and the Netherlands Bank (the central bank) had prevented this price rise by selling guilders and buying 50 million dollars. The FRBNY then drew $50 million worth of guilders on its swap line with the Netherlands Bank (NB) and used its newly acquired guilders to purchase 50 million dollars from the NB. The dollars purchased were 'uncovered dollars,' i.e., the Netherlands had no guaranty that these dollars could be sold at any particular price. The dollars acquired by the Netherlands in the swap, however, were 'covered' by the forward contract part of the swap which required the System to buy dollars (sell guilders), three months later, at the original exchange rate. The result of these two transactions was that the Netherlands had exchanged its 50 million uncovered dollars for 50 million dollars that carried an exchange value guaranty. Therefore, the Netherlands had no need to exchange its dollars for US gold in order to protect the value of its holdings. The transaction had at least delayed, and hopefully avoided, a purchase by the Netherlands of $50 million worth of US gold.[20]

Mr Anderson then proceeds to explain how the swap would be unwound three months later:

Now assume that the capital flow into the Netherlands was temporary, and reversed. To avoid a decline in the dollar price of the guilder, the NB then bought guilders and sold dollars. The NB would then have replenished its stock of dollars by purchasing some from the FRBNY, or what is the same thing, the FRBNY would have used dollars to buy guilders from the NB. Alternatively, the FRBNY might have bought guilders directly in the market, instead of indirectly through the NB. The FRBNY would then have used these guilders to repay the swap by performing the forward contract.

If the FRBNY hadn't acquired enough guilders to fully repay the swap, the portion of the swap not repaid might have been renewed to be paid in the future; alternatively, it might have been paid with guilders purchased from the International Monetary Fund. . .

or from some other source, but 'in actual experience a substantial majority of drawings have been repaid without resort to special means such as these'. (The amount of swap transactions outstanding is given in Table 8, page 114.)

An alternative device used by the US for offering another country's central bank immunity against exchange risk is the sale to it for dollars of securities denominated in the partner country's currency, for example lira bonds to the Bank of Italy:

The first line of defense against speculation provided by this strengthened swap network has been reinforced by negotiation of a series of Treasury issues of special certificates and bonds denominated in the currencies of the European central banks and treasuries to which they have been issued. Lira bonds taken up by the Bank of Italy now amount to $200 million in US dollar equivalents. Mark bonds placed with the German Federal Bank amount to another $200 million, while Swiss franc bonds and certificates acquired by the Swiss National Bank and the Swiss Confederation amount to $129 million. The precise purpose of each issue has varied somewhat from country to country, but one common characteristic is that these issues provide the foreign countries concerned with an advantageous investment medium for past or present balance of payments surpluses.[21]

Such securities are officially called 'nonmarketable US Treasury bonds and notes payable in foreign currencies', but are more commonly known as Roosa bonds, after Robert Roosa, the assistant secretary of the Treasury for monetary affairs in the Kennedy administration. The total of Roosa bonds outstanding at the end of 1962 and subsequently is shown in the final column of Table 8.

Table 8   *Drawings outstanding under the Federal Reserve swap network, and Roosa bonds outstanding, 1962–80 ($ million)*

End of year	Federal Reserve drawings on foreign banks	Foreign banks' drawings on the Federal Reserve	Roosa bonds
1962	230	0	250
1963	384	50	730
1964	295	200	1085
1965	135	475	1210
1966	280	550	340
1967	1775	1396	1045
1968	432	1667	1640
1969	330	650	1750
1970	810	0	1085
1971	2855	0	1825
1972	1585	0	1540
1973	1426	0	1460
1974	1462	0	1470
1975	1465	0	1600
1976	1065	150	1545
1977	1306	0	1170
1978	5615	0	345
1979	3188	0	0
1980	0	0	0

Source: *Federal Reserve Bulletin* (December 1976), pp. 1008–11, and subsequent issues; US Treasury *Bulletin*, table 1FS–4.

10 The IMF General Account in the 1960s

The United States has never made use of its drawing rights under the International Monetary Fund to meet deficits in its balance of payments. If and when appropriate, these rights should and will be exercised within the framework of Fund policies. The United States will also support continued efforts in the Fund to facilitate drawings by other members in the currencies of industrialized countries whose payments positions are in surplus and whose reserves are large. This will help to reduce the burden now borne by the dollar.

President Kennedy's message to Congress,
6 February 1961

Thanks to an increase in membership and to upward revisions in the quotas of existing members, including the large general increases in quotas in 1959 and 1966, the size of the General Account grew steadily in the 1960s. Total quotas, in billions of dollars, were 9.2 at end-1958, 14.0 at end-1959, 16.0 at end-1965, 20.6 at end-1966 and 21.3 at end of the decade. Drawing rights were widely used by members, as may be seen from Table 9 (page 116).

Two new facilities for specific purposes were introduced in the course of the 1960s, the facility for compensatory financing of export fluctuations (established 1963) and the buffer stock financing facility (established in 1969). The nature of these facilities, as of others introduced in the 1960s, is described in Appendix A (page 245). The other innovations in the 1960s were designed to widen the range of currencies drawn from the General Account, so as to prevent an excessive proportion of dollar drawings, and to institute new arrangements (the General Arrangements to Borrow) by which the resources available to the General Account from members' subscriptions could be supplemented by borrowing from ten members (the Group of Ten, as listed on page 117) and Switzerland.

Table 9   *IMF drawings, 1947–69 ($ million)*

	Gross drawings by members		Total
	In US dollars	In other currencies	
1947	461	7	468
1948	197	11	208
1949	101	—	101
1950	—	—	—
1951	7	28	35
1952	85	—	85
1953	68	162	230
1954	62	—	62
1955	28	—	28
1956	678	14	692
1957	977	—	977
1958	252	86	338
1959	139	41	180
1960	148	132	280
1961·	822	1656	2478
1962	109	475	584
1963	194	139	333
1964	282	1668	1950
1965	282	2151	2433
1966	159	1289	1448
1967	114	721	835
1968	806	2746	3552
1969	1341	1530	2871
	7312	12 857	20 169

Source: IMF, *International Financial Statistics* (July 1971), p. 12.

The General Arrangements to Borrow

An important turning point in the history of the IMF was the recognition by the United States that its balance of payments deficit had become a major problem. As a precautionary measure, President Kennedy stated in his 6 February 1961 message to Congress, quoted at the beginning of this chapter, that the United States would be prepared, whenever necessary, to draw on the IMF to obtain other currencies with which to mop up any excess of dollars held abroad. The United States's first actual transaction with the Fund, a relatively small standby facility, occurred in July 1963.

As a further precautionary measure, also dating from 1961, arrangements were devised whereby a group of larger and richer members should agree to lend their currencies to the Fund, whose charter conveniently permits it to borrow from members.[1] In the event the United States used other means to finance its deficit and the arrangements were in the 1960s activated solely for the benefit of other countries, including the UK; none the less, confidence in the dollar presumably benefited from the knowledge that the resources available to the Fund for a possible support operation had been considerably increased.

The arrangements in question, which became known as the GAB (General Arrangements to Borrow), were discussed at the annual meeting of the Fund in September 1961 and settled by the end of the year. They provided for ten industrial countries to make, if necessity arose, supplementary resources available to the Fund to meet drawings by the USA or the UK (and since 1968 also by the rest of the participants). The lending commitments of the so-called Group of Ten were arranged as follows:

	$ *million*
United States	2000
United Kingdom	1000
West Germany	1000
France	550
Italy	550
Japan	250
Netherlands	200
Canada	200
Belgium	150
Sweden	100
Total[2]	6000

In March 1963 the ten countries were joined by Switzerland, with a contribution of the equivalent of $200 million, as provided for in an exchange of letters with the IMF managing director. Suitable arrangements were made to deal with the difficulty that Switzerland is not a member of the IMF.

These supplementary resources are not available automatically, since use of them requires the approval of the Group of Ten. Broadly speaking, following a request to the Fund for a drawing or standby facility, made by one of the participants in the Arrangements, the Fund may make a call on the supplementary resources.

The participating countries, however, undertake to meet the call only if they agree, after consultation, as to the need for it. Then contributions are made by individual countries, possibly up to the maximum of their commitments, but only to the extent that their reserves and balance of payments positions permit. In this way any request for a drawing which may require the activation of the GAB is dealt with in accordance with the Fund's established policies and practices, though the agreement of the countries providing supplementary aid is necessary.

These arrangements came into effect in October 1962. However it was not until the end of 1964 that the scheme was first activated – in order to make possible a large drawing by the UK in December of that year.

Choice of currencies for drawing

The provisions of the Fund charter governing the choice of currencies to be drawn by a member, and the choice of those which the member may use for repayment, have always been rather complicated.[3] The most important provisions are, however, that no currency may be used for repayment unless

1 the Fund's holding of it is not in excess of 75 per cent (amended in 1978 to 100 per cent) of the quota of the country whose currency it is: thus sterling might not be used for repayment if the Fund's holding of sterling had (by virtue of prior drawings of other currencies by the UK) increased to more than 75 per cent (subsequently 100 per cent) of the UK quota, and
2 the country whose currency it is has emerged from the transitional provisions of Article XIV: hence sterling, and indeed the currencies of all the major powers except the US and Canada, might not be so used prior to the concerted move in February 1961 from Article XIV status to Article VIII status.

Prior to February 1961 the effect of these two conditions was to make the two dollars virtually the only currencies suitable for repurchases, and in practice no other currency was so used. As a result (and also because in the early post-war years many essential goods were readily obtainable only for dollars)

Fund members were most reluctant to draw any currency except dollars, since they would have to repurchase with dollars. . . .

But then things changed, as the main European currencies gradually became more useful to buy commodities with, and therefore more desirable. And in February 1961 the situation was transformed by the acceptance of the obligations of convertibility by nearly every country in Western Europe. Thereafter their currencies, as well as US dollars, could be used in repurchases. Consequently their currencies, as well as US dollars, became acceptable in drawings. . . . In these circumstances something had to be done to decide which currencies countries should draw, and in which they should repurchase. Otherwise there would be no way of influencing drawings and repurchases toward the ideal situation in which the Fund's holdings of each member's currency equalled 75 per cent of the member's quota. This problem . . . took a long time to solve, but in July 1962 the Board of the Fund took a comprehensive decision. . . .

As regards drawings, three factors were to be taken into account: the balance of payments of the countries whose currencies would be considered for drawing, their reserves, and the Fund's holdings of their currencies. Accordingly, drawings would be directed toward the currencies of countries whose balance of payments was good, and whose reserves were in good shape, provided that the Fund's holdings of the currency of that country were not being depleted too much. As regards repurchases, what would be watched would be the Fund's holdings of each currency compared with that country's quota, although some consideration would also be given to the country's balance of payments . . . the Fund could not accept in repurchases any currency of which its holdings were at or above 75 per cent of that country's quota, nor the currency of any country that had not accepted the obligations of convertibility.

From these general principles a regular procedure has been evolved, based on a quarterly forecast of the drawings that may be made in the ensuing quarter, and of the repurchases that may be expected during the quarter. A list is drawn up of countries whose balances of payments and reserves would permit them to provide assistance to other members. . . . If, however, the Fund's holdings of a particular currency in the list should fall very low, its use in drawings will be limited unless the Fund can borrow more of that currency under the General Arrangements to Borrow or otherwise.

The budget thus worked out is discussed in advance by the Managing Director with the Executive Directors appointed or elected by the countries whose names are on the list and, subject to any modification introduced as a result of this consultation, the list is used as a guide when advising members what currencies to draw.[4]

A consequence of these new arrangements was a marked swing away from drawing in US dollars in favour of other currencies (see Table 9).

11 Basle and Brussels

Over the years I have witnessed at first hand how well central bankers have learned to work together. The BIS . . . has long served as a vital forum in this respect.

Alfred Hayes,
lecture in August 1975[1]

Historical background

On the eve of the second world war, international liquidity took almost exclusively the form of the reserve assets held by central banks and with these assets taking the form of gold, US dollars and sterling. The only international institution concerned with liquidity arrangements was the Bank for International Settlements (BIS) set up in Basle in 1930 as the result of the same conference at The Hague which drew up the Young plan for dealing with German reparations; however, this institution had (after a very promising start) lapsed into virtual inactivity following the financial débâcle of 1931.

These liquidity arrangements of the late 1930s continued in the post-war period but were backed by new devices which supplemented the owned reserve assets of the three traditional kinds with new arrangements for drawing rights and other facilities. Such facilities were sometimes *ad hoc* and bilateral, but more frequently they were institutionalized. Much the most important institution for the provision of liquidity came to be the IMF, which began to do business in 1947, though on a modest scale until 1956. In the 1950s, however, there were important, though short-lived, Western European arrangements, notably the Intra-European Payments Agreements (Chapter 1) and the European Payments Union (Chapter 2).

The Bank for International Settlements also staged a spectacular recovery. It acted as agent for the West European arrangements just mentioned. Its monthly meetings at Basle also provided an occasion for the Governors of the central banks of the major powers to consult on matters of common interest.

The central banks represented on the BIS Board of Directors were those of the UK, France, Germany, Italy, Belgium, the Netherlands, Sweden and Switzerland, but in the 1960s other countries (including the United States as from 1961 and more recently Japan and Canada) have participated in the informal discussions at Governor level which are always held in conjunction with the monthly board meetings.[2] In the course of the 1960s the eleven countries just mentioned came to be known as the Group of Ten, with Switzerland as the eleventh associate member. The early history of this group, G-10 as it is usually called, will be described in Chapter 12. More or less the same group of countries had profited from their monthly meetings at Basle to concoct in 1961 the first of a succession of rescue operations, described below, which in due course came to be known as Basle-type operations.

Finally, the banking business of the BIS also began to thrive. The intention of the founders of the BIS was that it should be a bank for central banks, accepting deposits, making advances, discounting bills, exchanging currencies and indeed undertaking all kinds of banking business – but with a clientele limited to central banks, especially those in Europe and North America. After a promising start in 1930, this banking business later dwindled as a consequence of the 1931 financial débâcle, and did not begin to recover until the 1950s. By 1960 the balance sheet total of the BIS had reached the equivalent of nearly $1 billion; by 1970 it had grown to about $7 billion; and by March 1981 to about $38 billion. The development of the Eurodollar market (see Chapter 13) has opened up new opportunities for the BIS: in recent years it has operated extensively in this market, both on its own account and also on behalf of various central banks. It is a sign of the growing importance of the BIS as a bank that it participated as a principal in most of the Basle-type operations of the 1960s as well as providing the forum in which they were negotiated.

The Basle operations

The prototype Basle operation was provoked (as was the establishment of the Federal Reserve swap network) by the speculative capital flows which followed the German and Dutch revaluations, each by 5 per cent, in March 1961. The reaction of the major central banks to this dangerous situation began at the BIS monthly meeting at Basle, in the week following the German and Dutch revaluations.

The first action that the governors took was to state formally that the central banks represented, namely those of Belgium, France, Italy, the Netherlands, Sweden, Switzerland, the United Kingdom and Western Germany, were satisfied that rumours about further currency adjustments had no foundation: and as a practical earnest of this belief they announced that the central banks concerned were co-operating closely in the foreign exchange markets.

Details of the various techniques to be employed were left for agreement and in practice they varied widely, but the purpose was never in doubt. This was to ensure that, despite such pressures as might be generated in the foreign exchange markets during the heat of the day, no party to the so-called 'Basle Agreement' should be forced by speculative movement of funds to deviate from the declared policy.

Whilst no one could estimate for how long or in what volume these movements would continue, it was clear in the minds of all concerned that this was essentially an essay in short-term banking accommodation which would be reversed in a reasonably short space of time, either by a reflux of short-term funds or recourse in due time, if this reflux did not occur, to one of the international sources of longer-term financial accommodation. . . .

The pressures on sterling varied from month to month between the beginning of March and the end of July. The largest amount outstanding at any one time under the 'Basle Agreement' . . . was approximately £325 million.[3]

On 25 July 1961 measures were taken by the UK to reduce the pressure of home demand: among other things most indirect taxes were increased by a surcharge of 10 per cent, steps were taken to limit government expenditure, bank rate was raised from 5 to 7 per cent and various other monetary brakes were applied.

Immediately after the announcement of 25 July, arrangements were made for the equivalent of £536 million to be drawn in various currencies from the International Monetary Fund and a standby credit of £179 million was made available in case of need. This fortification of reserves both enabled the United Kingdom to repay the Basle credits and provided additional assurance to overseas opinion that the exchange parity of sterling would be maintained.[4]

From the beginning of August until the end of 1961, the pressure of home demand unmistakably abated, and at the same time the speculative pressure on sterling rapidly subsided. The subsequent improvement in the UK balance of payments permitted the repayment of the British drawing from the IMF to be completed by August 1962, though a standby of $1000 million was retained.

A second operation of the Basle type was undertaken by the UK in February and March 1963, a third in 1964 and thereafter from time to time. There was also a lira rescue operation in 1964 and one for the French franc in 1968, following the student riots and other political troubles in May and June.

The Basle Group Arrangements

In addition to periodic recourse to normal Basle-type arrangements, which were all in the legal form of three-month credits or swaps (though with the possibility of renewal) the UK benefited from two longer-term 'Basle Group Arrangements', as they were usually called. The first of these was negotiated in June 1966 (renewed in March 1967 and March 1968) and the second in September 1968 (likewise renewed at intervals until September 1973). The Basle Group Arrangements were unusual in being specifically intended to counter the threat to United Kingdom reserves arising from the possibility of the conversion of overseas-held sterling balances. Under the 1966 Group Arrangement the central banks of Austria, Belgium, Canada, Italy, Japan, the Netherlands, Sweden, Switzerland and West Germany, and the Bank for International Settlements collaborated in affording the United Kingdom swap facilities to offset most of any reduction in the United Kingdom reserves caused by fluctuations in overseas countries' sterling balances, whether held by monetary authorities or privately. Such fluctuations were to be measured by reference to a base date early in 1966.[5]

Continued nervousness about the pound after devaluation and about the stability of the international monetary system caused sterling area countries to speed up the process of diversifying their reserves (see Table 10, page 124); this led to another Basle Group Arrangement in 1968. This differed from its predecessor in relating only to sterling balances held within the sterling area; it also differed in that at the same time agreements were negotiated with the countries of that area whereby each undertook to hold a specified proportion of its reserves in sterling, and in return obtained a dollar-value guarantee covering the greater part of its sterling holdings. Twelve central banks[6] and the BIS provided a medium-term facility of $2000 million on which the United Kingdom could draw during a three-year period in order to offset fluctuations below an agreed base level in the sterling balances of sterling area holders, both official and private. Then a series of agreements, mostly for three years with provision for an extension to five, was negotiated between the United Kingdom and individual overseas sterling area countries, whereby each undertook to hold a specified proportion of its reserves in sterling and in return obtained a dollar-value guarantee on its official holdings of sterling in excess of 10 per cent of its total official external reserves. At the same time it was announced that the earlier facility, negotiated in June 1966, would be progressively liquidated and cease by 1971.[7]

Table 10   *Annual change in overseas sterling area holdings of gold and non-sterling currencies, 1958–69**

Year	£ million	Year	£ million
1958	15	1964	73
1959	65	1965	54
1960	−20	1966	335
1961	112	1967	266
1962	131	1968	712
1963	97	1969	198

* Excluding Eurodollars and other non-sterling currencies held in London.

Source: *Economic Trends* no. 191, p. liii, and no. 197, p. xxxix.

At the conclusion of the negotiations in 1968 the United Kingdom was entitled to draw some $600 million to finance earlier reductions in the sterling balances. In 1969 and 1970, when sterling holdings increased, the United Kingdom's net entitlement was correspondingly reduced. By mid 1969 almost all the amount outstanding under the 1968 facility had been repaid.[8] The facility remained in force until September 1973, when it lapsed. The United Kingdom continued its guarantee on most of the sterling reserves held by the sterling area countries, henceforth on terms which afforded compensation to the holders if the pound should, on average over the next six months, fall below $2.4213. At the end of the six months the UK's guarantee continued, but instead of being a dollar-value guarantee it was henceforth expressed in terms of a 'basket' of the major currencies (including the dollar) in fixed proportions. This guarantee ended at the end of 1974 and thereafter all sterling balances were subject to the risk of exchange-rate variations.

The European Economic Community

The Treaty of Rome, which came into effect in January 1958 and thereby established the European Economic Community, provides for the setting up of consultative machinery (including a Monetary Committee) for enabling the EEC Commission and the member countries of the Community to discuss and (if possible) co-ordinate their policies and activities in respect of international monetary questions. A Monetary Committee was duly set up and in 1964 the Commission gained the consent of the Council of Ministers to widen the powers of this committee and also to establish further Committees for Short-term and Medium-term Economic Policy, a Committee of Central Bank Governors and a Budgetary Committee. Of these committees, the important ones for monetary matters are the Monetary Committee and the Committee of Central Bank Governors. There are also periodic meetings of the finance ministers of the EEC. These consultative arrangements are in operation and there is no doubt that in consequence the member countries are prepared to discuss their affairs at Brussels in a more intimate and detailed fashion than is usual among sovereign states. It would, however, be premature to claim that they have yet reached the stage of being able to resolve differences arising between themselves in the field of monetary co-operation and thus to present a common front to the rest of the world.

The Rome Treaty envisages something more than mere consultation on monetary matters as between its signatories, in that one of the articles in chapter 2 (Article 108) provides for the possibility of a member of the Community being afforded 'mutual assistance' by 'the granting of limited credits by other member states, subject to the agreement of the latter'. The EEC has in fact since the late 1960s given a great deal of thought to plans for developing closer monetary integration within the Community, much the most ambitious and detailed of these being the final Werner Report of October 1970, which laid down a programme for the achievement by stages of complete European monetary union. This report envisaged the following reforms:

1   that the EEC countries should pool their reserves (of gold, dollars, IMF drawing rights, etc.) and settle their individual deficits and surpluses by internal EEC financial arrangements;
2   that the EEC members should agree a grid or matrix of exchange-rate parities as between their respective currencies

and keep their actual exchange rates very close to these parities
(as in the 'snake' scheme of April 1972, the *modus operandi* of
which is briefly outlined below, pages 157–8);
3   that these parities should be adjusted less and less frequently,
until finally as from the end of stage two (which the summit
conference of October 1972 ruled should be in 1980) the
parities should be fixed for ever;
4   that eventually the national currencies of the member countries,
originally six but increased to nine in 1973, should preferably be
replaced by a single Community currency.

Action to date has been confined to the first two of the above
proposals, on which significant progress was achieved with the
establishment in March 1979 of the EMS (European Monetary
System), described in Appendix B (page 253). Prior to 1979,
nothing had been done towards implementing the Werner reforms
except the snake scheme, and even this had a chequered history in
that defections from it were rather frequent.

Aside from the Werner proposals, the EEC has been able to
introduce useful, if modest, arrangements for mutual financial assis-
tance of the kind envisaged under Article 108. In February 1970
there was set up an agreement on short-term monetary support.
This facility is automatic and unconditional. There followed in
March 1971 an agreement on a scheme for medium-term financial
assistance: this facility is not automatic, but at the discretion of the
EEC, which may also impose conditions on the drawing country.
Both facilities were placed under the auspices of the European
Monetary Co-operation Fund, which came into existence in April
1973 but which otherwise was given nothing to do prior to the
setting up of the EMS in 1979. The only member country which has
thus far used these EEC financial facilities is Italy, which got a
short-term standby in June 1973 and drew in March 1974. The
drawing was about $1.9 billion. When the Italian short-term credit
expired on 18 December 1974 it was consolidated into a medium-
term credit (although the UK's contribution remained short-term).
Italy had repaid these credits by September 1978.

In October 1974 the Community finance ministers authorized the
issuance of EEC loans on the world market to 'rescue' member
countries in balance of payments difficulties. A total of $3 billion
was envisaged in the first instance. This authorization was duly
ratified by the member countries and the scheme was first activated
in March 1976, for the benefit of Ireland and Italy.

Three loans totalling $800m will go to the market on March 22 while a private placement of dollar notes for $500m with a duration of not more than four years will be made in April. . . .

The loans are raised under Community guarantee and $300m is destined for Ireland and $1 billion for Italy.[9]

This loan facility was reactivated in May 1983, in favour of France, following the devaluation of the French franc as part of the realignment of parities in the EMS on the preceding 21 March. France drew the equivalent of some $3½ billion under this arrangement over the period up to the end of September 1983. More recently, in December 1985, Greece was granted a rather smaller loan under the same facility.

12 Reform in the 1960s

Yet, the facts are that: during the past two years the traditional processes by which world reserves are increased have not yielded a growth of liquidity; such inadequate growth of reserves as has occurred in the past two years was due to *ad hoc*, uncontrolled and impermanent special factors, that cannot be projected to the future. . . . We can no longer take continued reserve growth for granted. Consequently, since we want our economies to continue to grow at healthy rates, there is no time to waste before we agree upon new means for adding to the world's ability to increase monetary reserves. We should therefore make it our conscious aim to arrive at agreement, in our negotiations during the next few months, on the structure and major provisions of a contingency plan for reserve creation, a plan sufficiently developed to be presented for approval to the Governors of the International Monetary Fund when they meet at Rio de Janeiro in September.

Henry Fowler,
US Secretary of the Treasury,
address in March 1967[1]

The Group of Ten

After the inauguration of the General Arrangements to Borrow towards the end of 1962 the finance ministers and central bank Governors of the participating countries, which came to be known as the Group of Ten, began in 1963 to hold regular meetings to discuss all important questions arising in the field of international monetary arrangements, and thus to usurp the intended role of the Board of Executive Directors of the International Monetary Fund. The influence of the group was reinforced by the fact that its membership nearly coincided with that of the so-called Working Party No. 3 (or WP3), a subcommittee set up by the Economic Policy Committee of the OECD[2] to review on a regular basis the monetary and fiscal policies of members in the light of current economic developments, with special reference to balance of payments disequilibria.[3]

By the smaller and poorer countries of the world, the Group of

Ten and WP3 came to be regarded, sometimes rather unfavourably, as alternative manifestations of the same rich man's club. Moreover, it did not pass unnoticed that the central banks of the same group of countries were represented at the monthly meetings at the Bank for International Settlements at Basle (see above, page 121).

The Group of Ten took its first major initiative in September 1963, at a meeting of Ministers and Governors at which it was decided to entrust a committee of officials, the so-called Group of Deputies, with the task of undertaking 'a thorough examination of the outlook for the functioning of the international monetary system and of its probable future needs for liquidity'. The Deputies were given wide terms of reference, except that they were not required to reconsider what was taken to be the proven value of a monetary system 'based on fixed exchange rates and the established price of gold'.

In June 1964 the Deputies duly reported back to the Ministers and Governors, who on the basis of the report agreed to sponsor two proposals for action and two for further studies. The first of the proposals for action was to support an increase in IMF quotas – an increase which was successfully negotiated in the course of 1965 and came into operation in 1966. The second proposal for action was to invite WP3 to engage in the 'multilateral surveillance' of the ways and means of financing balance of payments disequilibria, based on much improved statistical data to be collected from the member countries through the agency of the BIS. This 'multilateral surveillance' was duly brought into operation by WP3 before the end of 1964.

To turn now to the two studies sponsored by the Ten, the first was a study by WP3 of the 'balance of payments adjustment process', and this, as we saw in Chapter 5, duly appeared as an OECD publication in August 1966 called *The Balance of Payments Adjustment Process, a Report by Working Party No. 3 of the Economic Policy Committee*. The other study proposed by the Deputies in their report of June 1964 arose out of their discussions

concerning two types of proposal: one for the introduction, through an agreement among the member countries of the Group, of a new reserve asset, which would be created according to appraised overall needs for reserves; and the other based on the acceptance of gold tranche or similar claims on the Fund as a form of international asset, the volume of which could, if necessary, be enlarged to meet an agreed need.

These alternatives, 'reserve units' and 'drawing rights', differed in that the latter, like IMF gold-tranche drawings, would have to be repaid, and might even, like IMF credit-tranche drawings, be non-automatic and conditional; in contrast reserve units would be owned reserves, to be used entirely at the owner's discretion and without any obligation to repay or reconstitute. Both the alternatives, reserve units and drawing rights, were to be considered by an *ad hoc* committee of officials, reporting to the Group of Ten, under the chairmanship of the Italian member, Rinaldo Ossola. The Ossola Report was completed in May 1965 and published as the *Report of the Study Group on the Creation of Reserve Assets*. On receipt of the Ossola Report, the Ministers and Governors instructed their Deputies (who were at that time presided over by Dr Emminger of the Bundesbank) to 'determine and report to Ministers what basis of agreement can be reached on improvements needed in the international monetary system, including arrangements for the future creation of reserve assets, as and when needed, so as to permit adequate provision for the reserve needs of the world economy'. Thus the Ossola Report was followed by the Emminger Report, which was published in July 1966.

It is important to bear in mind that the two studies initiated by the Group of Ten (the study of the adjustment process by WP3 and of international liquidity by Ossola) were closely interrelated, especially in the minds of the Ministers and Governors from continental Europe, in the sense that the introduction of any new kind of international asset, far from being allowed to absolve deficit countries from the need to balance their accounts with the rest of the world, was intended to be matched by a firm resolve by all countries in deficit or surplus (but especially the former) to adopt, with greater alacrity than before, remedial policies appropriate to the treatment of the prevailing international disequilibria. At one time, indeed, it seemed that some of the continental members of the Group of Ten would be prepared to consider the possibility of a new kind of liquidity only as part of a package deal which would also prescribe certain unconditionally binding rules for remedial policies to be adopted by countries in balance of payments deficit. In due course, however, the view which prevailed was that remedies appropriate to all circumstances could not be prescribed in advance, and hence that prior agreement could reasonably be sought only for the acceptance of rather general guidelines. This was the line taken in the WP3 Report, as it appeared in August 1966.

Ossola, Emminger and Rio

The work of the Ossola Group was by intention only exploratory. The resulting report described and analysed the various proposals for new kinds of liquidity which were submitted for consideration by members of the Ten and by the IMF. The Emminger Group was intended to proceed to the next stage, that of making positive recommendations, but though it can claim to have made some progress, it was not able, in its 1966 report, to produce any generally acceptable scheme, and indeed one member (France) did not in the end accept that any scheme was necessary, even as a basis for 'contingency planning'. Hence the Ossola and Emminger reports have to be regarded as only the first stages of a long process of international negotiation, which until September 1966 was conducted almost entirely within the Group of Ten, though with the Fund's managing director in attendance and with the assistance of experts from the staff of the IMF, the BIS and the OECD. However, at the IMF annual meeting in September 1966 it was agreed to build on the foundations laid by the Emminger Report in a new forum, a joint group of the Deputies of the Ten and the executive directors of the Fund. This new body met for the first time in Washington in November 1966, and on three occasions in 1967. The Ten also continued to meet separately as did also the Common Market countries, so that in the twelve months between the IMF annual meetings of 1966 and 1967 three separate bodies were engaged in the same exercise. The result of all these deliberations was the 'Rio draft', an outline for a scheme for Special Drawing Rights, put before the IMF annual meeting at Rio de Janeiro in September 1967. The Rio draft was translated into draft Articles and then further amended at a ministerial meeting of the Ten in Stockholm in March 1968, whereupon it was accepted by the Executive Board of the Fund as the basis for a proposal for an extensive amendment to the Articles of Agreement, to be submitted to the member countries for ratification.

The amendment to the Articles of Agreement, which was submitted to member countries in 1968 and duly ratified in 1969 by the appropriate voting procedure, was the first amendment to the Fund's charter, as originally settled at Bretton Woods. The main purpose of the amendment was to entrust the IMF with the operation of a new Special Drawing Account, in addition to operating the General Account.

The main issues in the SDR negotiations

The four main issues arising in the prolonged negotiations of the Special Drawing Rights scheme were as follows:

Membership

It was not until towards the end of 1966 that it was accepted that contingency planning for a new reserve asset should be on the basis that membership of any new scheme would be open to all members of the IMF on an equal footing. Previously there had been considerable support within the Group of Ten for a much more restricted membership, comprising the Ten with the addition of other rich countries, such as Austria and Australia, should they wish to join. On this basis the developing countries would have been excluded from membership, though as a *quid pro quo* they might have been offered more favourable treatment in the IMF General Account, for example by an increase in their quotas (and hence in their drawing rights).

The 'Link'

The rights of the developing countries also came up for serious consideration, as from 1967,[4] in the guise of proposals, which had Italian support, that the issuance of any new reserve asset should be arranged so as to provide additional development finance for the Third World. Such proposals for a 'Link', as it came to be called, were not in fact incorporated in the SDR scheme, which was deliberately designed *not* to cause the permanent transfer of real resources from one member country to another.

The case for reform

The first issue which inevitably arises in any proposal for a new reserve asset is whether this is allegedly needed to supplement existing reserve media, to replace them, or to do both. Discussions on this issue got off to a bad start, since in February 1965 General de Gaulle made his famous pronouncement extolling the virtues of gold as compared with other reserve assets (see page 181). But in the course of the year the Ten seemed to have reached a consensus that for the time being it was not practical politics to replace the dollar and the pound as reserve currencies, and certainly not by gold.

Certain radical proposals ... such as the total exclusion of the foreign exchange component by transition to a pure gold reserve standard or the transfer of today's foreign exchange reserves to the IMF, accompanied by the transformation of the latter into a sort of world central bank, were rejected by the leading countries from the outset as being impracticable under the present circumstances.[5]

The alternative case for introducing a new reserve asset (namely to *supplement* existing reserve media) is the one which is seriously canvassed in the Ossola and Emminger reports. All the Ten except France agreed that (though there might be no immediate need for a new kind of liquidity) contingency planning should go ahead lest the need should arise in the not-too-distant future. When, then, should the creation of any kind of liquidity begin, and at what pace should it proceed? The Ossola Report stressed that the need for additional reserves could not be assessed by any simple formula. Instead, many symptoms would have to be taken into account:

An indication that reserves are inadequate might be found in a reluctance to extend inter-governmental credit, or in an increasing propensity to seek credit, in preference to parting with reserve assets. Clearer evidence of a general scarcity might be found in a marked tendency to make mainten-ance, increase or restoration of reserves an overriding objective of economic policy, taking priority over other fundamental objectives, such as economic growth, a high level of employment and freedom of international trade. .... Significant symptoms of strain would be a generalisation of trade and payments restrictions, instability of exchange rates, rising unemploy-ment and falling international prices.[6]

When would any of these 'symptoms of strain' appear? At the time of the Emminger Report the majority of opinion among the Ten was that they had not yet appeared. As the Bundesbank put it, in its *Report* for the year 1965,

It is true ... that the total holdings of monetary reserves have increased only slightly in 1965, especially when the statistics are adjusted for the influence of some temporary special circumstances. It is also true that new accruals of monetary gold in the Western world have, especially owing to persistent hoarding of gold, since the beginning of 1965 dwindled to very small proportions, which alone would never suffice to meet the world's demand for reserves in the longer run. On the other hand, however, this slow expansion of the world's monetary reserves has by no means pre-vented world trade from developing vigorously during the past year.[7]

Nevertheless, following the lead given in July 1965 by Henry

Fowler, the then Secretary of the US Treasury, in associating the US with the case for reform, the Group of Ten (except for France, which had not so far accepted the need for contingency planning) decided that it was prudent to work on the basis that the stagnation of world reserves in 1965 (a phenomenon which was repeated in a number of subsequent years) might betoken the end of the upward trend in total reserves of the traditional kinds, and that (even if this evidence was inconclusive) the upward trend would anyway 'come to a natural end since the creation of additional reserves by US balance-of-payments deficits, which in the past seven years accounted for more than half of the new gold and exchange reserves, would in the long run be neither desirable nor indeed possible'.[8] Hence prudence required, in the opinion of all the Ten except France, that contingency planning should go ahead for the introduction of some new kind of reserve asset. What kind, then, should it be?

What kind of reserve asset?

In the early stages of the discussions in the Group of Ten, that is, at least up to the time of the Emminger Report, the choice was taken to lie between a reserve unit scheme, which seems to have made the running up to 1967, and a drawing-right-type scheme, which came to the fore in the course of 1967 thanks to French support.[9]

As regards the former Dr J. J. Polak of the IMF, looking back at the end of 1967, wrote:

Three or four years ago, there was some groping for the creation of additional reserve assets by a further extension of the reserve currency concept. It was suggested, in particular, that half a dozen or so currencies other than dollars or sterling should also perform the functions of reserve currencies. Traces of this approach can also be found in the early suggestions for a composite reserve unit, which would make the value of this unit to some extent derive from the market value of the underlying currency balances. . . .

Although the discussions continued for a while in terms of a reserve asset 'backed' by currency balances, it became increasingly clear that the essential value of the new asset derived from the obligation of participants to accept it, in much the same way as the value of domestic fiduciary money derives from its status as legal tender. The acceptance obligation was gradually made more precise, and the balances of their own currency by which countries were originally supposed to acquire the new asset were increasingly seen as immaterial to the plan, and in fact they were dropped when we drafted the Outline.[10]

Thus by the time of the Outline, or the 'Rio draft' as I have called it, the negotiating statesmen and officials of the Group of Ten had settled for contingency planning on the basis of a fiduciary reserve unit, which would not be 'backed' by national currencies, gold, or any other asset. The only hesitant member of the group was France. It had agreed, at an important meeting of the Common Market countries at Munich in April 1967, to join the rest of the Ten in contingency planning only on the understanding that this planning would be for a drawing rights scheme. Now France found itself, later in the year, presented with an outline for a scheme whose label, 'Special Drawing Rights', suggested that it related to new drawing rights, but whose provisions were quite unlike the existing IMF drawing rights and instead provided for what was essentially a reserve unit; indeed the only concession in the new scheme in favour of the French point of view was the 30 per cent reconstitution provision (below, page 137) which may be regarded as a vestige of the French idea of a *repayable* drawing right.

Thus France had misgivings, which were not overcome at the Rio meeting in September 1967. Hence the necessity for calling the Stockholm meeting of the Ten in March 1968 (see page 131), and even this failed in its main purpose in that the French minister, M. Debré, persisted in his misgivings and reserved his position. It was not until September 1969 (after M. Pompidou had succeeded General de Gaulle) that France expressed willingness to participate in the SDR scheme, as provided for in the new Articles which had been adopted in the previous July.

Under none of the schemes considered in the Ossola and Emminger reports, nor under the one eventually adopted in the Rio draft, was the required annual increase in the new reserve medium to be brought into existence by making it available preferentially to countries that immediately needed it to finance deficits. The Emminger Report flatly rejected the possibility, in the foreseeable future, of entrusting an international agency with any such freedom of action. 'We are agreed', it states, 'that deliberate reserve creation should be neither geared nor directed to the financing of balance of payments deficits of individual countries.' Instead there would be a 'distribution of additional reserve assets to all participating countries in accordance with an agreed general formula', for example in proportion to IMF quotas.[11]

The adoption of the SDR scheme

In the course of the second half of 1969, the negotiations which had been under way since 1963 suddenly came to fruition. The Bretton Woods charter was amended, among other things by the inclusion of new Articles making possible the creation of a Special Drawing Account. The amendment entered into force on 28 July 1969 following acceptance by the required three-fifths of members representing four-fifths of total voting power. The 'club' for operating the SDR scheme came into existence on 6 August: by that day the Fund had received instruments of participation in the Special Drawing Account from members together having more than the required 75 per cent of total quotas. At the Fund annual meeting in September, agreement was reached as to the date of the initial creation of SDRs: this was to be at the beginning of 1970.[12] Agreement was similarly reached on the amount of the SDRs to be created in the first three years: $3.5 billion in January 1970 and $3.0 billion in 1971 and again in 1972. Agreement on activation in 1970 was possible only because the EEC countries were sufficiently impressed by the evidence of a growing shortage of international liquidity (which would be intensified by the improvement then wrongly forecast in the US balance of payments) not to insist on their earlier contention that activation had to be conditional, first, on a substantial improvement in the US balance of payments and, second, on the observance of stricter 'rules of the game' (more particularly by deficit countries) to expedite the adjustment process.

The SDR facility in outline[13]

SDRs are more readily available than the credit that the IMF provides through drawings in the credit tranches of the General Account. Any participating country is able to use SDRs whenever it has a balance of payments or reserve need to do so. Its exercise of this right is not subject to consultation or prior challenge nor contingent on the adoption of prescribed policies designed to restore balance of payments equilibrium. Moreover, the use of SDRs does not entail repayment according to a fixed schedule, as does the use of the resources of the General Account, although prior to 1981 SDR balances had to be partially reconstituted following large and prolonged use.

The scheme provides for the creation of specified annual amounts of a new reserve asset called SDRs, the value of which to any one participant rests basically on the obligation of other participants to accept them, up to a prescribed ceiling, in exchange for a national currency. The SDRs thus created are distributed among the participating countries in proportion to their IMF quotas. The amounts to be issued are for a 'basic' period of several years. The initial basic period was the three years 1970–1–2 in which a total of $9.5 billion was issued. This was followed by an interval of seven years, at the end of which there was a second basic period of three years (1979–80–1) during which a slightly larger amount was issued.

The cumulative total of all the newly created SDRs allocated to any participating country is known as its 'net cumulative allocation', and the ceiling to any participant's commitment to accept SDRs from other members, in exchange for a national currency, is set by the provision that no participating country can be required to hold more SDRs than three times its net cumulative allocation.

Any participating country which asserts its need to finance a balance of payments deficit[14] is entitled to use its SDRs to obtain currencies from other participants, though up to 1981 this right was subject to the limitation that over a five-year period a country's average holdings must not be less than a certain minimum percentage (initially 30 per cent but reduced to 15 per cent in 1979) of the average of its net cumulative allocation over the same period.

A participant entitled to make use of its SDRs may do so in either of two ways: *bilaterally*, to buy back its own currency from another participating country, if the latter is willing, or to effect certain other transactions specified by the Fund; or *through the Fund*, in which case the Fund designates other participants to whom the SDRs may be transferred in exchange for a national currency, and who must thereupon accept them up to the limit of their respective ceilings. In the latter case the Fund selects countries for designation on much the same basis as it selects currencies for drawings from the General Account (see Chapter 10).

The value of the SDR in terms of national currencies was initially set by the convention that one SDR equalled one-thirty-fifth of an ounce of gold, so that until the increase of the dollar price of gold in 1971 one SDR equalled one dollar. However, in July 1974 the convention was changed: thereafter the value of the SDR varied proportionately with that of a basket of sixteen (subsequently five) national currencies (see page 167).

SDRs in the 1970s

In the event, the decision to issue SDRs in 1970–2 could not have been more ill-timed. The US deficit did not disappear, as had been expected, but increased dramatically, and likewise the total of other countries' official reserves. Had these developments been correctly foreseen, the SDR scheme would certainly not have been activated in 1970. Hence it is not surprising that there should have been such a long interval between the initial issuance in the basic period 1970–2 and the second issuance beginning in January 1979.

13 The Eurodollar market

There is nothing new about banks taking deposits in foreign currencies. . . .
Canadian and Swiss banks . . . took US dollar deposits and placed them
through New York agencies in loans or investments here . . . these deposits
did not call for the coinage of a special name as long as they were covered by
loans and investments in New York. They were simply an appendage to the
American money market.

The something new that got added – and gave the market a dimension
that warranted a new name – was the innovation of lending or investing
dollar deposits in Europe. This practice, initiated by British overseas and
merchant banks in the middle 1950s, quickly spread to the European
continent, and attracted the participation not only of Canadian and Swiss
banks – on the base of their already existing dollar deposits – but also of
European offices of American, Japanese, and Russian banks.

Norris O. Johnson,
pamphlet dated 1964[1]

Europe acquired US dollars under the Marshall Plan, and later on,
as the US went into balance of payments deficit, the accumulation
of dollars proceeded further. European central banks converted
some billions of their surplus dollars into gold but they also reduced
restrictions on the private holding of dollars. Thereafter European
banks, merchants and industrialists accumulated short-term dollar
deposits, and it was this which opened the way for the development
of the Eurodollar market.

What distinguishes a Eurodollar deposit from a 'native' dollar
deposit is that it is the liability of a bank located outside the USA.[2]
Thus it is the location of the debtor bank and not of the holder (who
may possibly be a US resident) which makes a deposit 'Euro'.
Eurodollar deposits are, however, readily convertible into native
dollars, since they are all promises to pay dollars in New York: the
debtor normally settles by cable transfer on New York, which serves
as a clearing house for transfers of Eurodollar deposits, following
instructions from foreign centres.

In the simplest kind of Eurodollar business, banks located outside the US (which may be overseas branches of US banks) take (that is, borrow) dollar deposits, lend the dollars as Eurodollar advances, and earn a differential between average rate paid and average rate earned to cover expenses and produce a profit. In more common practice, however, foreign exchange transactions become involved: banks can obtain dollars for making Eurodollar advances by selling for dollars other currencies they have on deposit; while on the other hand banks receiving deposits of dollars can sell them for other currencies they want to use. Thus a bank's Eurodollar liabilities may be either less than or greater than its Eurodollar assets.

The risks of exchange-rate fluctuations – involved in taking one currency and lending another – can be minimized by 'swaps' – trading one currency for another in the present (spot) and contracting to reverse the transaction at an appropriate date in the future (forward). For example, a bank in London may obtain sterling to lend to (say) UK local authorities by taking dollars as interest-bearing deposits, selling them for sterling and covering forward.

Alternatively, the currency swap may be undertaken not by the bank but by its borrowing customer. For example, a London bank may lend dollars to a firm on the Continent. The firm may get the dollars at a lower interest rate than by borrowing local currency, and it may be that it is dollars that are needed for the firm's transactions. But if the borrower needs local currency, to be acquired by selling the dollars, he takes a risk that the local currency may be devalued in terms of the dollar, so that the amount of his loan, in local currency, will be increased. Unless he is prepared to accept this risk, he will obtain forward cover – that is, he will enter into a contract to buy dollars against the local currency on the date the loan matures. If the dollar is selling at a premium in the forward market, it will cost him something to cover the risk. If the cost of forward cover, expressed as an annual rate, is added to the interest rate on the dollar loan, the total cost of borrowing may still be competitive with the rate he would have had to pay on a local currency loan.

So much for the actual organization of the Eurodollar market. Let us now consider some of the reasons for its very rapid growth after about 1957.

1 On the demand side an important initial spur to the development of the market was the increase of the United Kingdom bank rate to 7 per cent in 1957 and the restriction then put on the use of

acceptance credits in sterling for the financing of trade between non-sterling-area countries. In consequence sterling was no longer available for part of its traditional uses, and not unnaturally London banks began to do business in another currency.

2   Also on the demand side was the diversion of borrowers from US to non-US sources of dollar finance, resulting from the imposition by the US authorities of the interest equalization tax and other restrictions on capital outflows over the period from 1964 until January 1974 (see page 105).

3   On the supply side of the market, there was a diversion of dollar deposits from US to Eurobanks (including the foreign branches of American banks) as the result of legal limitations on interest rates payable by banks located in the USA. Such banks were officially restricted (under so-called Regulation Q) as to the maximum rate payable on time deposits. In 1959, when limits of 2½ per cent at ninety days and 3 per cent at six months were in force, Regulation Q made American deposit rates uncompetitive with Eurodollar deposit rates and this has occurred again on various occasions. To alleviate this problem for US banks, certain *foreign*-owned deposit rates and this occurred again on various occasions. To USA were exempted from Regulation Q as from October 1962, but until June 1970 Regulation Q still applied to all other deposits at such banks. As from 24 June 1970, however, Regulation Q was suspended for thirty-day to eighty-nine-day certificates of deposit, issued by banks located in the USA, in denominations of $100,000 or more, and on 16 May 1973 for longer maturities.

4   On several occasions (particularly 1966 and 1968–9) when US banks have been short of reserves, those with foreign branches have been anxious to attract dollar deposits at these branches for on-lending to their US head offices. In this way they were able to improve their reserves at the expense of competitors who confined their banking operations to the United States. This form of competition was especially successful during the period when Regulation Q was effective, for then a bank could not offer interest on US deposits in excess of the prescribed ceiling rate, whereas Euro-deposits could be remunerated at an unrestricted rate. An additional advantage of taking deposits in foreign branches is that the reserve requirements imposed by the US authorities on US banks do not apply to Eurodollar deposits at their foreign branches, nor did they before 1969 to amounts on-lent by these branches to the US head office. As from October 1969, however, liabilities of

banks located in the USA to their foreign branches were subject to a 10 per cent reserve requirement; this has changed from time to time but at the present time (1988) it is 3 per cent.

Of the above advantages enjoyed by Eurodollar centres, that afforded by Regulation Q has been virtually inoperative since June 1970 and those afforded by the IET and other kinds of US restrictions on capital outflows were discontinued as from January 1974.

Since then many depositors and borrowers have been able to do their banking business indifferently as between New York and London, so that dollar interest rates in the two centres must now always be closely in line. Indeed if the Eurobanks are to be competitive their deposit and lending rates must lie *within* the spread between deposit and lending rates in New York; that is, the Eurobanks need to work on a narrower margin between deposit and lending rates than New York banks.

The Eurodollar market and official reserves

The Eurodollar market concerns the international monetary system, as treated in this book, mainly for its relevance to the dollar transactions of national monetary authorities. In the 1960s and subsequently it has been thus relevant in the following ways:

1   As will shortly be explained in this chapter, there was in the course of the 1960s a growth of Eurodollar deposits held in official reserves. Such deposits were negligible at the beginning of the sixties, but by 1970 they had reached a total of about $10 billion.

2   In the 1970s the amount of officially held Eurodollars increased even faster, mainly by the investment of the oil revenues of the oil-exporting countries, as will be explained in Chapter 19. By the end of 1977 officially held Eurodollars had reached the enormous total of $70 billion.[3]

3   The recycling of native dollars through the foreign branches of US banks back into their head offices, such as occurred in 1966 and again in 1968–9, temporarily mopped up the large amounts of dollars which otherwise would have found their way into reserves of other countries' central banks. This will be explained in Chapter 14.

4   As from 1973 there has been an enormous amount of public sector borrowing in the Eurodollar market, both by industrial countries, including the UK, and by many of the developing

countries, with the specific intention of replenishing official reserves. We shall return to this in Chapter 19.

Official holdings of Eurodollars

Although, as we saw in Chapter 3, changes in the total of *native* dollars in other countries' reserves are related, among other things, to transactions between these countries and the United States, the accumulation of official holdings of *Euro*dollars must be attributed to transactions undertaken by other countries' central banks with commercial banks located outside the USA. If these central banks, to prevent a rise in the value of their national currency, sell it in the market, what they acquire in exchange are native dollars. They only replace these by Eurodollars if they choose to deposit them at a Eurobank, which in turn will probably then on-lend them to a customer[4] who may well sell them for another currency, say marks,[5] which may force the Bundesbank, in order to prevent an appreciation of its currency, to sell marks in the market and thereby add to German dollar reserves. In such a case the Bundesbank may thereby be acquiring unwanted dollars, but if so no blame can be attached to the US authorities, who could indeed claim that their restrictions on capital outflows (above, pages 105–9) were designed precisely to prevent US residents from shifting their deposits from banks in the US to Eurobanks (and thereby adding to the dollar deposits already held at the latter by non-US central banks and other non-US investors). No, if any official authority is to be held responsible for the consequences of the growth in official holdings of Eurodollars, the responsibility must surely lie with the central bank which elected to on-lend its native dollars to a Eurobank. That such was the case was only gradually realized in the 1960s, so the US authorities came in for ill-founded criticism, but in June 1971 the point was taken in the Group of Ten, who reached an agreement to limit the amount of their recycling of reserves into the Eurodollar market. However, this agreement in no way committed the central banks of other countries, and official holdings of Eurodollars continued to increase, reaching a total of $21 billion at end 1973. After that date the *raison d'être* of the G–10 agreement substantially disappeared, since with the repeal in January 1974 of official restrictions on US capital outflows, Eurobanks could thenceforth attract dollar deposits on any scale they needed simply by offering depositors of whatever nationality slightly better terms than those obtainable at banks in New York. None the less, the G–10 agreement was specifically renewed in February 1979 – a case of carefully locking the back door even though the front door was now wide open.

Other Eurocurrency markets

Some of the factors which contributed to the rapid growth of the Eurodollar market later came also to apply in the case of other currencies, especially the pound sterling, the German mark and the Japanese yen. The countries concerned have had from time to time exchange control regulations designed to impede either capital outflows or capital inflows and hence to deny some categories of banking customers ready access to the domestic banking system; they also impose irksome regulations such as minimum reserve ratios on banking in the home currency. Hence in each case banking operations have developed in locations which escape the impact of such regulations: there is, for example, a Eurosterling market in Paris, a Euromark market in Luxembourg and a variety of Eurocurrency markets in London and in Switzerland. The growth in Eurocurrency deposits other than in dollars has been rapid, especially in the 1970s: identified official holdings alone, which amounted to the equivalent of only $0.4 billion at end 1970, had by end 1977 reached $15 billion.

14 The collapse of Bretton Woods convertibility

Since the major deficit country, the United States, could not adjust its exchange rate without endangering the operation of the system, and since most of the surplus countries were persistently reluctant to change their own rates, the disequilibrium in world payments increased through the latter half of the 1960s until it reached a breaking point in mid-1971. At that time, the disequilibrium became so large that speculative pressures caused billions of dollars to be exchanged for foreign currencies within a few days. These currency movements greatly increased US liabilities to foreign official institutions and further reduced the stock of US reserve assets. This brought to a head a problem which had been developing for some time: how to maintain convertibility as the stock of dollars held by foreign official institutions grew and the United States' own stock of reserve assets, mainly gold, shrank.

Report of the US Council of Economic
Advisers, January 1973[1]

In the late 1960s one of the earlier symptoms of disequilibrium, the persistent UK deficit, seemed to be yielding to treatment, aided by the devaluation of sterling (from $2.80 to $2.40) reluctantly undertaken by the British government in November 1967. However, other symptoms, particularly the persistent US deficit and the persistent surpluses of Germany and Japan, became increasingly acute. At the September 1968 annual meeting of the IMF, the managing director warned that 'continuing attention will have to be paid to the working of the adjustment process' and the G–10 finance ministers in conference at Bonn in November 1968 discussed the case for adjusting par values, including that of the mark. One of the two German ministers present, Strauss, was not averse to an eventual multilateral realignment of exchange rates (as happened at the Smithsonian conference in December 1971) but nothing of the kind was achieved at the Bonn conference, which was indeed a complete fiasco. So no action was taken for the time being, though in 1969

France devalued (in August) and Germany yielded to the pressure of events by unpegging the mark on 29 September and re-pegging it at a higher dollar value on 26 October.

The case for a reform of the Bretton Woods procedure for parity changes, so as to achieve greater flexibility, did not, however, go by default: as from January 1969 there were discussions on the subject by the IMF executive directors, meeting with elaborate precautions to ensure secrecy, while the IMF staff assisted with exploratory research. Later in the year the issue was aired in public: there was considerable discussion at the September 1969 IMF annual meeting about the desirability of greater exchange-rate flexibility, and the executive directors were commissioned to prepare a report, which duly appeared in August 1970 under the title *The Role of Exchange Rates in the Adjustment of International Payments*.

Then everybody lost interest in the subject: at the 1970 IMF annual meeting the French Governor, then Giscard d'Estaing, spoke against greater exchange-rate flexibility and there was no strong dissent from his view. One reason why the reforming mood of 1969 evaporated was that the US deficit, as measured by the US official reserve transactions balance, turned into a surplus in 1968 and 1969. Though in these years there was a marked deterioration of the export surplus on goods and services (see page 104), this was masked by an unprecedented upsurge in the recourse of US banks to the Eurodollar market,[2] mainly in the form of borrowing by New York banks of a high proportion of the dollars deposited at their foreign branches in London and other centres. Such borrowing was the New York banks' reaction to the stance of US monetary policy, which in its credit squeezes in 1966 and again in 1968–9 had engineered a shortage of Federal funds (the commercial banks' reserves at the Federal Reserve banks), while preventing, under Regulation Q, any competition for deposits *within the United States*. Under this regulation, as we saw in Chapter 13, a legal ceiling was set to the interest rates payable on deposits at banks in the United States. Once market rates had risen to this ceiling (as they had during the squeezes in question) US banks could no longer offer competitive rates on deposits taken in the United States; hence those which were fortunate enough to have London branches stole a march on their competitors by offering high rates to depositors in London. (Of course, US residents could not in many cases freely transfer their deposits from US centres to London, due to the US restrictions on capital outflows, but all the same high rates offered in

London did succeed in attracting substantial deposits from foreigners, and these were on-lent to head offices, in preference to on-lending to foreign borrowers.) Liabilities of US banks to their foreign branches rose from about $2 billion in the mid 1960s to $4 billion at the end of 1966, about the same at the end of 1967, and $6 billion at the end of 1968, reaching a peak of over $14 billion in September 1969 (see Table 11). Thereafter (thanks to a tightening of the US restrictions on capital outflows and a fall in US interest rates) the total declined – and especially rapidly after 24 June 1970, when Regulation Q was suspended for thirty-day to eighty-nine-day certificates of deposit in denominations of $100 000 or more.[3]

Table 11 *Liabilities of US banks to their foreign branches and foreign branch holdings of special US government securities, 1966–71 ($ billion)*

		Liabilities	Securities
1966	June 29	2.0	
	December 28	4.0	
1967	June 28	3.2	
	December 27	4.2	
1968	June 26	6.2	
	December 31	6.0	
1969	June 25	13.3	
	September 24	14.3	
	December 31	12.8	
1970	June 24	12.2	
	September 30	9.7	
	December 30	7.7	
1971	March 31	2.9	1.5
	June 30	1.5	3.0
	December 29	0.9	

Source: *Federal Reserve Bulletin* (January 1972), p. A88, table 21.

The consequence of the high interest rates offered on certain occasions in the 1960s by US banks on dollar deposits in London, and their practice of on-lending such deposits to their US head offices, was that non-residents' dollar receipts, which might otherwise have found their way into the reserves of foreign central banks, were instead recycled back to the United States, to the great benefit of the US balance on official reserve transactions, in the late 1960s.

Alas, the benefit was short-lived: indeed it was disastrously reversed in the early seventies, as the New York banks repaid their dollar borrowings from their foreign branches.[4] Moreover, the Eurodollar market now came to be used on a large scale for transactions which had just the opposite effect from the recycling operations of the late 1960s: speculators borrowed dollars in the Eurodollar market and promptly sold them for other currencies, so that foreign central banks found it necessary to buy dollars on a large scale in order to prevent the undue appreciation of their currencies in relation to the dollar. There was also in the early 1970s massive switching out of dollars into other currencies by corporate treasurers anxious about the possibility of a depreciation of the former in relation to the latter. Finally, there was a perverse movement in the leads and lags in payments for US exports and imports: US exporters, fearing a fall in the value of the dollar, readily gave their customers extended credit, while US importers settled their accounts with unwonted alacrity. Thus it was that the US balance on official reserve transactions swung wildly from a surplus in the late 1960s to the enormous deficits in the early 1970s: of the order of $10 billion in 1970 and $30 billion in 1971, to which corresponded only slightly smaller increases[5] of respectively $8 billion and $27 billion, in US liabilities to foreign official holders.[6]

Reactions to the dollar flood

The immediate reaction to the dollar flood was the imposition of controls, by most developed countries, to stop the inflow of short-term capital. These controls operated in three main ways:

1 They sought to discourage non-resident bank deposits in the local currency, for example by preventing the payment of interest on non-resident deposits, or by imposing penal reserve requirements against such deposits.
2 They restricted the ability of non-residents to acquire securities denominated in the local currency.
3 They penalized borrowing abroad by resident companies, as for instance under the German Bardepot scheme.

The imposition of such controls was not the remedy favoured by the United States, which hoped for a revaluation of the surplus countries' currencies, and in particular of the German mark and the

Japanese yen; however, under the Bretton Woods procedure it was the United States's partners that had to take the initiative, so that all the USA could do was to exercise persuasion. In the event, however, though some other countries did take the required initiative, they acted so belatedly and inadequately as to arouse in 1971

increasing apprehension of a loss of United States competitive strength in world markets. As the weekly figures of dollar reserve gains abroad confirmed the generalized weakness of the dollar and the prospect that the United States deficit was rising well above the abnormally high level of 1970, overt speculation began to appear in the exchange markets in March, further swelling the torrent of dollars flowing to foreign markets.

Although the developing weakness of the dollar was generalized across the European currency exchanges, the German mark was particularly exposed to speculative buying pressure . . . [as also was the Japanese yen].

Early in May, a report by the main German economic research institutes, recommending either a floating of the mark rate or revaluation as the best solution to this and other policy dilemmas, was greeted sympathetically by certain high-ranking German officials. The market seized on this apparent shift of policy, and speculative funds flooded into Germany. The Bundesbank was forced to buy dollars in mounting volume, more than $1 billion on May 3–4 and a further $1 billion in the first forty minutes of trading on May 5, at which point it withdrew from the market.

To protect themselves against the backwash of the German move, the central banks of the Netherlands, Switzerland, Belgium, and Austria similarly terminated official support of the dollar that same morning. Over the weekend, the Swiss franc and the Austrian schilling were revalued by 7.07 per cent and 5.05 per cent, respectively, while the German mark and Dutch guilder were allowed to float. . . . The revaluations of the Swiss franc and Austrian schilling did little, however, to bring about a spontaneous return flow of speculative funds as the foreign exchange markets remained highly nervous. In particular, the flotation of the mark and guilder aroused widespread fears in the market that other countries might take similar action. Furthermore, as the mark and guilder floated upward they tended to become barometers of weakening confidence in the dollar. Meanwhile, current statistics on the performance of the United States economy failed to measure up to earlier hopes, and the foreign trade balance slipped into a deepening deficit in April and subsequent months. . . .

On Sunday, August 15, President Nixon announced a major new program of domestic and international economic measures. . . . With respect to international payments, the President introduced a 10 per cent temporary surcharge on dutiable imports into the United States, and announced a temporary suspension of convertibility of the dollar into gold and other assets.[7]

The purpose of this drastic step was to force other countries to unpeg their currencies from the dollar, and in this it was successful. Whether they were then re-pegged at higher parities in relation to the dollar (as in fact happened in December) or whether they continued to float, was for the United States at this stage a matter of secondary importance which could be discussed in due time, after its partners had accepted the inevitability of a substantial appreciation of the dollar value of their currencies. In the US view, foreign statesmen and officials could be made to give up the defence of their existing pegs only if the dollars they would thereby acquire were made inconvertible into gold and so less desirable to hold. Hence the US decision to suspend convertibility for a 'temporary', but all the same indefinite, period. In any case, the US decision announced on 15 August 1971 would very soon have been imposed by the pressure of events, since the growing lack of confidence in the dollar would soon have produced a run on the US gold reserve on a scale such as would have quickly led to its exhaustion. So the suspension of dollar convertibility was inevitable in the absence of a major appreciation of other currencies, which in turn was not negotiable so long as the dollar remained convertible: this was the impasse from which Mr Nixon hoped to extricate his country in his speech of 15 August, and he succeeded. A cynic might point out that the President must also have been mindful of the political advantages of a move which, by making the foreign-currency price of US goods more competitive, would reabsorb some of the US unemployed – though only on the beggar-my-neighbour basis of increasing unemployment elsewhere. By all accounts, however, this was no more than a welcome side-effect: the decision was taken for essentially monetary reasons.

Part Four

From pegging to floating, August 1971 onwards

15 The dollar standard, December 1971–March 1973

The external measures announced on August 15 . . . [by] the US Government suspended the convertibility of dollars held in foreign official reserves into gold and other reserve assets. Other actions taken – imposition of a temporary 10 per cent surcharge on dutiable imports and the limitation of tax relief for capital expenditures to domestically produced capital goods – were intended to emphasize the seriousness with which the US Government viewed the need for exchange rate adjustments.

Federal Reserve System, *Annual Report,* 1971[1]

After Mr Nixon's announcement on 15 August 1971, the major European governments

sought to develop some joint policy response to the United States measures. These negotiating efforts failed. . . . The exchange rate structure thus emerging after August 15 was, in most instances, the product of controlled rather than free floating. Many central banks continued to intervene on an *ad hoc* basis, while the market was further strongly influenced by a wide variety of new exchange controls, the United States import surcharge, and sharply conflicting official appraisals of an appropriate realignment of parities.[2]

The initial stance of the United States after 15 August was to wait and see, in the belief that the pressure of events would ensure the degree of exchange-rate alignment that John Connally, the then Secretary of the Treasury, thought necessary for the improvement he wanted in the US balance of payments. However, a policy of wait-and-see had its disadvantages. In the first place, controls on capital movements were proliferating, contrary to the philosophy of free capital movement which the US favoured and believed to be in its national interest.

There was a spate of new measures to limit short-term capital inflows in 1971 in connection with the upheaval in exchange markets. The floating of the German mark and the Dutch guilder in May 1971 led to some measures to limit short-term inflows in those countries,[3] and also in Belgium and France. Then the US measures announced

on August 15, by generating massive flows out of the dollar into a number of European currencies and the Japanese yen, caused the authorities in the United Kingdom, Switzerland and Japan to act to prevent speculative inflows, and prompted additional moves in France and the Netherlands to the same end. . . .[4]

In the second place, the US soon found that its import surcharge imposed on 15 August was having its severest impact on the country which was least unsympathetic to the case for a realignment of exchange rates – Germany. So, after temporizing for several months, Mr Connally showed a greater willingness to negotiate.

The Smithsonian agreement

The negotiations, which took place in the G–10 forum, were the first ever conducted to adjust exchange rates on a multilateral basis,[5] in place of the one-at-a-time procedure of the 1960s: they were also novel, and indeed unique, in proceeding by an attempted reconciliation of the participating countries' respective balance of payments objectives – very much on the lines of the procedure recommended in the WP3 Report of August 1966 (see pages 74–5). It cannot, however, be said that this procedure was *readily* adopted by the governments of the main countries concerned; rather it was forced on them by the initiative of officials in the IMF and OECD, whose statistical exercises came to be the basis of the G–10 discussions. Nor can it be said that these discussions were enabled by the new procedure to advance smoothly and amicably to an agreed realignment of dollar pegs. Such an alignment was indeed achieved, but the debates which preceded it were protracted and increasingly acrimonious. Mr Connally made no secret of his exasperation at the readiness of EEC members of the Group to reject his own proposals, though apparently unable themselves to agree on an alternative. They in turn were equally uncomplimentary about the tough line adopted by the US. In the end, however, in the Smithsonian building in Washington, on 18 December, a deal was concluded. In return for the ending of the 10 per cent surcharge and the other unwelcome measures imposed by Mr Nixon on 15 August, the other members of G–10 agreed to re-peg on the dollar at target rates ('central' rates, as they were now to be called) which amounted to a substantial depreciation of the dollar, though a smaller one than Mr Connally had wanted. The changes made in dollar rates are shown in Table 12. In addition to these changes in target rates, pegging was henceforth to be less precise than under the Bretton Woods arrangements, the permitted margin of 1 per cent each side of parity being now replaced by one of 2¼ per cent each side of the central rate.

Table 12 *Smithsonian agreement, 18 December 1971: percentage revaluation of currencies in terms of the US dollar*

Country	Per cent
Belgium	11.6
Canada	(floating)
France	8.6
Germany*	13.6
Italy	7.5
Japan	16.9
Netherlands*	11.6
Sweden	7.5
United Kingdom	8.6

* Increase as compared with par value in effect prior to May 1971.

An ingredient in the Smithsonian package was an increase in the official price of gold from $35 to $38 an ounce. This change was without operational significance in that the dollar was no longer officially convertible into gold, but it enabled the change in pegged rates to be represented as more in the nature of a depreciation of the gold value of the dollar than an appreciation of the dollar value of other currencies. This was a diplomatic setback for Mr Connally (who had previously been asserting that the dollar price of gold would on no account be increased),[6] but for some European central banks it had the advantage of maintaining the local-currency value of their reserve assets.[7]

After the Smithsonian agreement, the US dollar retained its role as intervention currency, even though the US authorities made it clear that they were for the time being much less ready to engage in swap transactions with other central banks; indeed the swap network was put into cold storage from 15 August 1971 until July 1972 and even afterwards was put to only little use until July 1973, as is apparent from Table 13. Even less were the US authorities prepared to mop up unwanted dollars by converting them into gold.

Thus the post-Smithsonian regime may properly be described as a dollar standard, under which $n-1$ currencies were convertible into the dollar, without the latter being itself convertible into any other reserve asset.

Table 13   *Federal Reserve swap network: gross drawings, quarterly, 1971–5 ($ million)*

Quarters		By USA	By other countries and BIS
1971	1	615	21
	2	555	6
	3	2395	—
	4	—	3
1972	1	—	8
	2	—	6
	3	10	1
	4	35	4
1973	1	104	11
	2	—	23
	3	489	36
	4	24	46
1974	1	255	26
	2	130	76
	3	9	245
	4	366	129
1975	1	861	45
	2	169	1
	3	—	305
	4	250	199

Source: *Federal Reserve Bulletin* (December 1976), pp. 1009–11.

It seemed reasonable to hope at the end of 1971 that the world would peacefully settle down to an improved version of the monetary regime of the 1960s – the improvement being that a technique had now been found to re-peg exchange rates by multilateral agreement, and thereby to escape from the difficulty that the special role of the dollar deprived the United States authorities of the ability to devalue. However, as we shall see, things did not in fact go so smoothly for the dollar standard, which progressively gave way to a floating regime, beginning with the floating of sterling in June 1972.

The snake in the tunnel

We have seen that the Bretton Woods pegging arrangements, as they operated up to August 1971, required each country other than the US to keep the market value of its currency within a 'tunnel', the ceiling of which was 1 per cent above its dollar parity and the floor 1 per cent below. The Smithsonian conference of December 1971 enlarged the tunnel to 2¼ per cent above and below the dollar parity (or central value, as it was now termed). Hence a European country's currency could fluctuate (from ceiling to floor, or vice versa) by 4½ per cent in relation to the dollar. But if one European currency rose from floor to ceiling while another fell from ceiling to floor, their relative fluctuation would be 9 per cent. Such a large fluctuation as between two European currencies was repugnant to the EEC's aspiration to move by successive stages to eventual European monetary union, as mapped out in the Werner Report of October 1970. In this report, EEC central banks had been 'invited, from the beginning of the first stage [that is, as from January 1971] to restrict on an experimental basis the fluctuations of rates between Community currencies within narrower bands than those resulting from the application of the margins in force in relation to the dollar'. There would follow in the course of the first stage a 'progressive narrowing of the margins of fluctuation between Community currencies' and such a convergence of economic and monetary policies that in the course of the second stage, which would begin in January 1974, member states would 'no longer have to resort on an autonomous basis to the instrument of parity adjustment'. At the end of stage two, autonomous parity changes would be totally excluded, and indeed the hope was that parities between EEC members would thereafter be immutable: moreover the permitted fluctuation of actual exchange rates above and below parity would become nominal or even zero, thereby facilitating the creation of a single currency for the whole of the EEC (above, page 126).

In the light of the Werner plan, which was approved in principle by the Community's Council of Ministers in February 1971, the widening of the 'tunnel' accepted by G-10 at the Smithsonian conference was naturally seen as a step backwards, and as a challenge to EEC members to inaugurate specifically EEC arrangements for keeping fluctuations as between member countries' currencies within narrower limits. This was the purpose of the 'snake in the tunnel'. The dollar value of the member countries' currencies would be kept within the wide tunnel provided for in the Smithsonian agreement, and supervised by the IMF; at the same time they would have their *relative* movements confined within a narrower EEC snake.

The essential characteristic of the snake scheme is that whenever the 'strongest' EEC currency's percentage premium over its parity plus the 'weakest' currency's[8] discount on its parity (expressed in terms of a common *numéraire*) reaches a predetermined limit (2¼ per cent, or half the amount permitted by the Smithsonian tunnel) then someone buys the weakest currency with the strongest. The 'someone' may be either the weak-currency country (debtor intervention) or the strong-currency country (creditor intervention) or both together. With creditor intervention, the intervening country buys the weak currency in the exchange market with its *own* currency, which it can make available as required; hence the only problem which arises is what to do with the weak currency which has been purchased. With debtor intervention, the intervening country has first to borrow from its partner the strong currency needed for purchasing its own weak currency in the market: hence the need for the so-called 'very short-term' credit facility which was incorporated in the EEC scheme.

Whether the intervention is by the creditor or by the debtor country, a settlement arrangement is needed, by which periodically (monthly, in the EEC scheme) the creditor countries can exchange their accumulation of weak currency for a more acceptable reserve asset, and at the same time obtain repayment of their 'very short-term' credits, likewise in terms of an acceptable reserve asset. The snake scheme provided that the monthly settlements should be effected by the transfer by the debtors to the creditors of a mixed bag of reserve assets selected on an agreed formula.

The Community snake came into operation for the original six members in March 1972. The new members (the UK, Denmark and Eire) joined in May 1972 but defected in June, when sterling was floated; Denmark rejoined in October 1972, but the UK and Eire remained outside the scheme. Italy left the snake in the February 1973 crisis (see below); France left in January 1974, rejoined in July 1975, but left again in March 1976. On the other hand, two non-EEC countries joined: Norway in May 1972 and Sweden from March 1973 to August 1977. On the eve of the establishment of the European Monetary System in 1979 (see

Appendix B, page 253) the snake membership comprised Germany, Benelux, Denmark and Norway.

The crisis of June 1972

Following the devaluation of sterling in 1967, the British balance of payments improved, if only very belatedly, and 1969–70–1 were all years with reassuring export surpluses on goods and services. In 1972, however, the balance began to deteriorate and the export surplus was in the course of the year transformed into deficit. Mr Barber, the Chancellor of the Exchequer, reacted to the situation by announcing on 23 June that the pound would be allowed to float and also that the UK exchange control on capital transactions would henceforth be applied to the sterling area in much the same way as it applied to other countries, as we saw in Chapter 6. The UK float provoked a crisis in that it was not clear until 27 June whether other countries would follow suit. In the end, nobody (except Eire, which continued to peg on the floating pound) followed the UK's example. The crucial international meeting, at which the decision not to follow the UK's example was taken, was an EEC meeting of the non-defecting members of the snake – one of the earliest cases where the EEC has provided the forum for successfully taking decisions in international monetary affairs.

The consequences of Mr Barber's decisions proved to be more far-reaching than appeared at the time, in that in retrospect they are now seen to mark the end of the sterling area. Of the sixty-five or so overseas sterling area countries which had previously pegged their currencies on sterling, only about a dozen (mainly small ones) continued to do so thereafter, and subsequently the number has dwindled still further. Moreover the tendency for the former sterling area countries to diversify their reserves accelerated considerably, with sterling forming a diminishing proportion, and the dollar and other currencies an increasing proportion, of their total reserve holdings.

The misfortunes of the dollar standard

By floating sterling in June 1972, Britain withdrew not only from the snake but also from the tunnel. In the nine months that followed, her example was followed by other countries. At the end of March 1973 the snake survived with reduced membership, but the tunnel had been abandoned, in the sense that none of the United States' G–10 partners was any longer pegging on the dollar. This, then, was the end of the regime of the dollar standard.

Why did the Smithsonian agreement fail to achieve the stability that might reasonably have been expected of it? What seems to have happened is that the knowledge that the dollar had been devalued, and could presumably be devalued again at any time by the Smithsonian technique, led to a lack of confidence (as witnessed by the rapid rise, shown in the chart below, in the free market price of gold)

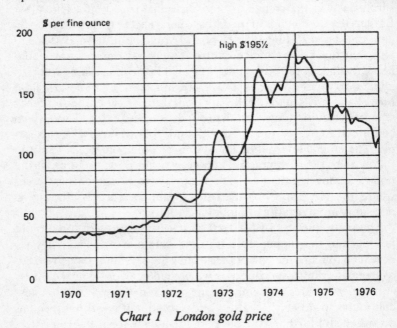

Chart 1   London gold price

in the future stability of the Smithsonian central values. There was also the knowledge that these target rates were the outcome of hard bargaining between the United States and its fellow members of G–10, in which the US had maintained that larger changes would be needed to restore equilibrium. It was known too that some influential Americans felt no commitment to central values of any kind and were perfectly ready for a transition to floating. As regards the other G–10 countries, it was known that those central banks which were the legal owners of their country's reserves[9] were liable to legal and political embarrassment if they made book losses on the local-

Table 14   *Foreign exchange reserves, 1969–73 ($ billion)*

Month-end	Industrial countries*				All other countries
	Germany	Japan	Other	Total	
1969 Dec.	2.7	2.6	12.0	17.3	15.1
1970 Dec.	8.5	3.2	14.4	26.1	19.3
1971 Dec.	12.6	13.8	24.5	50.9	28.4
1972 Dec.	17.2	16.5	27.4	61.1	43.0
1973 March	25.0	16.1	30.4	71.5	47.3
June	25.1	13.1	32.7	70.9	52.0
Sept.	28.1	12.7	31.6	72.4	54.6
Dec.	25.1	10.2	30.9	66.2	56.5

* G–10 plus Switzerland, Austria, Denmark and Norway.
Source: IMF, *International Financial Statistics* (April 1976), p. 24.

currency value of their dollar holdings, and hence were increasingly reluctant to accumulate stocks of what might prove to be a wasting asset. Even more important, it was known that the central banks of both Germany and Japan, in pegging at the Smithsonian central values, were accumulating reserves (Table 14) at a pace which they could clearly not tolerate much longer, if they were to retain any control over the liquidity of their commercial banks.

The great increase in the exchange reserves of these two countries, and in a smaller proportion of other industrial countries, as shown in Table 14, corresponds very closely with the very large US deficit requiring to be financed by official reserve transactions (Table 15).[10] Why did the US official reserve transactions balance fare so badly? In the first place, and partly no doubt because of the J-curve effect, the US export surplus on goods and services did not respond with alacrity to the relative depreciation of the dollar effected at the Smithsonian conference: indeed the surplus regularly achieved in 1970 and previous years developed in 1971 and 1972 into a substantial deficit (Table 15). Additionally, and more important, the lack of any confidence in the permanence of the Smithsonian central values set the scene for a speculative run on the dollar, which undermined confidence still further, and hence became self-justifying and self-perpetuating.

The immediate reaction of the surplus countries, particularly Germany and Japan, to the dollar flood, was recourse to restrictions on capital inflows.

Most of the post-August 15 measures were rescinded shortly after the December 18 Smithsonian meeting which produced a general exchange rate realignment. But in February and March of 1972, Belgium, the Netherlands and Japan experienced undesirably large reserve increases and instituted new regulations to limit short-term inflows. In late June of 1972, following the floating of the pound sterling, Germany, Japan and Switzerland acted to limit inflows of speculative funds . . .[11]

and these controls were retained, with occasional temporary relaxations, until well after the March 1973 crisis: dismantling did not begin seriously until early 1974, although then it proceeded rapidly.

Another important reaction to the difficulties encountered in the operation of the dollar standard was that statesmen and officials in the major countries, and especially in the UK, began to take an interest in possible alternative regimes, in which the dollar would no longer have such a different role from other national currencies. To this we shall return in Chapter 16.

Table 15 *US balance of payments, quarterly, 1970–3, seasonally adjusted ($ billion)*

Quarters		Export surplus or deficit (−) on goods and services	Deficit (−) financed by official reserve transactions
1970	1	1.3	−3.2
	2	1.6	−2.1
	3	1.7	−2.0
	4	1.0	−3.3
1971	1	1.4	−6.1
	2	0.5	−6.4
	3	0.9	−12.0
	4	−0.5	−6.0
1972	1	−0.7	−3.8
	2	−0.6	−0.8
	3	−0.2	−4.8
	4	−0.4	−1.6
1973	1	0.8	−10.0
Total		6.8	−62.1*

* Of these $62.1 billion official reserve transactions, $54.8 billion comprised an increase in US liabilities to foreign official agencies.

Source: Survey of Current Business (June 1979), pp. 38–9.

The crises of February and March 1973

The mounting dollar flood breached the dykes on 10 February 1973, when the Japanese authorities closed the exchange market and suspended their market support for the dollar. The crisis was resolved, like that of 1971, by a multilateral negotiation of new central values for the main currencies, though the lira and the yen were left floating, along with the Canadian dollar (which had been floating since June 1970), the UK and Irish pounds (since June 1972) and the Swiss franc (since January 1973). The negotiations in this case comprised a whirlwind trip by Paul Volcker, then US Under Secretary of the Treasury for Monetary Affairs, to major capitals including Tokyo, followed by a meeting at Paris on 12 February under the French finance minister, Giscard d'Estaing, of the representatives of five countries: the US, the UK, France, Germany and Italy. The revised pegs agreed at Paris achieved a general appreciation in relation to the dollar by repeating the Smithsonian gimmick of raising the official dollar price of gold, this time from $38 to $42.2 an ounce, while leaving unchanged the gold value of other currencies.

Alas, the dollar flood still continued, and a further crisis broke in March 1973. It lasted longer than the February one, from 2 to 19 March. Its outcome was also more crucial to the evolution of the monetary system, since it marked the abandonment (only temporarily, it was wrongly thought at the time) of pegging on the dollar by the major industrial countries. Once again the forum for resolving the crisis was not the G–10; this time, however, it was larger than the Ten, namely the eleven countries of the G–10, including the associate member Switzerland, plus the three smaller EEC countries: Denmark, Luxembourg and Eire. This group of fourteen met twice, on 9 and 16 March, on both occasions in Paris. Of the fourteen countries represented, the EEC countries in the snake (France, Germany, Benelux and Denmark) agreed to proceed with a joint float, in which they were joined by their snake partners, Sweden and Norway. (Germany at the same time revalued in relation to the other snake members by 3 per cent.) The other EEC countries continued to float individually, as did Canada, Japan and Switzerland. None of these countries any longer pegged on the US dollar; thus for the fourteen countries concerned this was the end of their experiment with the dollar standard. As regards the other hundred or so members of the IMF, they followed a variety of practices. A few, mainly small countries, continued with the old sterling area practice of pegging on sterling. Many continued to peg on the dollar. Several pegged on synthetic monetary units, comprising 'baskets' of a number of major currencies in fixed proportions. The varying practices of the IMF members, as at mid 1975, are shown in Table 16, taken from the IMF *Annual Report*, 1975.

Table 16   *Exchange rate practices of Fund members, June 1975*

	Number of currencies	Percentage share of trade of Fund members*
Currencies that float independently	11	46.4
Currencies pegged to a single currency, of which:	81	14.4
(a) Pegged to US dollar	*54*	*12.4*
(b) Pegged to French franc	*13*	*0.4*
(c) Pegged to pound sterling	*10*	*1.6*
(d) Pegged to Spanish peseta	*1*	—
(e) Pegged to South African rand	*3*	—
Currencies pegged to a composite of other currencies, of which:	19	12.4
(a) SDR	*5*	*5.0*
(b) Other	*14*	*7.4*
Currencies pegged to others but that change the peg frequently in light of some formula	4	2.0
Currencies in the EEC snake	7	23.2
Total	122	98.4

* Imports plus exports, 1974.

Source: IMF *Annual Report* (1975), p. 24.

16 The Grand Design, 1971–3

In my view, a plan for reform could be built round three central points, which I will now state.

First, the SDR could become the *numéraire* in terms of which parities are expressed and in relation to which currencies are revalued or devalued.

The second point is that the SDR could become the main asset in which countries hold their reserves. Already today most countries hold their reserves in gold, in currencies, and in SDRs. The proportions vary, but in most cases currencies are the major element. Eventually – it would no doubt take time – the SDR could become the major element, with currency holdings largely confined to working balances.

Thirdly, arrangements would be needed to provide for the controlled creation of adequate but not excessive world liquidity without reliance on the deficit position of one or more countries. This was indeed the intention of the existing SDR scheme. We need to carry this forward to make it effective.

Anthony Barber,
at the IMF annual meeting, 1971[1]

The Barber plan

The dollar flood of the early 1970s provoked two kinds of reactions from the monetary authorities of the major powers. There were *ad hoc* reactions to the pressure of events: these have been considered in Chapter 15. There was at the same time a reaction against the regime of the 1960s, which now seemed to be breaking down, and a readiness to consider the possibility of a completely new world monetary order, with a new charter to replace Bretton Woods and a new international currency.

The first statesman of the G–10 countries publicly to advocate proposals for major reform was Anthony Barber, in his speech at the annual meeting of the IMF in September 1971, the gist of which is conveyed in the quotation at the beginning of this chapter. The immediate reaction to the speech was anything but enthusiastic, but with the replacement of John Connally by George Shultz at the US Treasury in 1972 both the US and the IMF showed more interest in the possibility of a 'Grand Design' (as it subsequently came to be called) to rewrite the Bretton Woods charter. The Executive Board of the IMF prepared a report, *Reform of the International Monetary System*, which was presented to the Board of Governors in August 1972. Mr Shultz's address to the Governors at the IMF annual meeting in September 1972 dealt at some length with a possible Grand Design, though without disclosing any clear US position on the critical issues involved. The Governors set up an *ad hoc* committee, the Committee of Twenty (which was in due course to meet at official level under the chairmanship of Jeremy Morse) and the US government prepared for its guidance a memorandum dated November 1972, setting out US views, though still in a noncommittal way.

What then were to be the main provisions of the Grand Design? The various proposals which were drafted in 1971 and 1972, and which I have just mentioned, were far from being in agreement, but it is possible to draw from any one of them a list of the main issues which the Committee of Twenty was intended to consider. The following is such a list, based predominantly on Mr Barber's plan, but not attempting to follow his presentation or priorities.

Numéraire

Mr Barber's first point in the passage I quote above takes for granted what was in 1973 to become a controversial issue, namely that a system of adjustable parities should continue, in preference to floating rates. In such a system the *numéraire*, in terms of which parities are expressed, may be one of the national currencies, say the dollar, as had indeed been *de facto* the case throughout the post-war period. Alternatively it could be, as Mr Barber preferred, an independent unit, like the SDR, which had the advantage that the procedure for establishing parities could then be made identical for all the national currencies. Another such independent unit was gold, but in September 1971 the relative claims of gold and SDRs to serve as *numéraire* were not an important issue, since the value of SDR was then (by its initial definition in 1969) equal to one-thirty-fifth of an ounce of gold (the same as the dollar at the then official price of gold). However, the transactions value of the SDR could be redefined in some other way, as indeed it was from July

1974, when it became equal to a basket of stated, fixed quantities of each of sixteen national currencies;[2] and Mr Barber's preference was for a *numéraire* unit the value of which had such a capability for redefinition from time to time, rather than one defined specifically in terms of gold.

Multicurrency intervention

Mr Barber envisaged that central banks' market transactions would continue to be in national currencies, but that a 'wider use might develop of currencies other than the dollar'. What the Barber plan supposed was that the G–10 and a number of other major countries might operate a scheme for multicurrency intervention on the lines of the EEC snake scheme then under discussion (and which was to become operational in March 1972). The essential characteristic of such a scheme is that excessive deviations from parity are corrected by the purchase (by either of the two countries concerned) of the weakest currency with the strongest. Intervention is then multicurrency, in the sense that the currency bought is whichever happens at the time to be the weakest, and the currency used to buy it is whichever happens at the time to be the strongest.

Asset settlement

At intervals (of one month in the case of the EEC snake) the weakest-currency country would need, in some acceptable way, to settle with the strongest-currency country for the amount of the intervention that has been done in the market. Under the Barber plan, the preferred method of settlement was to be by a transfer of SDRs from the debtor country's central bank to the creditor country's central bank.

Adjustment

The obligation of SDR settlement imposed on weak-currency countries meant that any deficit country without exception (since this provision would apply to the United States, the same as to everybody else) would be subject to pressure to take steps, which might include devaluation, to close its deficit. The pressure on surplus countries to adjust would, however, remain inadequate (as it always has been, in the British view, in the whole post-war period) unless a suitable reform could 'provide for, and indeed promote, appropriate adjustment by all countries – those in surplus as well as those in deficit – in order to maintain equilibrium, and so avoid one of the unsatisfactory features of the present system'.

Sanctions

What kind of reform would be needed to stimulate adjustment, by surplus no less than by deficit countries, was not specified in the Barber Plan, but some kind of sanctions would presumably need to be used, or at any rate threatened, and in subsequent discussions a number of fines or 'charges' and other penalties were proposed[3] by the United States, whose recent experience as a deficit country made her especially anxious to impose on surplus countries a greater responsibility for adjustment. In these discussions about sanctions, the United States argued for the adoption of statistical *indicators* (as they were called) to trigger presumptively the imposition of sanctions, or at any rate to establish a prima facie case that sanctions should be applied. 'The type of indicator favoured for these purposes related to reserve levels rather than reserve flows.'[4]

Substitution

If official transactions in the exchange markets were to be in many national currencies, rather than in dollars only, and if foreign currencies acquired by such transactions were then to be redeemed in SDRs, the main role of the existing reserve currencies would have been usurped by the SDR. What then would happen to the *overhang* (as it was called) of official holdings of dollars and, incidentally, of sterling? Some arrangement would be needed for 'substitution', by which was meant the substitution of SDRs for existing reserve holdings of national currencies. Such substitution could be optional or mandatory, immediate or over a period of time, and the various possibilites offered scope for endless discussion. What Mr Barber himself favoured seems to have been a more or less complete substitution 'by stages' of reserve currencies by SDRs, with SDRs becoming the 'major element' in reserves, and 'currency holdings largely confined to working balances'. To this end a Substitution Account should be established by the IMF, which would issue SDRs in exchange for the deposit of reserve currencies – mainly dollars but also possibly sterling. He said:

Next, there is the question whether existing official holdings of reserve currencies should be converted into SDRs and, if so, how fast. This would be a matter in which the different views of holders of reserve currencies about the composition of their reserves would be of primary importance. But if some of the problems created by the existence of reserve currencies are to be removed, it would be desirable to move in the direction of conversion of existing balances on a considerable scale, probably by stages.

So what I envisage is a gradual conversion over a period of time. Primarily I have in mind the problem of existing holdings of US dollars, but these general principles could also provide a way of running down over time the reserve role of sterling, which is already envisaged by the British government.

One thing which the machinery for a conversion operation, or series of operations, would have to ensure is that as SDRs were issued for this purpose they would be matched by actual retirements of reserve currencies. One possible method would be to set up a new account in the IMF to which special issues of SDRs would be made, equivalent to the expected maximum amount of conversion. . . .

As these conversion operations would merely replace currency balances by SDRs, they would not add to international liquidity. Decisions about the desirable quantity of liquidity would be separate.

Reserve growth

Apart from issuing SDRs in substitution for the overhang of national currencies, the IMF would make further issues from time to time (as it had already begun to do in 1970 and 1971) 'to provide for the controlled creation of adequate but not excessive world liquidity without reliance on the deficit position of one or more countries. This was indeed the intention of the existing SDR scheme. We need to carry this forward to make it effective.'

The Committee of Twenty

In July 1972, the Governors of the Fund decided to set up a committee at ministerial level, containing one member and two associates for each of the twenty constituencies that chose an executive director of the Fund, and charged this Committee of Twenty (C–20) to advise and report on all aspects of reform of the international monetary system. They also set up a committee at Deputy level to formulate proposals for approval by the Ministerial Committee and in September Jeremy Morse, of the Bank of England, was appointed chairman of the Deputies. Finally, the chairman and four vice-chairmen of the Deputies, sometimes described as the Bureau, formed a high-powered secretariat to draft these proposals for approval by the Deputies.[5]

Then, in Mr Morse's own words, in June 1974:

We set out in September 1972 to consolidate all that earlier work and to build, as at Bretton Woods, a complete design for an international monetary system that would last for twenty-five years. This effort was envisaged to take about two years: in the first year, the establishment and resolution of the main issues; in the second year, the working out of detail and – about now – the translation of it all into legal form by way of amendments to the Articles of Agreement of the Fund. The first big wave to hit us was the double-headed exchange crisis of February/March 1973 which broke the fixed rates restored at the Smithsonian [meeting]. Having weathered that, we went fast, and by the end of that summer we had an Outline which did indeed set out all the main issues. However, after a promising meeting in July, the C–20 decided in Nairobi in September that it would not resolve these issues. Instead, the Deputies were asked to go on and work out the detail for the unresolved alternatives, in the hope that this would make resolution easier. Then the second, and more unexpected, wave hit us – the towering rise in oil prices with its threatened disturbance of the whole balance of payments structure. The C–20 meeting in January, in Rome, changed tack. Recognizing that the return to par values and all that goes with it was likely to be delayed, they decided to switch to a more evolutionary process of reform, and to concentrate now on those aspects that were most relevant to the present situation. So, since then, the Deputies have been collecting their work on the reformed system, principles and details, into a final version of the Outline which still leaves some issues open for later decision, and have also been preparing a package of immediate steps to deal with current problems.[6]

So the Grand Design, as Mr Morse called it, on which he and his fellow Deputies had lavished so much time and trouble, was in due course published: it appeared as Part I, 'The reformed system', of C–20's final *Outline of Reform*, dated 14 June 1974.[7] 'The reformed system', at the time it was made public, was alas of historical interest only: Philippe Simonnot of *Le Monde* appropriately described it as Jeremy Morse's 'mummy'.[8] Not only had it been left stranded by the course of events subsequent to the Nairobi meeting (Chapter 17, below), but even at the Nairobi meeting it had been clear from Governors' reactions to the 1973 draft of the Outline that the 'reformed system' was not negotiable. All the efforts of Mr Morse and his colleagues had not succeeded in reaching a consensus on major issues, and no further progress towards a consensus was achieved between the 1973 draft Outline and the final version of June 1974. Philippe Simonnot's post-mortem in *Le Monde* indeed lists no less than nine issues on which, he claimed, the Twenty had been unable to reach agreement. Though his harsh verdict may need to be somewhat tempered, there can be no doubt that some at least of the differences he lists were at all times very far from being reconciled.

First, although the recourse in early 1973 to floating exchange rates, in place of the parity system, was ostensibly only temporary, there were senior statesmen and officials, particularly in the United States, who were determined to continue the experiment indefinitely, partly because they saw in floating the best protection against a renewed overvaluation of the dollar, such as had developed in the 1960s.

Second, the Americans who did not reject out of hand a return to a parity system were all the same quite clear that such a return must be conditional on the adoption of an agreed procedure for sanctions, triggered by statistical indicators, against countries in persistent surplus, to force them to play a fuller part in the adjustment process. The continental European countries would not accept this aspect of the Grand Design: they short-sightedly cast themselves permanently in the role of surplus countries and the US in the role of deficit country, and so regarded sanctions and indicators simply as gratuitous concessions to the special interests of the US.

Third, there was no solution to the overhang problem which was acceptable both to the US and to the holders of her currency. The latter were not prepared that the US should redeem the unwanted dollars in goods, by undervaluing the dollar and thereby running a large and persistent export surplus: such a treatment was wholly unacceptable to the industrial interests in Europe which would suffer the increased US competition. Nor was it any more acceptable to replace the overhanging dollars by redeeming them in SDRs, which amounted to getting the IMF members as a whole to take over liabilities which hitherto had been specifically American.[9] So at no stage in the C–20 deliberations was a solution to the dollar overhang problem in sight. (The fate of the sterling overhang, though of vital importance to the UK, was clearly subsidiary to that of the dollar overhang, and hence never came up for serious consideration.)

As Mr Morse tells us in the passage already quoted, C–20 in January 1974 had abandoned further work on the Grand Design and concentrated instead on 'immediate steps', as they are called in Part II of their final *Outline* of June 1974. The most important of these, from the point of view of subsquent action by the IMF and its member countries, were:

1 The establishment of a new committee, with the same constitution as C–20 meeting at ministerial level, as a new IMF forum. (Such a committee was in fact duly established, the so-called Interim Committee, which met for the first time in October 1974.)
2 The method of valuation of the SDR should be changed, and based on a basket of national currencies. (As already noted, this change was in fact made as from July 1974.)
3 There should be further international study of the Fund arrangements for gold, leading if need be to a modification of the Articles.
4 The Articles of the IMF should also be amended to regularize the recourse by members to floating rates of exchange.
5 The serious difficulties then facing many developing countries required new arrangements to increase the flow of concessionary funds.

Of these five issues, the first two proved uncontroversial and were acted upon in 1974. The third and fourth proved to be highly controversial, as we shall see in Chapter 18, but agreement was eventually reached at the meeting of the Interim Committee at Kingston, Jamaica, in January 1976, and embodied in the second amendment to the Fund's Articles. The Fund's financial facilities were also modified in various ways for the benefit of the developing countries.

Forums

The controversies and negotiations went ahead in many forums. The G–10, which went out of favour with the United States as from the time of its famous Smithsonian meeting in December 1971,[10] and faded into the background during the period of C–20's deliberations, staged a comeback in 1974,[11] though it has never resumed the crucial role it enjoyed in the 1960s. There were bilateral meetings of heads of state, as for example the important meeting between Presidents Ford and Giscard d'Estaing in December 1974 in Martinique. There was the new Interim Committee of the IMF, which met at intervals as from October 1974. There were meetings at ministerial and official level of the EEC member countries. But as from the time of the IMF annual meeting at Nairobi in September 1973 the really important forum came to be G–5, comprising the finance ministers of the United States, Japan, France, Germany and the UK. It met first at Nairobi when finance ministers were also meeting as IMF Governors and as members of C–20; then at Giscard d'Estaing's invitation in November 1973[12] and again in January 1974 at the Château d'Artigny and in September 1974 at Champs-sur-Marne; it met on board the US Presidential yacht *Sequoia* in the summer of both 1974 and 1975; also from time to time when finance ministers assembled for C–20 meetings. G–5 appears to have usurped in the 1970s the role assumed by G–10 in the 1960s.[13]

Like the G–10, which in some of its manifestations met with a membership of eleven, the G–5 sometimes brought in an additional member, Italy. For example, Italy was brought in for part of the deliberations at Champs-sur-Marne. Thus the important meeting of six heads of government at Rambouillet on 17 November 1975 may be regarded as a summit meeting of the 'stretched' version of G–5.

The case for G–5 as a forum was that bargaining proceeds best in the smallest group which can bring together all the parties whose agreement is needed, and for international monetary affairs this is a group of five or six. In the words of Paul Volcker, then president of the Federal Reserve Bank of New York: 'The central problem primarily concerns a small number of major countries – if their currencies are reasonably stable, the rest can fall in place.'[14]

17 The dollar recovers, 1973–5

Many feared that resort to floating without clearly defined rules of behaviour would undermine international economic integration and interfere with trade and investment. Some went further. They felt that what they saw as a total breakdown of the monetary order was responsible for much of the instability in the world economy and carried the seeds of political and economic chaos.

But the worst has plainly not happened. Flows of international trade and investment – while recently affected by recession – have been well maintained. Controls on trade and payments have not proliferated. Resort to 'beggar my neighbor' policies – one source of concern to those pushing comprehensive reform – is so far notable mostly by its absence.

Paul Volcker,
address in November 1975[1]

Though there had from the end of the 1960s been a growing body of influential opinion, especially in the United States, which maintained that floating was in principle better than pegging, and hence welcomed the course of events in the first quarter of 1973, to most statesmen and officials responsible for international monetary affairs in the G–10 countries the transition to floating was something that had been forced on them by the pressure of events, a leap in the dark which caused them deep forebodings. Many viewed with misgivings a system in which none of the national currencies was officially convertible into gold, or indeed into anything else. If currencies were permitted to float freely, without any official market transactions, the day-to-day fluctuations in market rates would be too violent for bankers and traders to carry on their normal business. If, on the other hand, currencies were managed by official market intervention, countries might intervene at cross purposes – central bank X selling its currency to keep its relative value down, central bank Y buying it to keep its relative value up: moreover with floating rates the Bretton Woods rules of good behaviour, designed to prevent beggar-my-neighbour remedies for unemployment, would no longer be applicable, since they presupposed pegged rates; hence one must expect rounds of competitive exchange depreciation, such as occurred in the 1930s.

However, even in the course of 1973 floating was seen to be working better than had been expected. One sign of this was the reassuring behaviour of the spread between the buying and selling rates quoted by dealers in the foreign exchange markets. According to the IMF,

An initial consequence of the greater short-term volatility of exchange rates that has characterized the floating period was an increase in the spread between buying and selling rates for currencies. Subsequently, the situation seems to have improved in these respects, although for most currencies spreads remain wider than before the adoption of generalized floating. For example, the spread between quoted buying and selling rates in New York for spot sterling in terms of the dollar was approximately twice as wide during March–April 1975 as it was in June 1971. A similar tendency can be observed, in greater or lesser degree, for most other major currencies that had been observing par values in June 1971. It should be noted, however, that the wider spread in spot quotations is a trivial element in the cost of financing international trade, and probably has its main effect on financial flows of a reversible character.[2]

For a more general appraisal of how floating was working in practice I quote the verdict of Dr Otmar Emminger, of the Bundesbank: 'The floating of currencies has functioned better, in certain respects, than many people thought. . . . It would be premature to go back now to a regime of fixed or stabilised parities, the conditions for whose satisfactory operation not being present' at the end of 1973.[3]

The event which began to build up confidence in the floating regime, and led more and more statesmen and officials to regard it as viable for an indefinite period and not just a temporary expedient, was the realization that the dollar could rise, as well as fall, in the market. There was 'a rising rate for the dollar against European currencies after July 1973'.[4]

The proximate cause of the dollar's improvement was the decision, taken in the first week of July by a G–10 meeting of central bank Governors at Basle, to resume official transactions in support of the dollar (see page 216), but the more fundamental cause was the improvement in the US trade balance. The US export deficit on goods and services became a modest surplus in the first quarter of 1973 (see Table 17) and improved dramatically in the rest of the year. The medicine of exchange depreciation was at last working:

the combined effect of the exchange-rate adjustments at the Smithsonian conference and again in February 1973, together with the depreciation of the dollar in the free-floating regime, had by July 1973 reduced the dollar's value in terms of a weighted average of fifteen major currencies by 19 per cent as compared with mid 1970 (Table 18) and US prices of manufactures were getting distinctly more competitive. In addition there occurred in 1973 a rise in the prices of many primary products of which the US is a net exporter, and this too helped the trade balance.

Table 17   *US export surplus or deficit (−) on goods and services, quarterly, 1972–5, seasonally adjusted*

Year	Quarter	$ billion	Year	Quarter	$ billion
1972	1	−0.7	1974	1	3.8
	2	−0.6		2	2.3
	3	−0.2		3	1.4
	4	−0.4		4	1.8
1973	1	0.8	1975	1	4.4
	2	1.7		2	6.4
	3	3.8		3	5.6
	4	4.7		4	6.6

Source: *Survey of Current Business* (June 1979), pp. 38–9.

Oil prices and the dollar

Then later in 1973 came the OPEC decision to jack up the price of oil. This produced a vast increase in the demand for dollars, and to a lesser extent for sterling, as the currencies in which the greatly increased oil bills had to be paid. Almost overnight, the problem of the dollar overhang disappeared, or at any rate became far less acute. As Alfred Hayes, until July 1975 president of the Federal Reserve Bank of New York, put it in his Per Jacobsson Foundation lecture on 31 August 1975:

Before the eruption of the oil crisis in October 1973, the so-called dollar overhang loomed large among the pressing international issues. Then, as oil importing countries found their large dollar-reserve cushions a blessing rather than a burden, this issue seemed to dissolve. . . . If there is a dollar overhang, it probably is not as large as it seemed a few years ago.

The rise in oil prices which occurred as from late 1973 operated in two distinct ways to alleviate the problem of the dollar overhang. In the first place it contributed to the rapid rise in commodity prices, which meant that the great increase in world reserves as between end 1970 and the spring of 1973, mainly through the build-up of dollar reserves (see Table 14, page 161), was soon overtaken by an even more rapid rise in the dollar value of world imports:

in 1971–2, the ratio of reserves to [international] trade, one simple though incomplete measure of reserve adequacy, sharply reversed the long decline that had persisted over the postwar period. But the ratio of reserves to world imports then dropped again in the two years after 1972. For a sample of sixty countries, that ratio at the end of 1974 stood at 24 per cent. That was the lowest point ever recorded since the series started in 1954, when the ratio stood at just over 70 per cent.[5]

Table 18 *Percentage depreciation of the US dollar's effective exchange rate in the 1970s, relative to pre-June 1970 parities*

	January	April	July	October
1970	0	1	2	2
1971	3	3	3	6
1972	9	10	11	10
1973	10	15	19	18
1974	12	16	16	14
1975	16	16	14	12
1976	12	11	12	12
1977	11	11	11	11
1978	14	15	17	19
1979	18	17	18	16

Source: Morgan Guaranty Trust Company, *World Financial Markets* (August 1976), pp. 6 and 7, and subsequent issues. The percentage exchange-rate changes are in each case *vis-à-vis* a group of fifteen major currencies weighted according to bilateral trade.

In the second place, the oil-exporting countries (mainly members of OPEC) did not increase their imports in line with the increase in the value of their exports, as we see from Table 20 on page 179. The oil exporters' identified cash surplus, in $ billion, was no less than 53.2 in 1974 and 35.2 in 1975. These vast surpluses had to be settled in the first instance in dollars and sterling, predominantly the former, and were thereupon heavily invested in dollar-denominated assets, as we see from Table 19. Hence in most oil-importing countries there arose an enormous demand for dollars to pay for their oil. Oil-importing countries with large dollar reserves drew them down: those less well provided borrowed heavily:

For oil-importing countries their willingness in many cases to engage in substantial official borrowing to maintain reserve holdings does not support the idea of an enormous surfeit of world reserves.[6]

Table 19   *Identified deployment of oil exporters'* annual cash surpluses, 1974–80 ($ billion)*

	1974	1975	1976	1977	1978	1979	1980
United Kingdom							
Government securities	3.6	−0.5	−1.0	−0.2	−0.1	0.4	1.8
Sterling bank deposits	1.7	0.2	−1.4	0.3	0.2	1.4	1.4
Non-sterling bank deposits (mainly $)	13.8	4.1	5.6	3.1	−2.0	14.8	14.8
Other non-sterling debt	1.2	0.2	0.8	0.2	—	0.2	−0.5
Equity and other	0.7	0.3	0.5	0.4	0.1	0.4	0.1
Total UK	21.0	4.3	4.5	3.8	−1.8	17.2	17.6
United States							
Government securities	5.5	2.5	3.2	3.4	−2.4	2.2	9.7
Bank deposits	4.1	0.6	1.7	0.4	0.8	5.0	−1.2
Other	2.1	6.5	7.2	3.5	2.5	−0.4	6.0
Total US	11.7	9.6	12.1	7.3	0.9	6.8	14.5
Other countries and international organizations	20.5	21.3	19.2	20.6	15.5	36.6	54.4
Total cash surplus	53.2	35.2	35.8	31.7	14.6	60.6	86.5

* 'Oil exporters' here means OPEC plus Trinidad and Tobago, Bahrain, Brunei and Oman – seventeen countries in all.

Source: Bank of England *Quarterly Bulletin*, June 1980, p. 159, September 1980, p. 293 and June 1981, p. 185.

As we shall see in Chapter 19, much of this vast official borrowing served to recycle OPEC oil revenues, a considerable amount of which was invested in oil-importing countries, either directly or as deposits at Eurobanks on-lent to public sector agencies in the countries concerned. In consequence the total foreign exchange reserves of non-OPEC countries remained roughly stable in the course of 1974 and 1975.

Table 20 *Oil exporters: current account balance, 1973–80 ($ billion)*

	1973	1974	1975	1976	1977	1978	1979	1980
Trade balance	19	84	54	64	65	44	112	160
Services and transfers	−13	−17	−25	−29	−38	−45	−46	−54
Current balance	6	67	29	35	27	−1	66	106

Source: Bank of England *Quarterly Bulletin*, June 1980, p. 154, September 1980, p. 294 and June 1981, p. 185. For a reconciliation of annual totals of Tables 19 and 20 see Bank of England *Quarterly Bulletin*, September 1980, p. 294.

A symptom of the greatly improved status of the dollar as from early 1974 was the dismantling of restrictions on short-term capital flows out of the dollar into other currencies. The US restrictions imposed on outflows in the 1960s (described in Chapter 9) were all abolished in January 1974; those imposed by other countries on inflows (see pages 148, 153, 161) were all greatly liberalized, if not removed completely, in the course of the same year.

With the overhang problem in abeyance, perhaps even disposed of for good, and with so many countries preoccupied with the immediate problem of financing their oil deficits, everybody lost interest in C–20's Grand Design. In December 1973, according to *The Financial Times*:

The energy crisis, combined with the rapid improvement in the US balance of payments, has now raised serious doubts about the chances of an agreement on world monetary reform by the July 31 deadline next year that was set by the Finance Ministers at the Nairobi IMF meeting in September . . . the sharp turn-around in the US balance of payments has given both sides less interest in reform and made the US more determined than ever only to settle on its own terms.[7]

What were these terms? Briefly they were that the displacement by the SDR of the dollar, in its international roles, or most of them, as proposed in the Barber plan, should not be proceeded with; that gold (the only other rival to the dollar in its international roles) should as far as possible be demonetized; that to this end measures to be adopted for the benefit of the developing countries should involve the sale of part of the IMF's gold holding; and finally that the floating-rate experiment, inaugurated in March 1973, should be continued for an indefinite period. The first of these aims, the abandonment of new roles for the SDR, was in effect achieved by the deadlock in the negotiations of the Grand Design. The other US objectives, with respect to gold and the modification of the IMF Articles so as to authorize floating, took rather longer to negotiate, as will be described in the next chapter.

18 From Bretton Woods to Jamaica

The new system which was adopted at the Jamaica Conference was not the outcome of the long drawn-out reform discussions of earlier years. The IMF Ministerial Committee simply acknowledged the existing realities concerning exchange rates and gold, as they have evolved since the breakdown of the Bretton Woods System in 1973, and legalized them.

Otmar Emminger,
address in February 1976[1]

The role of gold

The Barber plan of September 1971 (pages 165–9) was not the first official proposal to displace the dollar from its international role: General de Gaulle had in February 1965 extolled the virtues of gold[2] as against the dollar, and was known to be sympathetic towards the proposals of Jacques Rueff to double the official price of gold and invite the US to draw on its own gold reserves, thus revalued, in order to redeem the then dollar overhang[3] – which was then under $16 billion, as against $45 billion at the time of the Barber plan.[4]

Nothing came of de Gaulle's comments on gold, but the initial French position in the SDR negotiations betrayed the French preference for gold. Thus in the mid 1960s, at the time of the early discussions of the G–10 Deputies on the functioning of the international monetary system, the French put forward a proposal for official settlements to be made in units comprising a basket of gold and national currencies in fixed proportions.[5] When this was discovered to be not negotiable, the French at first opposed the introduction of any new type of international liquidity, and then, when (at the Munich meeting of the EEC finance ministers in April 1967) they at last conceded the case for contingency planning, they insisted that the plan had to be for the eventual introduction of a drawing facility, rather than a reserve asset, the presumption being that the reserve asset role ought eventually to be played by gold.[6]

Gold reappeared on the diplomatic scene at the time of the

Smithsonian conference in December 1971, when the French were insistent that some part of the readjustment of currency parities should be achieved by a change in the relative value of the dollar and gold – which could be taken to imply that parities were now being fixed in terms of gold, instead of being (as was *de facto* the case in the 1960s) in terms of the dollar. Since this was not the only argument for changing the official price of gold,[7] the US negotiators gave way to French insistence and agreed that the official dollar price of gold be increased from $35 to $38 an ounce, which meant seeking Congressional approval to a modification of the Bretton Woods Act.[8]

With the subsequent abandonment of pegging in favour of floating, the choice of *numéraire* ceased to be a live issue, but it seems to have been accepted that should pegging ever be resumed, the *numéraire* will be the SDR (which since mid 1974 has been valued in terms not of gold but of a basket of national currencies).

Apart from its possible role as *numéraire*, gold also came to be a bone of contention in respect of its use in official transactions. The Washington conference of March 1968, which dissolved the gold pool, agreed on a ban (which lasted until November 1973) on official market transactions in gold (see page 110), but central banks were always free to buy and sell gold as between themselves. But at what price should they do so? As the result of decisions taken in December 1971 and February 1973, the official price of gold (the maximum price for official purchases under the Bretton Woods charter) had been increased from $35 to $38 and then to $42.2 (see pages 155 and 163) an ounce, but this was still much below the free market price at which private-sector buyers and sellers dealt in the London market. No central bank would in these circumstances want to part with its gold at the official price, so official transactions in gold had dried up altogether ever since the ending of the dollar's official gold convertibility in August 1971.

The US attitude for some time thereafter was simply that the Bretton Woods charter prohibited official purchases at above the official price, and the charter should be respected. France on the other hand wanted authorization for official transactions at the free market price as a preliminary to fixing a higher, 'more realistic', official price, at which gold would assume an active role in inter-central-bank settlements as an alternative to the dollar. The United States reacted by a shift of position, conceding the case for inter-central-bank transactions at the free market price, but with the intention (diametrically opposite to France's) that such transactions should continue indefinitely at a fluctuating price, which would in due course discredit gold as a monetary asset and possibly lead to its eventual demonetization.

In the negotiations which followed in 1974, in the forums already noted on pages 172–3, various changes were made in official arrangements for gold but none gave much indication as to which of the rival scenarios would obtain in practice. However, negotiations in 1975, validated by the communiqué of the Jamaica meeting of the IMF Interim Committee in January 1976, settled decisively for the US scenario.

Three things were already settled in 1974. It had been agreed by the G–5 finance ministers, at their meeting on board the *Sequoia*, that gold may be valued for collateral purposes, in inter-central bank loans, at any mutually agreeable price, and in December the same year a Germany-to-Italy loan was negotiated, whose provisions made use of this device. Then at the meeting of the French and US Presidents at Martinique on 16 December 1974, it was agreed that central banks might in their balance sheets value their gold stocks at market price instead of at $42.2 an ounce; and as from 6 January 1975 the Bank of France duly revalued its gold. Finally, the US authorities decided that the legal prohibition on US residents holding gold should be repealed and a modest amount of gold from the US reserve be offered for auction to ensure that the new private demand should not bid up the market price: the necessary change in US law became operative as from 1 January 1975 and the first gold auction was held on 6 January.

The really fundamental issue on gold, whether inter-central bank transactions were to remain constrained by the official price of gold, took longer to settle. It had already been raised in an international forum in April 1974, on the occasion of a meeting of EEC ministers at Zeist, in Holland. There France had attempted to persuade her partners to support her advocacy of inter-central bank transactions in gold at the free market price, instead of at $42.2: however, the most they would agree to was not to oppose French advocacy of this course should the IMF charter at some future time come up for revision. More than a year later, at the end of August 1975, at a meeting of G–5 finance ministers, once more on board the *Sequoia*, the Zeist resolution was accepted by the Americans, but only as part of a package whose contents owed as much to US as to French initiative. For early in 1975 the US had got substantial agreement in the G–10 that the gold transactions of the Ten should be such as to prevent any increase in the weight of the total gold reserves of the G–10 countries plus the IMF, which *taken as a whole* would not therefore make net purchases in the free market and thereby afford support to the free market price. This agreement was to be for two years, at the end of which it would be reviewed, with participants then being free to terminate their adherence if they so wished.[9] At about the same time the French launched a proposal that the IMF should return part of its gold reserves to member countries, in proportion to their quotas, while the US countered with a recommendation that a part should be auctioned for the benefit of the developing countries which would get the proceeds of the auction, minus the book-value of the gold, valued at its former official price of $35 an ounce.

Here, then, were the ingredients in the *Sequoia* package,[10] which would seem to go as far as the US could realistically hope for in the direction of demonetizing gold and was by the same token a setback for the French. It was duly accepted by the IMF Interim Committee, which met in September 1975 in Washington, and then by the IMF Board of Governors:

In September, at the IMF annual meeting in Washington, key understandings in principle were reached regarding the role of gold in the monetary system and upward revisions in Fund quotas. The understanding on gold involved abolishing the official price of gold and ending the obligation to use gold in transactions with the Fund. In addition, a sixth of the Fund's gold holdings would be returned to members in proportion to their quotas and another sixth sold, with the differential between the former official price and the selling price being used to benefit developing countries. Under an agreement subject to review after two years, the Group of Ten also barred any increase in the total stock of gold possessed by the IMF and the monetary authorities of the ten countries. Moreover, they agreed not to peg the market price of gold, which dropped in London to about $140 per ounce at the end of 1975 from the all-time high of $195 a year earlier.[11]

Exchange rates

After the abandonment of pegging in March 1973, the floating which replaced it was initially intended to be temporary only, and Jeremy Morse and his colleagues in C–20 went ahead with drafting their Grand Design, which incorporated a revised version of the par value system. In Europe the opinion remained widespread that floating should be only temporary, and this point of view was forcibly represented by France on behalf of 'Franco-Europeans'.[12] However, by the time of the Nairobi discussions in September 1973 on the C–20's draft Outline, US opinion was moving in favour of a continuance of floating, and Anthony Thomas, of *The Times*, reported in October 1973 that 'the chances of the United States acceding to the European demands for a return to "fixed but adjustable exchange rates" in a reformed world monetary system are receding fast'.[13]

As time went by there were European converts to the US opposition to a return to a par value system: moreover the improvement both in the US balance of payments and in the standing of the dollar ensured that the US view should carry more and more weight. The issue was settled at the summit conference of the Group of Five plus Italy at Rambouillet on 15–17 November 1975 (above, page 173). Already in August 1975 the Monetary Committee of the EEC had failed to agree to support the French case for a return to fixed parities,[14] while in October an address by Giscard d'Estaing at the Ecole Polytechnique had indicated a certain shift in the French position, for so long attached to the principle of fixed exchange rates: he had suggested that floating rates should be replaced not by fixed rates but by a certain 'viscosity' of exchange rates.[15] This implied a readiness by France to come to terms with the US at Rambouillet, so as to permit the forthcoming meeting of the IMF Interim Committee in January 1976 in Jamaica to settle new IMF rules for exchange rates, in place of the par value system in the Articles of the original Bretton Woods charter.

And so indeed it happened. The Rambouillet summit agreed several things about exchange rates (see page 216) but its contribution to the drafting of new IMF Articles on exchange rates was that France gave up her insistence on the eventual re-establishment of a system of fixed but adjustable rates. Instead, the establishment of such a system would require an 85 per cent affirmative vote in the IMF, which with the IMF's weighted voting would give the US an effective veto. Moreover, under the amended Articles pegging could never be at parities expressed in terms of gold.

Amendment of the IMF Articles

In addition to the amendments to the IMF Articles concerned with gold and exchange rates (mainly Article IV) it had also been agreed earlier in 1975 by the IMF Interim Committee that there should be a one-third overall increase in members' quotas, with some proportionate redistribution of the total as between different members, and this was supported by a resolution passed by the Board of Governors. Then at the Jamaica meeting in January 1976 it was further agreed that members' potential access to the IMF's resources under each of the four IMF credit tranches should be increased by 45 per cent until the quota increases became effective – as they did in due course, after an interval of several years. (This and subsequent increases in quotas raised the total to about $90 billion in 1984.)

The position reached at the time of the Jamaica meeting was summarized by the Federal Reserve Board as follows:

With the Interim Committee's meeting in January 1976, 4 years of intensive international monetary negotiations reached a conclusion. These discussions had started at the time of the Smithsonian Agreement in December 1971, and they continued under the auspices of the IMF's Committee of Twenty in 1972–4. They were carried out during a period of dramatic upheavals in the international economy and in international monetary arrangements. The result of the 4 years of negotiations is not a complete blueprint for a new international monetary system, such as had been expected when the Committee of Twenty started its work. However, when the proposed amendments to the IMF Articles of Agreement are formally approved by at least 77 countries holding at least 80 per cent of the total votes in the 128-member IMF, the Fund will become a stronger and more flexible institution.[16]

The second amendment came into effect as from 1 April 1978.

19 Oil prices and adjustment, 1973–80

The members of the Organization of Petroleum Exporting Countries have developed a huge surplus on goods and services with the rest of the world as a result of the quadrupling in oil prices since late 1973 and their inability promptly to spend on imports all the subsequent enlarged export receipts. This surplus, estimated at about $60 billion in 1974, can be reduced only by the following means, alone or in some combinations: (1) a reduction in oil prices; (2) a reduction in demand for OPEC oil by importing countries; (3) an increase in imports of goods and services by members of OPEC.

Robert Solomon[1]

The OPEC export surplus

The raising of oil prices in late 1973 by the members of OPEC (Organization of Petroleum Exporting Countries) faced the post-1958 international monetary system with its biggest-ever disequilibrium, and one which was unusually intractable to adjustment. According to the Bank of England's statistics for 'oil exporters' (comprising the thirteen OPEC countries and four others), their export surplus on trade in 1974 turned out to be no less than $84 billion, as against $19 billion in 1973 (Table 20, page 179). Netting out their deficit on services and transfers, their current account surplus was somewhat less than their trade surplus – $67 billion in 1974 and $6 billion in 1973 – but its increase from one year to the next was none the less enormous and of course implied a corresponding decrease in the current balance of oil *im*porters.

What happened subsequently? With the help of hindsight, we are now able to answer the questions raised by Robert Solomon in 1974, in the passage quoted above.

1   The real price of crude oil, as measured by its price relative to the price of manufactures exported from the major industrial countries, was fairly steady up to 1978, following the first round increase in 1973. Then there was a further big second round rise in 1979–80 (see Table 21).

Table 21   *Real price of crude oil**

Year	1st quarter 1974 = 100
1972	41
1973	46
1974	104
1975	103
1976	111
1977	110
1978	98
1979	129
1980	185

* Index of OPEC oil prices, deflated by index of prices of manufactures exported from the major industrial countries.

Source: Bank of England *Quarterly Bulletin*, December 1980, p. 404.

2   Although in the 1970s the industrial countries' appetite for oil was somewhat mitigated by a slowing down in their trend rate of economic growth, by economies in their use of oil, and by the increase in the output of their own oil fields, for example in the North Sea, there was, prior to 1980, no sustained reduction in demand for OPEC oil by oil-importing countries.

3   There was a somewhat faster increase in imports of goods and services by OPEC members than appeared plausible in 1974. Nevertheless, according to the Bank of England, the oil exporters' surplus on current account took until 1978 to disappear, and then rose again, to no less than $66 billion in 1979 and $106 billion in 1980, thanks to the second round increase in oil prices (Table 20, page 179).

4   Thus the OPEC surplus resulting from the first round increase in relative oil prices yielded only slowly to the operation of the adjustment process: in consequence over the period beginning in 1974 the disequilibrium was to a considerable extent being *financed* rather than *cured*. And as from 1979 the disequilibrium was back to square one.

   Why did the adjustment problem prove so intractable? Ironically, the unpegging of exchange rates in 1973, which should have permitted the adjustment mechanism to respond more promptly and effectively to an unforeseen shock, was in this instance wholly irrelevant to the problem at hand. For virtually all the international trade and payments of the biggest oil exporters are in terms of the currencies of the oil-importing industrial countries, in particular the United States dollar: in relation to the oil problem, the oil exporters' domestic currencies are just small change for local transactions, which can be ignored without seriously falsifying any of the relevant issues. Hence variations in exchange rates can have no important part to play in dealing with the OPEC surplus in total: all that such variations can do is to influence the distribution of the corresponding deficits as between one oil-importing country and another.

Moreover, even if there had been a relevant exchange rate between OPEC and the oil-importing countries, neither the trade balance nor the flow of capital as between the two groups would have been at all sensitive to changes in the exchange rate:

The rate at which the current surplus of the OPEC countries can be compressed is limited by their ability to absorb imports. Given the economic characteristics of these countries, the price elasticity of their aggregate demand for imports must be very low and therefore devaluation of OECD currencies relative to OPEC currencies would do little, if anything, to curtail the OPEC surplus. And, since the major capital and money markets are in OECD countries, OPEC members have little choice but to invest their surpluses somewhere in OECD, regardless of exchange rates.[2]

Let us then forget about exchange rates until we come to the subsidiary problem of how the overall oil deficit was shared among the different oil-importing countries, and consider what other aspects of the adjustment mechanism might operate to alleviate the overall OPEC surplus. If the OPEC countries become richer, as occurs automatically with the rise in their oil revenues, they will import more: unfortunately, however, the structure of some of the oil-exporting economies is such that their capacity to absorb imports is very severely limited, especially in the short run, so here the income effect could clearly not be relied upon to produce quick results. Nor could the income effect in the oil-importing countries. If the oil-importing countries become poorer, as automatically occurs with the rise in the cost of oil imports (which is equivalent to a tax, the proceeds of which are not available for spending by the oil-importing country's government), their demand for imported oil will fall off, as will their demand for goods in general; but since fuel is such a necessity, its usage will tend to be cut less drastically than the consumption of goods in general.

This pessimistic conclusion is not greatly upset, except in the longer run, by the effect on the pattern of consumption in the oil-importing economies due to the rise in the price of oil relative to other goods. When oil is more expensive, its users switch to alternative fuels, but this takes time; they also economize more on fuel than on other goods, but this also takes time. Finally the high price of oil must in the long run encourage the more rapid exploitation of non-OPEC sources of supply, but here again the relevant time-lag is clearly a long one.

So the mechanism of automatic adjustment operating to reduce the OPEC trade balance was exceptionally sluggish and in practice did not show significant results until the 1980s. It could perhaps have been speeded up by recourse to discretionary devices, to be adopted by the governments of the oil-importing countries; they could, for instance, have adopted measures of fiscal and monetary deflation. However, in the 1970s the stance of their fiscal and monetary policies was by and large aimed at mitigating, rather than aggravating, the fall in real income caused automatically by the rise in the cost of imported oil. (Their reaction in the 1980s to the second round increase in oil prices was completely different, and markedly deflationary, as will be described in Chapter 23; moreover economies in the use of oil per unit output also began to depress oil consumption in the 1980s.)

Financing the oil disequilibrium

Given that adjustment proceeded so slowly after the first round of increases in the real price of oil, it is not surprising that a very large 'oil disequilibrium' needed to be financed in the years 1974 to 1980 – something well in excess of $300 billion, according to Table 20. How was it possible to finance a disequilibrium on such a scale?

In a sense financing is automatic, in that 'OPEC members have little choice but to invest their surpluses somewhere in OECD':[3] failure by OPEC members to take any initiative in the matter of investment would simply result in the accumulation of their oil revenues in dollar or sterling deposits at banks in the OECD (and more particularly in the G–10) countries. The only way the OPEC countries could avoid investing in the OECD countries would have been to cut off the supply of oil, but events early in 1974 suggested that this was not in fact going to be a serious danger.

Yet the proposition that OPEC members had little choice but to invest *somewhere* in the OECD did not dispose of the whole financing question, since there remained the recycling problem, which inevitably arose when the places where OPEC members chose to invest did not correspond to the places that were incurring the deficits that had to be financed. If, to take an imaginary example, all the OPEC deficit in 1974 had taken the form of a like increase in OPEC-owned dollar deposits at American banks, this would not of itself have settled the oil bills confronting other oil-importing countries with inadequate dollar reserves.

My illustrative example of 100 per cent investment in US bank deposits in 1974 is, of course, an unrealistic nightmare: as may be seen from Table 19 (page 178) oil exporters' investments in the US in that year were only $12 billion. Yet recycling on a grand scale was needed in 1974 and on a considerable scale in subsequent years.

The recycling of oil revenues

The recycling problem could in principle have been alleviated by the operation of the adjustment mechanism. Though this mechanism necessarily works badly, or at any rate very sluggishly, in remedying a disequilibrium as between oil-exporting and oil-importing countries as a whole, there is no reason why it should not perform normally as regards the distribution of this overall disequilibrium as between one oil-importing country and another. However, as was explained at the end of Chapter 15, the transition in the early 1970s from pegged to floating exchange rates was confined to the developed industrial countries: the non-oil developing countries mostly continued to peg and devalued only reluctantly and belatedly, so that changes in their exchange rates did little either to assist the adjustment process, or (it follows) to alleviate the amount of recycling required to finance their deficits.

At all events, the amount of recycling which had to take place was enormous in 1974–80. This amount is, however, intrinsically impossible to quantify with any precision. Let us begin by looking at what figures are available from the oil exporters' end of the recycling process: these are conveniently summarized in Table 22, below. We see that of the $317 billion cash surplus of the oil exporters in 1974–80 $14 billion was recycled via the IMF and IBRD, $47 billion went to the developing countries (directly or via regional development agencies) and the balance mainly to industrial countries, including a very large amount ($147 billion) deposited with private-sector banks (including Eurobanks), which on-lent on an enormous scale both to developed countries, such as the UK and Italy, and to non-oil developing countries. Of course, from the very nature of banking business, one cannot establish at all exactly how much of these OPEC deposits were on-lent to the monetary authorities of deficit countries, either directly or via other public-sector agencies such as the nationalized industries: the deposits taken by banks from all sources are pooled before being on-lent to borrowing customers and one cannot perform the statistical equivalent of unscrambling an omelette. None the less, it is safe to say that the lending to deficit countries by the Eurobanks was on a scale which would have been out of the question without OPEC deposits.

Table 22 *Deployment of oil exporters' cash surpluses* * in the seven years 1974–80*

	$ billion
Bank deposits	147
US and UK government securities	28
Finance supplied to IMF and IBRD	14
Finance supplied to developing countries†	47
Other capital flows	81
Total (seven years)	317

* Defined as in Table 19, page 178.

† Including subscriptions to regional and international development agencies, other than IMF and IBRD.

Source: Bank of England *Quarterly Bulletin*, June 1980, p. 158, September 1980, p. 293 and June 1981, p. 185.

At the other end of the recycling process are the deficit countries. Here we have an estimate by Weir M. Brown of the US Treasury of $15–$17 billion[4] in 1974 by industrial countries alone. The corresponding figure for most subsequent years would be much smaller, but in addition there was enormous external borrowing by the non-oil developing countries – estimated by the IMF at $267 billion[5] over the seven years, 1974–80, of which the amount coming from financial institutions (mainly banks) was, by a statistical fluke, almost the same (at $139 billion) as the amount deposited at banks by oil exporting countries; see Table 22. (It may be noted that 1981 saw the end of the recycling of 'petrodollars' by banks; the oil exporting countries added very little to their bank deposits in that year and then drew on them to the tune of $15 billion in 1982 and again in 1983, and even more in subsequent years.)

Until 1981 the Eurobanks on-lent massively to the monetary authorities of deficit countries (whether directly or via other public-sector agencies); in addition banks in the US, freed since January 1974 from the ceiling on their foreign lending (see Chapter 9 and page 179), made large loans of a similar kind for the same purpose. The monetary authorities of deficit countries were now utilizing a kind of official reserve transaction which had hardly ever been used before 1973. Before 1973 deficit countries frequently needed help to replenish their depleted reserves, but if so they solicited a rescue operation from the monetary authorities of other countries or from an international institution such as the IMF: it was thus an *official* rescue operation. Now deficit countries were instead replenishing their reserves by borrowing foreign currencies in the market from private – sector banks.

The preference for recycling through the market arose from the deficit countries' desire to avoid the politically unacceptable constraints on domestic economic policies frequently imposed on official rescue operations (in the form, for example, of a letter of intent to the IMF). So instead they borrowed in the market, even at the cost of a higher interest charge. It was not, however, just the deficit countries that came to prefer recycling through the market: their change in borrowing practices harmonized with the evolution of US government opinion, which in the 1970s became increasingly inclined to take a leave-it-to-the-market approach to international monetary questions.

This confidence in the market proved to be justified in respect of the aftermath of the first round increases in the real price of oil. However, although the private-sector banks began to play an equally important role in the aftermath of the second round oil price increases in 1979–80, they soon ran into serious difficulties, as will be seen in Chapter 23.

20 The principles and practice of floating

The Group of Ten countries, including Switzerland, can be divided into two main categories so far as their intervention policies [in the foreign exchange markets] are concerned, according to whether they limited themselves to intervention designed merely to smooth out day-to-day market conditions or whether, in addition, they operated in the markets in a way that brought about substantial changes in their net official reserves, including official, or officially inspired, borrowing . . . the United States belongs in the first of the categories mentioned above, as did Canada until the November 1976 provincial elections in Quebec, while all the other Group of Ten countries, including Switzerland, belong in the second. Germany, however, may be said to have a foot in both camps, belonging with the United States so far as the Deutsche Mark/dollar rate is concerned but with its fellow participants so far as interventions within the framework of the European joint float are concerned.

BIS *Annual Report*, 1977

Two schools of thought

The decision to abandon pegging on the dollar was taken at meetings in Paris in March 1973 attended by fourteen industrial countries (including all the EEC members) at which it proved impossible to agree new parities whose viability would seem credible to market operators (above, page 163). The hundred or so countries not represented at these meetings almost all opted against floating, as is apparent from Table 16 on page 164; moreover the fourteen at the meetings included the EEC members then floating jointly in the snake (above, pages 157–8) as well as Eire (which pegged on sterling until joining the modified snake arrangements introduced with the establishment of the European Monetary System in March 1979). So the number of countries operating the floating regime, whose peculiar problems are the subject of this chapter, were (and have since remained) relatively few. They comprised those of the fourteen which have at no time been in the snake since they unpegged from the dollar (the US, the UK, Canada, Japan and Switzer-land) together with (from time to time in the 1970s) the temporary defectors from the snake, namely Italy from February 1973 until March 1979 and France from January 1974 to July 1975 and again from March 1976 to March 1979.[1] Finally there is Germany, which though a member of the snake nevertheless viewed its exchange rate with the dollar in much the same light as the independent floaters viewed theirs: as the BIS put it in its 1977 *Annual Report* (quoted at the head of this chapter) Germany 'may be said to have a foot in both camps'. To summarize, then, the countries which had to make up their minds how to operate a floating regime, in place of a pegged-rate regime, were the US, the UK, Canada, Japan, Switzer-land and Germany; plus in earlier years Italy and France.

Subsequent to the transition to floating, the policy decisions which have had to be taken in these countries involve much the same considerations as under pegging, but they now came to the attention of ministers and officials in a somewhat different form. Whereas under the pegged rate regime the symptom of weakness or strength of these countries' currencies had been official transactions undertaken in the foreign exchange market, the corresponding symptom now became a rise or fall in market exchange rates. So when the authorities found their currency rising or falling in the market, they had to decide: shall we just let it rise or fall (a policy which came to be called 'benign neglect'), or shall we seek to influence the rate? And in the latter case, *how* do we want to influence it? Do we want to hold it at some target level or 'unofficial peg'? Or do we merely want to moderate or temporarily arrest its rise or fall – a policy of 'leaning against the wind'? Might we ever want to do the opposite and aggravate a rise or fall ('drive the rate')? In practice, the preferred alternative to benign neglect was almost always (though not invariably) leaning against the wind, either as an automatic reaction or (more usually) on a discretionary basis.

So there have effectively been two rival prescriptions for floating – benign neglect and leaning against the wind – and each has had its adherents, as the quotation at the head of this chapter clearly shows. At the time to which the quotation refers – the early part of 1977 – the DM/dollar rate exemplifies a policy of benign neglect, whereas the other floating currencies (sterling, the Canadian dollar, the French and Swiss francs, the lira and the yen) were being actively managed by the countries concerned. The two rival schools of thought identified by the BIS have both enjoyed a more or less continuous existence throughout the period of floating rates, though (as in the Thirty Years War) some of the protagonists have changed their allegiance from time to time, as will be described in Chapters 21 and 22.

Leaning against the wind

The kinds of official action that can be taken to implement a decision to lean against the wind are conventionally classified as four 'instruments of policy', all of which were familiar enough to the responsible officials, who had been using them to peg exchange rates in the 1960s and early 1970s:

1 Exchange controls on international capital movements, and regulations with equivalent effect.
2 Fiscal policy, in the sense of achieving an appropriate balance between taxation and government expenditure.
3 Official transactions in the foreign exchange markets, mainly comprising (as under the pegged rate regime) purchases or sales of US dollars by the United States' partners, though now from time to time also including purchases or sales of DM (and to a lesser extent yen and Swiss or French francs) by the US authorities.
4 Official transactions in the home-currency financial markets, especially the domestic money market, for the purpose either of raising interest rates (thereby attracting a capital inflow and supporting the home currency in the foreign exchange market) or alternatively of lowering interest rates (with the opposite consequence). .

Unfortunately, as officials well knew from their past experience with pegging, all these policy instruments had shortcomings, whether on account of their limited efficacy or on account of their side effects (which might be desirable but were all too frequently undesirable).

Exchange controls were from time to time imposed on capital inflows, to moderate an excessive appreciation of the exchange rate, though they leaked badly and were widely condemned for obstructing the optimum allocation of resources. In particular, they were imposed by a number of European countries and Japan on two occasions when there were speculative capital flows out of the US dollar: first at about the time of the transition from pegging to floating (see above, page 162) and again in 1977–8 (see below, pages 224–5). However, in the 1980s they have been little used by the floating currency countries. Exchange controls on capital outflows have likewise gone out of favour with these countries.

Fiscal policy also went out of favour in the countries in question, at roughly the same time, as an instrument for influencing the exchange rate. In the 1960s fiscal policy had been generally regarded as an effective instrument of adjustment for use by countries with persistently weak or persistently strong currencies: a weak currency would be strengthened by an increase in tax rates or a cut in government expenditure (both of which would reduce the pressure of domestic demand for goods and services and thereby improve the balance of trade); and conversely a strong currency would be weakened by a more expansionary fiscal policy. However, confidence in the plausibility of this story was eroded as attention came increasingly to be focussed on the effect of fiscal changes on international capital movements (as opposed to international trade). The alternative viewpoint was advanced that an expansionary fiscal stance, involving heavy government borrowing, would attract a capital inflow and hence strengthen (rather than weaken) the currency concerned. This line of argument was frequently used in the years 1981 to 1986 to relate the large US budget deficit to the simultaneous massive capital inflow into the United States and the consequential rapid appreciation of the US dollar. As Henry Wallich, an eminent member of the US Federal Reserve Board, put it in an address to the List Gesellschaft, on 6 April 1984:

In the case of the dollar, it has been at least an open question whether the strong fiscal expansion would appreciate or depreciate the currency. Two econometric models with which I am acquainted give opposite answers to this question. The reason is very simple. Strong fiscal expansion, given a stable money-supply policy, raises interest rates but also increases imports. Whether the capital-account effect (operating through higher interest rates) or the current-account effect (operating through a larger deficit) will predominate is not *a priori* obvious. In the American experience, to be sure, there is some evidence that the capital-account effect seems to be stronger than the current-account effect. In cyclical expansions, which have had the result of raising both interest rates and imports, the United States has tended to gain exchange reserves under the old fixed-rate system and to experience a rising dollar under the floating system.

Uncertainty as to how fiscal policy impacts on the exchange rate led in the early 1980s to a serious lack of confidence by decision-makers in the floating-currency countries that fiscal changes are an appropriate instrument for leaning against the wind in the foreign exchange market.

The remaining two policy instruments for influencing the exchange rate comprise *official transactions in the financial markets*. These differ in detail from one country to another, but they virtually always amount in practice to the equivalent of official sales of foreign exchange and/or home-currency securities (to support the home-currency's market value) or purchases of foreign exchange and/or home-currency securities (to depress the home-currency's market value). Such official transactions are intended to exercise an immediate influence on the exchange rate through capital inflows or outflows, whether on official account (when the central bank itself deals in the foreign exchange market) or on private-sector account (through influencing the level of home-currency interest rates relative to foreign-currency interest rates).

Official purchases in any of the financial markets operate to depress interest rates, and official sales to raise them, but at the same time they have an important (but frequently unwanted) side effect on the domestic banking system. Official purchases, if from non-banks, are immediately reflected as an increase in the monetary liabilities of the banking system, which comprise the main component of the money stock. Moreover, whether the purchases are from banks or from non-banks they invariably serve to make the banking system more liquid and hence ready to supply credit on more favourable terms to would-be borrowers[2]: this indeed is an essential part of the mechanism for depressing the level of interest rates. Thus official purchases, whether of foreign exchange or of home-currency securities, necessarily imply a more reflationary stance in monetary policy, and conversely official sales imply a more deflationary stance. When this side effect is unwanted, there is the possibility of insulating the banking system from the consequences of official transactions in foreign exchange by buying in one financial market and simultaneously selling in the other; that is, the Bank of England might for instance try to support sterling with no contractionary side effect on the UK banking system by selling a million pounds' worth of dollars and simultaneously buying a million pounds' worth of sterling securities. But such a tactic of 'sterilization', as it is called, came to be considered to be of limited efficacy, and for two reasons. First, though the Bank of England could undoubtedly match its purchases of dollars with a like amount of sales of sterling securities, with no net effect on the liquidity of the commercial banks, it may not be so easy for the Bank to ensure that the sterling securities it sells are taken up by nonbank investors, so full sterilization (in the sense of *completely* insulating the banking system from the Bank's dollar purchases) may not be achieved. Second, the impact of sterilized intervention on the exchange rate relies solely on the central bank's own transactions in the foreign exchange market, without inducing any supportive private-sector transactions in the market (since sterilized intervention exerts no pressure on interest rates). Hence it has come to be accepted that sterilized intervention cannot have a strong and sustained influence on the exchange rate: in the words of the Jurgensen Report, prepared in 1983 by officials at the behest of the Versailles Summit the previous year:

the Working Group felt that intervention had been an effective tool in the pursuit of certain exchange rate objectives – notably those orientated towards influencing the behaviour of the exchange rate in the short run. Effectiveness was found to have been greater when intervention was unsterilised than when its monetary effects were offset . . . There was also broad agreement that sterilised intervention did not generally have a lasting effect, but that intervention in conjunction with domestic policy changes did have a more durable impact.[3]

If the impact of sterilized intervention is as uncertain as the Jurgensen working group concluded, it follows that the monetary authorities can make a substantial impact on the foreign exchange market only by accepting a change in the stance of monetary policy: supporting the exchange rate requires a more deflationary stance, depressing it requires a more reflationary stance. The more deflationary stance has the advantage of giving additional weight to the official support of the exchange rate (since a deflated economy buys less imports), but may well be unwanted for its adverse effect on output and employment. Conversely a more reflationary stance helps further to depress the exchange rate (since a reflating economy sucks in more imports) but it may well be unwanted for its adverse effect on the price level. Ministers and officials who opt for leaning against the wind therefore expose themselves to the possibility of having to face an awkward dilemma.

The role of fiscal policy

Economists of the Keynesian school have seen an escape from this dilemma in a suitable adjustment to the stance of fiscal policy: any unwanted deflationary consequences of monetary policy could be offset by a more reflationary fiscal policy, and vice versa. But in practice the use of fiscal policy to offset the unwanted deflationary or reflationary consequences of a monetary policy aimed primarily at influencing the exchange rate has so far remained no more than a theoretical possibility, and for three reasons:

1   In a majority of the floating-rate countries (though not in Britain) the law or convention prescribes a separation of executive responsibility such that monetary policy and fiscal policy are in different hands, so that coordination of the two is difficult to achieve. Such is especially the case in the United States.

2   The adjustment of the stance of fiscal policy is normally an annual event, so that it is difficult to 'fine-tune' fiscal policy in line with changes in monetary policy.

3   Thanks to the influence of Professor Milton Friedman and his followers, monetary policy came to be regarded as much the most important instrument of policy for keeping an economy on course; hence it was concluded that the role of fiscal policy (if indeed it is considered to have a role) is to *support* monetary policy, not to *offset* it.

In consequence, fiscal policy was not adopted by those in authority as a possible escape from the dilemma that using monetary policy to lean against the wind in the foreign exchange market might well mean *mis*-using it in its role of keeping the domestic economy on the right course.

Benign neglect

Milton Friedman and his followers gave policy-makers a clear lead in this matter by advising them to refrain from leaning against the wind and instead to opt for benign neglect in an extreme form, with 'clean' floating (that is, no official transactions at all in the foreign exchange market) and an unchanging stance of monetary policy, which was identified with the achievement of a prescribed steady rate of growth of the money stock. Friedman's extreme views were however countered by a number of arguments:

1   Dr Oort's political analysis (above, page 72) still remained valid: a rise in the exchange rate reduces the international competitiveness of home industries and hence antagonizes the

workers and employers who are adversely affected, a fall in the exchange rate provokes a rise in the cost of living and may thereby lose the housewife's vote. Hence the practising politician likes to let sleeping dogs lie, in the sense of holding the exchange rate *de facto* stable, even in the absence of any official commitment to peg it.

2 International flows of short term capital, induced by the same so-called 'speculative' motives as under Bretton Woods, were even larger and more volatile post 1973 than in the 1960s. Friedman argued that under 'clean' floating speculation would not be seriously disequilibrating, but central bankers often feared serious 'bandwagon effects' leading to 'overshooting', which could be avoided only by official 'smoothing transactions' in the foreign exchange market.

3 Overshooting might also arise due to the J-curve phenomenon (above, page 66). The initial impact of an exchange-rate depreciation on external trade may be perverse in value terms, with the trade balance in value terms initially diminishing, before eventually increasing. If such is the case the depreciation will continue to the point where it is arrested by a capital inflow, motivated by the belief that the currency has become so undervalued that it must henceforth recover in the market and hence afford a capital gain to its holders. In other words, the combination of the J-curve phenomenon with benign neglect signifies that the balancing of supply and demand in the exchange market *requires* overshooting. This is so not only following an initial depreciation, but also *mutatis mutandis* following an initial appreciation.

4 The experience of the 1970s somewhat undermined the belief that a change in exchange rates can effect more than a temporary change in the relative prices of goods and services in different countries. As the then Governor of the Bank of England put it, in his Henry Thornton Lecture in June 1979,[4]

Recent experience has indeed suggested that there are now serious limitations to the role flexible exchange rates can play in promoting adjustment than was earlier believed. . . . First, changes in costs arising from exchange rate movements appear nowadays to feed through into an economy more quickly and completely than used to be the case. . . . At the same time many economies have become significantly more open, more vulnerable to price and demand developments in their trading partners.

The result of these two developments appears to have been that adjustment in nominal exchange rates can no longer be relied upon to yield, for more than a relatively short period, as large an adjustment of real exchange rates as could once have been anticipated – in other words, exchange rate adjustment is, beyond the short-term, now likely to be less effective as a means of changing international competitiveness.

5 Though the advent of floating had not brought about the disastrous consequences that were feared by many statesmen and officials (above, Chapter 17), the advocates of benign neglect found it difficult to justify, or even to explain, the large fluctuations in exchange rates which from the start characterized the floating-rate regime, and which proponents of leaning against the wind thought could and should be mitigated by official action. Though the issue of leaning against the wind versus benign neglect remained controversial, it came to be accepted on both sides that the volatility of exchange rates did impose real economic costs on the economies concerned, for reasons which the Deputy Governor of the Bank of England explained in an address quoted at the end of this chapter.

Intervention in the 1970s

In the light of the above considerations, it is not perhaps surprising that since the transition from pegging to floating no country has opted throughout for benign neglect in the extreme form commended by Milton Friedman. However, there have been wide differences of practice as between one country and another, and also as between one time and another in the same country, varying from something very close to benign neglect on the one hand, to determined and prolonged leaning against the wind on the other. And in the latter case there have also been differences in the mixing of the two ingredients of official action:

1 Official intervention in the foreign exchange market.
2 Official transactions in the market for home-currency securities (or other official action in the money market having equivalent effect).

As regards the former, the quotation on page 194 from the BIS *Annual Report* 1977 gives a useful survey of the policies of the different floating currency countries in the first half of that year. Briefly, and ignoring minor complications, the position up to that time had been as follows:

1   Completely clean floating, as recommended by Milton Friedman, had no adherents among the countries concerned.
2   The crucial DM/dollar rate was, however, only lightly managed: both the US Federal Reserve and the German Bundesbank were prepared to undertake official transactions to steady what they identified as a disorderly DM/dollar exchange market (as in July 1973 and February 1975), but their interventions were typically unwound after a period of a few months and were on a scale not exceeding about $1 billion on the part of each partner. (A 'disorderly' market in this context implies an unwillingness on the part of professional traders to cushion the pressures hitting the market by absorbing buy or sell orders into their positions.)
3   All the other exchange rates concerned came to be managed in a much more determined manner, with persistent and large scale intervention in the foreign exchange market. The intervention currency used was almost invariably the US dollar, but the requisite market transactions were almost always undertaken not by the Federal Reserve but by the central bank responsible for the other currency concerned; thus it was the Bank of England which intervened in the sterling-dollar market, the Bank of Italy in the lira-dollar market, and so on. Intervention was on both sides of the market. The Bank of England bought sterling heavily over the three and a half years beginning mid 1973 and sold no less heavily in 1977. Italy did much the same with the lira, except for differences of timing. The Japanese authorities bought yen heavily after the rise in oil prices at the end of 1973, but were soon selling yen even more heavily. Both France and Canada also showed themselves ready to intervene heavily on both sides of the market. The Swiss authorities were, as from February 1975, prepared to intervene heavily.

Thus there came to be, among the exponents of official transactions in the foreign exchange market, two schools of official thought. First, there was the US view, which the German authorities were prepared to go along with for the time being, and which favoured only light and occasional intervention. Second, there was the alternative view, which favoured persistent and large scale intervention. Such was the state of play up to mid 1977. Thereafter, however, the adherents of the rival views in some cases changed sides, as will be shown in the next two chapters.

Monetary policy in the 1970s

As we have seen, a policy of leaning against the wind can be implemented by official transactions in the home-currency financial markets (in particular the money market) as well as in the foreign exchange market. Official transactions in all these financial markets vary in precise form from country to country, but they all have equivalent effect to official sales (or purchases) of paper assets of one kind or another. Official *sales* of paper deplete the commercial banks' deposits at the central bank and so produce a tighter stance of monetary policy, with the following symptoms:

1 A higher level of interest rates.
2 A capital inflow and hence a higher exchange rate.
3 A slower growth of bank lending and of the money stock with a deflationary effect on the real economy.

Official *purchases* of paper have the opposite effect.

The dilemma facing the floating-currency countries (above, page 199) has been whether to set the stance of their monetary policy for its effect on the exchange rate or for its effect on the domestic banking system and the home economy. Up until the early 1980s the countries in question usually opted for the latter alternative: they preferred to reserve monetary policy for use in influencing the state of the home economy – in particular to keep the growth of the money stock on a pre-determined path. Nevertheless there were a number of cases where the setting of monetary policy was made more deflationary specifically to support a weakening currency, or more expansionary specifically to prevent the further appreciation of a strengthening currency. Examples of the former include, in the case of the United States, President Carter's package of measures in November 1978 and, in respect of the UK, the Bank of England's jacking up of sterling interest rates in September and October 1981 (as described below in Chapter 21). Examples of the latter are the decisions taken by both Germany and Switzerland in 1978, and again in 1983,[5] to allow their monetary aggregates to exceed the target growth rates, rather than permit a further appreciation of their currencies in the market. Germany's experience was described by Dr Emminger as follows:

We in Germany have always applied this monetary targeting in what we call a pragmatic sense and not in such a dogmatic sense as has for some time been prevalent in the United States. . . . This means we have never believed that one could be a slave of monetary targets over a short period, say three months or six months, or even one year, if other very important considerations come into conflict with that. So, we have played it in such a way, for instance, that . . . when the change in exchange rate seemed to damage our domestic economy or our stability and so on then we looked more to the change in exchange rates than to the money supply.[6]

In the course of the 1980s, there came to be a shift in official opinion in the floating currency countries in favour of paying increased attention to the exchange rate as an objective of monetary policy. To this we shall return in Chapters 21 and 22.

Fluctuations in exchange rates

Despite the intermittent attempts (sometimes only half hearted but sometimes more determined) by the floating currency countries to lean against the wind, their efforts have not prevented very large changes in exchange rates as between the relevant currencies. Partly this was because the 1970s saw a rapid acceleration of inflation, at different rates in different countries, but even so *real* exchange rates were highly volatile, as is shown in the chart (page 206) taken from the BIS *Annual Report* for 1987. It is difficult to resist the conclusion of a study in 1983 by John Williamson,[7] that there have been many *prima facie* cases of over-shooting (the yen in 1978, the pound in 1980, the US dollar in 1983) and of undershooting (sterling in 1976, the US dollar in 1978, the DM as from 1982).

While it remains highly controversial whether the volatility of exchange rates which has obtained under the floating-rate regime could, or should, have been mitigated by official action, it is generally accepted that it has imposed real economic costs on the economies concerned, for reasons which the Deputy Governor of the Bank of England explained in an address in November 1983:

In trying to assess the extent of the costs of this volatility, it is necessary to distinguish between short run instability, where changes in exchange rates are quickly reversed, and major and lasting swings. Short run instability

Chart 2   Real bilateral exchange rates of selected currencies against the US dollar, 1972–87*

Fourth quarter 1975 = 100.

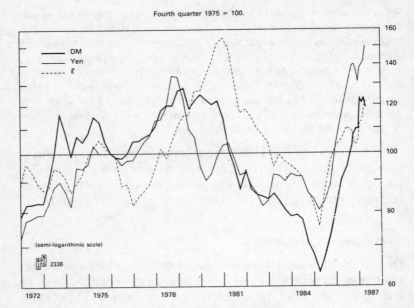

Note: Data prior to September 1986 are quarterly averages; thereafter, monthly figures are shown.
* Adjusted on the basis of movements in relative unit labour costs.

may give rise to considerable inconvenience to traders and consumers; and it may, because of such obvious arbitrariness in what is for everyone such an important price, bring the system into a sort of disrepute. But it seems unlikely to impose important economic costs, if only because sophisticated and efficient financial markets appear largely to have provided an answer. Forward cover is available in most major currencies at maturities long enough to cover the production process of the great bulk of goods in international trade, and provides insurance against exchange risk at what seems to be a remarkably low cost.

It seems likely, however, that major and more lasting exchange rate movements can impose real costs on national economies. Since wages, reflecting entrenched inflationary expectations, are slow to adjust, sustained movements in nominal exchange rates have generally been reflected in sustained changes in cost competitiveness. In modern conditions of high fixed capital costs and intense price competition, much of the strain is forced on to profit margins. There may follow scrappings of capital stock, lay-offs of labour and failures of firms that go further than required for fundamental adjustment but which, because of rigidities and imperfections, may not be reversed when conditions change.

On the other side of the coin, countries with undervalued exchange rates may undertake investment which later proves not to be viable at more normal levels of competitiveness; and may be subject to inflationary pressures while output is growing at a rapid rate.[8]

21 The floating pound

What we had to do earlier this year was to allow the exchange rate to fall because of the sharp collapse of the oil price. There clearly had to be a step change in the exchange rate and that duly occurred . . . So we are back to the policy of having an exchange rate which is exercising a financial discipline and that means that I do not wish to see it fall further.

Nigel Lawson
20 November 1986[1]

Benign neglect in the UK

The countries where Milton Friedman's recipe of benign neglect was most influential were the US and UK – partly, no doubt, thanks to the persuasiveness of monetarist literature but even more on account of the traumatic experience, in much of the 1960s, of having to live under the Bretton Woods system with an over-valued currency. The end of pegging in the early 1970s seemed like an escape from an irksome straitjacket: henceforth fiscal and monetary policy could be set by reference to the health of the internal economy, and a floating exchange rate would dispose of what had come to be considered a *self-inflicted* balance-of-payments problem. The central bankers concerned did not readily fall prey to such easy optimism but crucial policy decisions are taken by ministers rather than by central bankers.

In Britain's case, benign neglect has held sway in two periods since sterling was floated in June 1972 – namely in the first twelve months after June 1972 and again from October 1977 to September 1981 – and even then the Friedmanite doctrine of clean floating was tempered on both occasions by recourse to modest official transactions in the foreign exchange market to iron out what were identified as temporary fluctuations.

The origin of the UK practice of using official transactions in foreign exchange to iron out temporary fluctuations in the exchange rate dates back to the 1930s. Following the abandonment in 1931 of the official convertibility of sterling into gold at a fixed price, there had been set up in 1932 a Treasury account, administered by the Bank of England – the Exchange Equalization Account – specifically to deal in the market to iron out short-term fluctuations in the value of sterling. This account had always remained in existence. During the pegged-rate regime it had provided the resources for the Bank of England's market transactions to keep the pound pegged on the dollar, but after June 1972, with the floating of the pound, it reverted to its earlier role of smoothing out short-term fluctuations. Its resumption of this role was simply not called into question.

The first period of the UK version of benign neglect came to an end with the weakening of the pound as from mid 1973. The Bank of England then began to support sterling in the market, and continued to do so, on an increasing scale, until the autumn of 1976; moreover shortly afterwards, in July 1973, the Bank brought about 'a sharp upward shift in short-term rates in London' with the 'objective of stabilising the sterling exchange rate'.[2]

Then with OPEC's increase in oil prices towards the end of 1973 the decision was taken to support sterling in the market for as long as the UK remained an oil importer – that is, pending the coming into production of the North Sea oilfield. However, prolonged official support in the market was viewed by market operators with increasing misgivings, which reached crisis proportions in 1976, until Mr Healey's deflationary package towards the end of the year succeeded in restoring confidence.[3] Thereafter, thanks to this remedial treatment and then a growing awareness of the implications of North Sea oil, the pound strengthened rapidly. The authorities continued to lean against the wind, but now in the opposite direction. They sold sterling on a massive scale, using the dollars thereby acquired partly to replenish the official reserve, partly to repay some of the dollars they had borrowed over the years 1973–6. In addition, the Bank of England allowed a rapid fall in money market interest rates, the Treasury bill yield falling from 14 per cent at end 1976 to 4½ per cent at end October 1977.

Then in October 1977 the decision was taken to discontinue leaning against the wind, and the pound was allowed to rise in the market. Apart from April 1978, when the pound was temporarily weak and was strongly supported, the scale of the Bank's market transactions was appreciably reduced from October 1977 onwards, as may be seen from Table 23. Moreover, short term interest rates

Table 23   *Monthly movements in the underlying level* of UK international reserves $million, 1972–87*

	1972	1973	1974	1975	1976	1977	1978	1979	1980	1981	1982	1983	1984	1985	1986	1987
J		+12	−310	−685	+15	+1,894	+238	+59	+509	+308	+62	−359	−111	−282	+132	+72
F		+53	−232	−109	−14	+331	+259	+168	+368	−4	+96	−171	+40	−218	+112	+287
M		−6	−204	−10	−1,277	+1,075	−281	+1,017	+249	+51	−146	−328	−188	+259	+278	+1,785
A		+7	−237	−26	−1,486	+514	−2,115	+675	+242	−26	−394	+166	−155	+191	+264	+2,919
M		+289	−160	−716	−464	−605	−650	+303	+292	+278	−363	+233	−128	+223	+138	+4,760
J	−2,637	−12	−321	−519	−1,510	+891	−52	+599	+3	−388	−151	−178	−135	+124	+291	−230
J	−283	−685	−41	−26	−268	+1,794	+328	+1,356	+159	−418	+159	+70	−268	−9	−4	+499
A	+23	−388	+13	−285	−526	+962	−151	−146	+213	−29	+122	+28	−71	−36	−141	−457
S	−2	−463	−49	−181	−722	+1,768	+63	−431	+233	−677	+209	−76	−76	−97	−372	+380
O	−230	+22	−133	−153	−455	+3,036	+107	−417	+291	−225	+55	−61	−32	−324	−668	+6,700
N	+36	−130	−888	−301	−151	+183	−332	+7	+121	+254	−352	−73	+12	−201	+35	+31
D	−92	−367	−1,140	−113	+426	+257	+155	+493	+38	−96	−856	−195	+36	−416	+96	+3,740

* Excluding valuation changes, SDR issues and the capital element of all public sector, IMF and central bank debt transactions.

were steadily pushed upwards, especially after the advent of the Thatcher administration, even though this must have greatly aggravated the appreciation of sterling: they reached a peak of 17 per cent in November 1979.

Why the U-turn in 1977? Clearly official concern had switched from the sterling exchange rate to the need to keep the growth of the money stock, as measured by £M3, within its targeted ceiling. Official sales of sterling in the foreign exchange market in the earlier part of 1977 were seen as contributing to excessive growth of £M3; likewise the low interest rates in the autumn of 1977 were thought liable to aggravate the growth of bank lending which also was contributing to the growth of £M3. So a policy of leaning against the wind gave way to one of benign neglect, though mitigated by the Bank of England's traditional readiness to deal in the foreign exchange market to iron out temporary fluctuations.

A policy shift occurred in the opposite direction in the course of 1981, with the progressive weakening of sterling in the foreign exchange market. Though in 1980 and 1981 £M3 was overshooting its target, it was becoming increasingly discredited as the guiding star for UK monetary policy: hence official policy came to favour a lowering of interest rates from their high peak in November 1979.[4] But in September and October 1981 the Bank dramatically intervened in the money market to *raise* rates by some four percentage points,[5] in a (successful) attempt to hold the sterling rate against selling pressure in the market. Something similar may have happened on 26 November 1982 and 12 January 1983, but in these cases the initiative was taken by the clearing banks and the Bank of England followed. Much the same thing happened again on 9 May 1984, with the rise of ½ per cent (or in several cases ¾ per cent) in banks' base rates. The *Financial Times* then commented as follows:

The British authorities made it clear that they saw no domestic reason for Wednesday's rise of base lending rates to between 9 and 9¼ per cent, nor any immediate need for a further increase.

The Bank of England reluctantly followed market rates up by raising the rates at which it supplied funds to the banking system by ½ a percentage point. If it had not done so, it was feared sterling might have been pushed into an unwelcome sharp slide.[6]

In July 1984 there was an analogous episode. The *Financial Times* of 7 July reported that 'Clearing banks raised their base lending rates by ¾ of a percentage point to 10 per cent yesterday in the face of a further speculative run against the pound. The move, which was endorsed by the Bank of England, had an immediate steadying effect on sterling. . . . The rise in interest rates is a setback for the authorities who 10 days ago said they saw no domestic reason for an increase'. Five days later, on 12 July, the *Financial Times* reported a further increase in interest rates, this time of no less than two percentage points: 'Britain's major banks yesterday announced a sharp 2 percentage point rise in their base lending rates up to 12 per cent, halting the recent run on sterling on foreign exchanges. The move, led by Barclays and endorsed by the Bank of England . . . clearly marks a setback for the Government'.

By the beginning of 1985 short-term rates had been eased down to 9½ per cent, but a weakening pound provoked on 11 January a rise of one per cent in base rate – a rise which was later endorsed by the Bank of England by an equivalent increase in the rate on its own money market transactions. Then on 14 January the Bank jacked up rates to 12 per cent, and a further rise to 14 per cent followed on 28 January.

The House of Commons Committee on the Treasury and Civil Service took evidence from the Chancellor on these increases in interest rates in January 1985. It reported:[7]

In contrast to the previous position, where the concept of misaligned exchange rate was 'something of a metaphysical question', the Chancellor has now said that the pound is undervalued 'against the dollar and therefore against the basket of currencies because that is heavily weighted to the dollar'. Moreover, on the Wednesday following the first two of the most recent rises in UK clearing bank base rates, the Prime Minister was reported to have said: 'In my view, it's down too far and I do not like it sliding any further . . .'.[8] Later in a television interview the Prime Minister stated: '. . . people are undervaluing sterling very considerably'.[9] Despite this, the Chancellor denied that there has been any change in the Government's exchange rate policy . . . we have always found this stated policy somewhat difficult to reconcile with actual events and official action affecting the exchange markets. . . .

In paragraph 18 the Committee gave its own conclusions about the evolution of UK policy. It reported:

Nevertheless, in the light of recent history and the Prime Minister's statements that she considers sterling is undervalued and would like it to rise, we think it is becoming increasingly implausible for the Chancellor to maintain that the Government has no target or floor for sterling. These statements do seem to us to be at least superficially incompatible.

Apart from a temporary rise in January 1986, the course of short-term rates as from March 1985 was steadily downwards until 14 October 1986, when they were once again jacked up – this time from 10 to 11 per cent – and the Chancellor's explanation to the Committee was as reported in the quotation at the head of this chapter. In this quotation he in effect acknowledges that UK policy had completed a U-turn: beginning with a stance of very near to benign neglect in 1979 it had evolved into one very near to an unofficial, adjustable peg on the DM. Moreover, it was not only interest policy that was directed to this end: after the Louvre meeting in February 1987 (below, page 223) official transactions in the foreign exchange market were being undertaken in a much more determined fashion, to stabilise the exchange rate, than on any previous occasion in the 1980s (see Table 23). In March, April and May 1987 the Bank of England bought no less than $9.5 billion and in October a further $6.7 billion, not all of which was successfully sterilised by sales of sterling securities to non bank investors: hence there resulted an increase in the monetary liabilities of the banking system for the reasons explained above, (pages 198–9). In its report on the Autumn Statement, 1987, the House of Commons Committee on the Treasury and civil Service criticised the resumption of such large-scale official intervention in the foreign exchange market, implying that the management of the sterling exchange rate would have been more appropriately implemented by making bigger cuts in interet rates.[10]

22 The floating dollar

In July 1973 the Federal Reserve was called upon by the US and European governments to resume exchange market intervention, backed by a major enlargement of the Federal Reserve swap network. The very announcement of this policy shift from a free to a managed float of the dollar brought about an immediate recovery of dollar rates. But the dollar remained only lightly managed, the US government seemed to show little concern over the fate of the dollar, and the feeling persisted that benign neglect was indeed US policy.

Alfred Hayes
address in August 1975[1]

Benign neglect in the United States

As we saw in Chapter 20, the five years following the transition to floating was characterized by a policy in respect of the DM/dollar rate that was closely akin to benign neglect, with the US authorities firmly committed to this policy and the German authorities prepared to follow the US lead. However, the other floating-currency countries did not at this time subscribe to the same point of view. How can we account for the difference? What at the time most differentiated the United States from other countries with floating currencies was the US economy's greater degree of self-sufficiency. This explains the tendency in the United States to think of domestic and international economic policy as distinct, and as the latter as the tail on the dog.[2] The US attitude had two implications for US policy.

1 It signified that the instruments of monetary and fiscal policy should be used solely in the interests of the internal economy (interpreted as from 1970 to mean a prescribed rate of growth of the money stock) and should not be used for purposes of correcting an external disequilibrium. This aspect of US policy goes back a long way and had been departed from on only rare occasions. (The only occasions in the 1960s were the 1968 tax

increase, when concern for the dollar became a clinching argument for a reluctant Congress; and 'operation twist' earlier in the decade, when the Federal Reserve's open market operations were geared to getting short rates higher in relation to long rates, in order to attract international short-term capital to New York.)

2   It also meant that exchange rate changes were the appropriate means for correcting external disequilibria. This proposition did not have such a long US history, since we know that in the sixties the US authorities pressed the Wilson government to avoid devaluing sterling, lest this should call into question the whole pattern of parities then prevailing. But once the international monetary system had survived the eventual British devaluation in November 1967, the US became an advocate of readily adjustable parities and later (once pegging had given way to floating) of minimal intervention in the exchange markets.

What did other countries think of benign neglect on the part of the US? Briefly, they did not like it, at any rate when the US was seen to be complacent about the dollar depreciating; moreover (because of the widespread use of the dollar as a reserve currency) they were much more concerned about a depreciation of the dollar than about the depreciation of any other currency. They took the view that once the US authorities ceased, in August 1971, to deal in gold, they ought instead to have been prepared to deal in the foreign exchange market. A country whose currency has as wide an international clientele as that for the US dollar ought to show, in deeds as well as words, that it has a concern for foreign holders' interests. The fact that the US economy was so self-sufficient as to be little affected by the terms on which its exports exchanged against imports made foreign holders of dollars only more anxious to be reassured that the US was mindful of their interests as well as her own. One is left with the impression that the floating regime from March 1973 until 1978 was characterized by almost continuous disappointment on the part of the United States' trading partners that the US intervention in the foreign exchange market was so infrequent, so *ad hoc* and on such a restricted scale. On three occasions – in July 1973, in February 1975 and again at Rambouillet in November 1975 – hopes were raised of US conversion to a policy of more determined intervention, but always this proved to be a misunderstanding.

On the first of these occasions, the resumption of official intervention was decided upon at a G–10 meeting of central bank Governors in the first week of July 1973 (page 175). Thereafter, however, the dollar was only very lightly managed, at any rate by the US authorities, until the next concerted intervention in February 1975:

From July 1973 to January 1975, Federal Reserve operations in the dollar exchange market were confined to day-to-day smoothing operations, with little if any resistance to market pressures continuing over several weeks' time. In late January 1975, however, agreement was reached between representatives of the Swiss National Bank, the Bundesbank and the Federal Reserve on more determined and forceful intervention.[3]

This tripartite agreement in early 1975 was negotiated in a period, beginning in early September and ending in February–March 1975, when the dollar was temporarily weak. It was weak

owing largely to very active capital flows in all directions associated with US trade credits, the removal of US measures restraining capital export, the arrival and recycling of 'petrodollars', and the rapid fall in US interest rates relative to those in other major centres. The dollar fell 15 to 20 per cent against the currencies of the common float and by 5 per cent against other industrial-nation currencies. Net US official sales of foreign currencies during the six months ending in February 1975 were about $1.1 billion, not to mention the corresponding market operations by foreign authorities.[4]

The 1975 *Annual Report* of the Federal Reserve Bank of New York takes up the story after March 1975:

By March, the atmosphere in the exchange markets had improved and the dollar began to appreciate, as the United States trade balance moved into substantial surplus and interest rate differentials shifted in favour of New York. A desire for greater stability with major trading partners was exhibited in mid-July, when the French franc rejoined the snake. This was followed in November by the Rambouillet agreement between the United States and France, affirming the desirability of greater economic and exchange rate stability and calling for improved cooperation to counter erratic exchange rate fluctuations within the context of a system in which major countries have floating exchange rates.

We now see that the Franco-American agreement[5] at the Rambouillet conference had two aspects: on the one hand (see page 185) France gave up her insistence that any amended IMF charter must provide for the eventual re-establishment of a system of fixed (though adjustable) exchange rates. On the other hand, the

US agreed to a communiqué which committed the six countries at
the conference (G–5 plus Italy) to a statement that they intended 'to
work for greater stability in underlying economic and financial
conditions in the world economy. At the same time, our monetary
authorities will act to counter disorderly market conditions or erratic fluctuations in exchange rates.' However, this form of words did
not commit the United States to more forceful intervention in the
exchange markets. The US Secretary of the Treasury, William
Simon, made it clear that there would be no parities or bands of
fluctuations for the dollar against other currencies, and it subsequently became apparent that the US authorities would give a
narrow interpretation to 'disorderly market conditions' and 'erratic
fluctuations', so as to justify only very limited market intervention.
Fortunately for international harmony, dissatisfaction with benign
neglect was muted by the reasonably satisfactory performance,
most of the time, of the US dollar. Criticism flared up only on those
occasions when the dollar was falling in the market and/or when it
would have fallen (or would have fallen more sharply) but for
massive purchases by other countries' central banks. Such occasions
occurred on a serious scale only twice in the 1970s, first in the early
years of the decade and then again in 1977 and 1978 (see Table 18
for the dollar exchange rate and Table 24 for the US deficit
financed by official reserve transactions, on pages 177 and 218
respectively). In the former period the US rode the storm with
effectively no concessions to the critics of benign neglect, but in
1978 there were signs, especially in the last quarter, with President
Carter's package of measures, that US policy was changing
direction.

Benign neglect in abeyance, 1978–80

Exchange markets became unsettled during the last week of September 1977, and the US dollar remained under heavy selling
pressure during the remainder of the year, largely due to growing
concern about the size of the ongoing and prospective deficits on the
US trade balance. In a statement on 21 December 1977, President
Carter noted the emergence in the past year of a large deficit in the
US trade and payments position, stating that 'the two main causes
appear to be: large oil imports by the United States and relatively
slow economic growth in Japan, Germany and other countries'. The
deficits, he said, 'have contributed to some disorder in the exchange

Table 24   *US balance of payments, annually, 1969–80 ($ billion)*

Year	Export surplus on goods and services	Deficit (−) financed by official reserve transactions*	
		including OPEC's official $ holdings in the US	excluding OPEC's official $ holdings in the US†
1969	3.4	+2.7	+2.5
1970	5.6	−10.7	−11.1
1971	2.3	−30.5	−31.1
1972	−1.9	−11.0	−9.4
1973	11.0	−5.2	−4.5
1974	9.3	−8.8	+2.1
1975	23.0	−4.4	+2.7
1976	9.6	−10.5	−0.9
1977	−9.5	−35.0	−28.7
1978	−9.2	−33.5	−34.7
1979	4.9	+9.9	+15.4‡
1980	7.1	−9.0	+3.7

* Excluding from US official reserve assets the increases due to the allocations of SDRs and the proceeds of the issues of Carter bonds in Germany and Switzerland in 1978–80.

† The case for excluding OPEC official holdings of US dollars is that (unlike other countries' official reserves) they are not predominantly held for use in official transactions aimed at influencing the course of the exchange rate.

‡ Most of this reflects dollar reserves sold by the Japanese authorities in market operations to support the yen.

Sources: Report of the US Council of Economic Advisers, January 1980, pp. 316–17; Federal Reserve *Bulletin*, April 1981, p. A52 and p. A53, and previous issues; *Survey of Current Business*, June 1973, p. 46, and June 1975, p. 48, items 53–6 (which for the years 1969–73 have been taken as an approximation for OPEC's official dollar holdings).

markets and rapid movements in exchange rates'. He went on to say that 'while some exchange rate adjustment has been understandable in the light of economic developments in Germany, Japan, and the United States, recent exchange market disorders are not justified'. 'In the discharge of our responsibilities', he added, 'we will, in close consultation with our friends abroad, intervene to the extent necessary to counter disorderly conditions in the exchange markets.'

In the wake of Mr Carter's pronouncement, the German Bundesbank issued a statement on 5 January as follows:

An agreement was concluded between the US Treasury and the Deutsche Bundesbank on 4 January 1978, under which the Bundesbank has extended a credit line to the Treasury's Exchange Stabilization Fund, which can be drawn on for intervention in the dollar market. This new credit line is in addition to the existing mutual credit arrangement between the Bundesbank and the US Federal Reserve System. Intervention will be conducted in close co-operation between the US Treasury, the Federal Reserve System and the Deutsche Bundesbank. It is to be directed against speculative excesses and for the securing of orderly conditions in the foreign exchange market.

To support the steps taken on 4 January 1978, further cooperative steps were announced on 13 March. These included a doubling – to the equivalent of $4 billion – in the amount of the reciprocal currency arrangement between the Bundesbank and the US Federal Reserve System, thereby bringing the total of such swap lines between the Federal Reserve and fourteen central banks and the Bank for International Settlements to $22 billion. In addition, the US Treasury arranged for the sale of 600 million SDRs to purchase Deutsche marks. The announcement of 13 March also pointed out that the United States had a reserve position in the International Monetary Fund of some $5 billion 'which it will draw if and as necessary to acquire additional foreign exchange'.

Following the 4 January announcement, the Federal Reserve Bank of New York, acting for the Treasury and the Federal Reserve System, had moved to a more open and forceful approach in the exchange market. In due course it reported official US sales of foreign currencies, in the quarter ended 31 January 1978, equivalent to $1.5 billion – a record amount for a three-month period – in the New York exchange market. (The previous record quarterly currency sales by the US authorities were in February–April 1975, when currencies equivalent to $793 million were sold.) Since however the official intervention in the DM/dollar market at this time was a joint US–German operation, the scale of the operation can better be judged by the market support given to the dollar by *both* countries' authorities. Table 25 shows that, in the half-year ended end-March 1978, such support amounted to DM17 billion, or about $8 billion, a scale of official intervention which surely indicates a significant shift of policy from the 'light-intervention' stance in 1976 and early 1977, as described by the BIS in the quotation at the beginning of Chapter 20. In April 1978 the Carter administration announced its intention to sell gold, from the US official reserve, at a rate of 300,000 ounces a month (subsequently raised to 750,000 ounces a month).

Table 25   *US and German official support for the US dollar* (DM billion)*

Year	Period	DM billion
1977	quarters 1 and 2	0.7
	quarter 3	1.3
	quarter 4	9.3
1978	quarter 1	7.8
	quarter 2	−1.5
	1 July to mid October	1.8
	mid October to end December	16.0
1979	January to April	−9.9
	May to 13 June	−4.1
	mid June to 23 September	+18.6
	24 September to end December	+2.8
1980	January to mid April	−13.9

* Market purchase of US dollars by the Bundesbank plus sales of DM by the Federal Reserve Bank of New York.

Source: *Reports* of the Deutsche Bundesbank for 1977, 1978 and 1979.

Following these measures, a temporary recovery of the dollar occurred between early April and late May 1978, but towards the end of May began the largest and most general decline since the introduction of floating in March 1973. Essentially it resulted from a lack of confidence, due to an obvious reluctance on the part of the US authorities to deal with the crisis in the most direct way possible, by announcing their readiness to intervene in the exchange market on whatever scale might be necessary. Their attitude was widely interpreted as a reversion to the doctrine of benign neglect in an extreme form, and confidence was not restored, despite various anti-inflation measures adopted in October, until Mr Carter announced the massive support arrangements in his 1 November 1978 package.

Mr Carter's package

The October anti-inflation measures were announced on the 24th of the month. They called for restraint by unions on wages, by companies on prices, and by the federal government itself on spending. Wages and fringe benefits were not to rise by more than 7 per cent a year; groups of workers which complied with the 7 per cent pay guideline would get a tax rebate if the rate of inflation exceeded 7 per cent. Companies were asked to cut their price rises by 0.5 per cent below their average increases in 1976 and 1977; they could pass on 'unavoidable costs' and raise prices beyond this level, but only if their profit margins before tax did not widen as well. The budget for the fiscal year 1979/80 would pare spending to 21 per cent of gross national product, down from 23 per cent in 1975/76.

There followed the package of 1 November 1978. President Carter intended it to be a 'major step' in the anti-inflation plan that he had announced in the previous week. Mr Blumenthal, who presented the details of the package, said that the US would now 'intervene in a forceful and co-ordinated manner' on the foreign exchange markets, in co-operation with the West German, Swiss and Japanese central banks, to correct the 'excessive recent decline in the dollar'. Adequate means for intervention – to the tune of about $30 billion – would be assured by the following devices:

1   The currency swaps with central banks of Germany, Japan and Switzerland would be increased from a ceiling of $7.6 billion to $15 billion.
2   US Treasury gold sales would be increased from 750,000 ounces to 1.5 million ounces a month from December.
3   The US would draw $3 billion from its entitlement at the International Monetary Fund.
4   The US would sell to other countries' central banks $2 billion of its Special Drawing Rights allocation from the IMF.
5   The US Treasury would issue up to $10 billion of foreign currency denominated negotiable bonds – so-called Carter bonds. (In the event, $6.4 billion were issued.)

In addition, the following steps were taken to raise interest rates and tighten monetary policy:

6   The Federal Reserve increased its discount rate from 8½ per cent to 9½ per cent.
7   The Federal Reserve imposed on commercial banks 2 per cent

supplementary reserve requirements on deposits of $100,000 or more.

President Carter's package of fiscal and monetary measures in October and November 1978 were defended, as might be expected, as being necessary for the efficient operation of the US internal economy, but the arguments deployed by the US authorities also leant heavily – and to a wholly unprecedented extent – on the need to reinforce the international standing of the dollar. Moreover we find in the course of 1978 that references to the external position of the dollar begin to appear in the monthly instructions issued by the Federal Open Market Committee. By November the instruction is unambiguously relating open market policy to the dollar's market value – it reads 'in the short run, the Committee seeks to achieve bank reserve and money market conditions that are broadly consistent with the longer-run ranges for monetary aggregates cited above, *while giving due regard to the program for supporting the foreign exchange value of the dollar . . .*' (my italics).

The support for the dollar in the foreign exchange market undertaken by the US and German authorities as from mid October to the end of 1978 amounted to DM16 billion (see Table 25), or about $8½ billion. In addition the US authorities were buying dollars for Swiss francs and (for the first time ever) also for yen: in November and December 1978 these purchases totalled about $1 billion. At the same time, the Swiss and Japanese authorities were also buying dollars in the market, to the tune of over $4 billion and $2 billion respectively in the two months. As from early in 1979 the tide turned, and by about the end of May the authorities of the countries concerned had been able to unwind their support operations, though in June the dollar weakened again and support was resumed on a substantial scale, as is clear from Table 25.

The dollar strengthens

Though the annual summit meetings of heads of governments initiated in 1975 aimed at co-ordinating the pressure of demand in the major industrial economies, achievements fell well short of intentions. In 1977–8 the US raced ahead of its partners, with the result that its normal export surplus became a big export deficit (Table 24 on page 218) and the dollar weakened as described above. Then Germany went into the lead, with the result that in 1980 the dollar strengthened at the expense of the DM: the Bundesbank now needed dollars to support the DM in the market and obtained them by unwinding the support it had afforded the dollar in the three preceding years.

Then in 1981 the transition from the Carter to the Reagan administration brought a reversion to benign neglect. Mr Donald Regan, the Treasury Secretary, announced in April 1981 that official transactions in the foreign exchange market would be limited to 'emergency situations', such as the then recent shooting of President Reagan, and that the US authorities would henceforth 'not intervene to support the dollar in the foreign exchange markets as a regular practice'. At the same time overriding priority was to be given in monetary policy to keeping the growth of the money-stock on target, even if this should lead (as in due course it did) to US interest rates so high as to attract a massive capital inflow and bid the dollar up to a level seemingly unsustainable in the longer run.

Two periods of dollar weakness

As we have seen (above, page 217) the evidence of Tables 18 and 24 (pages 177 and 218) points to two periods of dollar weakness in the 1970s, an earlier period up to mid 1973 and then again in 1977–8. Other evidence points in the same direction:

1   Both periods witnessed a sharp upsurge in the market price of gold.
2   There was in both periods a revival of interest in European monetary schemes, reflecting a desire to reduce the international role of the dollar. The earlier period of dollar weakness saw the birth of the snake in 1972 (see page 158), the later period the agreement in December 1978 to establish the European Monetary System (see Appendix B, page 253).
3   There was also in both periods active consideration of possible ways of modifying the role of the IMF, again so as to reduce the international role of the US dollar: in the earlier period there was the Committee of Twenty's 'Grand Design', in the later period a revival of interest in one of its components, the proposed Substitution Account (see page 168). At the annual meeting of the Fund in 1978, the Interim Committee (the successor to the Committee of Twenty) considered a proposal that the second issue of SDRs might be made through the mechan-

ism of a Substitution Account, whereby a like amount of dollars would be taken out of national reserves. This proposal was rejected in favour of having a second issue, to be distributed in the same way as the first issue; nevertheless the committee did not dismiss the possibility of setting up a Substitution Account *as well*, and instructed the executive directors to keep the matter under review. Subsequently, at its meeting on 7 March 1979, the committee expressed broad support for active consideration of a Substitution Account. Though the committee's professed interest in the matter derived from the desirability of enhancing the status of IMF Special Drawing Rights, a contributor to *Le Monde* of 10 March plausibly suggested that the committee's attitude may also have reflected a certain lack of confidence in the dollar. The committee's interest continued for another twelve months, but at its March 1980 meeting, in Hamburg, it had to face the fact that for the time being the Account seemed no more readily negotiable in 1980 than it had been in 1973 (above, page 171).

4   The earlier period of dollar weakness had been characterized by the imposition of exchange controls on capital inflows, especially by Germany, Japan and Switzerland (see pages 148, 153 and 161), and there was renewed recourse to such measures in 1977–8. In December 1977 the German authorities discontinued authorizing the acquisition by non-residents of domestic bonds with more than two but less than four years to maturity, and in January 1978 they imposed increased minimum reserve ratios on non-resident deposits at German banks. The Japanese authorities in November 1977 imposed a high reserve ratio (initially 50 per cent but increased in March 1978 to 100 per cent) on most non-resident deposits at Japanese banks; also in March 1978 they introduced a ban on the purchase by non-residents, in the over-the-counter market, of domestic securities maturing in less than five years and one month. Switzerland had not followed the example of Germany and Japan in repealing more or less completely in 1974–5 the restrictions imposed earlier in the 1970s; none the less Swiss restrictions were tightened up in February and March 1978: a ban was reimposed on investment by foreigners in Swiss franc securities, and likewise a ban on the sale by entrants into Switzerland of foreign bank notes against Swiss francs in amounts exceeding SF20,000; moreover, the rule imposing a negative rate of interest on

privately-held non-resident deposits at Swiss banks was extended to cover official holders too. However, with the recovery of the dollar later in 1978 and early 1979, all three countries (Germany, Japan and Switzerland) discontinued in 1980 and 1981 the restrictions newly imposed in late 1977 and early 1978.[6]

These various features of the two periods of dollar weakness in the 1970s give no clue as to why US policy changed course in the later period but not in the earlier one. Can we then identify circumstances which were *different* in the two periods? There are at least three such circumstances.

In the first place, though the oil industry has traditionally been a dollar industry, using the US dollar for pricing, invoicing and finance, and though the dollar has traditionally been favoured as an investment medium by the OPEC countries, the loyalty of some of the big oil producers to the dollar was in 1978 becoming somewhat strained. As the *Financial Times* reported on 2 March 1978:

The fall in the dollar has resulted in increasing concern in recent weeks in the oil-producing states and action by them to raise their prices seems probable after the latest Kuwait move.

After a meeting with the Emir, Sheikh Ali Khalifa al Sabah, Minister of Oil, was quoted as saying: 'In case the current slippage of the dollar continues, Kuwait will take the initiative in calling for an emergency meeting of Oil and Finance Ministers to discuss the dollar's position as well as whether to continue the current freeze of oil prices or to decide on price hikes.'

In the second place, there were growing US misgivings about the efficacy of exchange rate changes *alone* to achieve adjustment, on account of the J-curve effect. As Paul Volcker put it:

For one thing, we have learned that even large exchange rate changes have not been nearly as effective as hoped in achieving adjustment of long-standing imbalances in current account positions. Where clear improvements have been made, they can be traced mainly to changes in relative demand pressures, or to structural changes such as North Sea oil. I do not doubt that trade and current account positions will in time shift in response to real exchange rate changes, but I believe we are learning that the process takes a number of years – possibly even a decade – to work its way fully through the economic structure.

At the same time, there is little evidence that floating exchange rates have substantially dampened the tendency for changes in business activity in one country to affect the trade of others. Changes in income continue to dominate current account balances in the short-run. The shifts in current account positions may exert a pronounced influence on exchange rates, but the exchange rate movements will not, in turn, have much impact on cyclical imbalances. Indeed for extended periods, J-curve effects may be perverse.[7]

In the third place, the US economy was in the 1970s becoming progressively less self-sufficient: this was dramatically so in respect of oil, but so it was also of a wide range of other goods, including manufactured products such as motor cars. Thus the dollar exchange rate was becoming an increasingly weighty element in the internal price structure, and in particular in the price level of goods entering into personal and household expenditure. Hence a falling exchange rate came to have political implications in the US – as it had had in most other countries throughout the post-war period.

The dollar overshoots

The transition from the Carter administration to the Reagan administration in the early 1980s saw the adoption of a more expansionary fiscal policy and a more deflationary monetary policy, with large budgetary deficits and high interest rates (Tables 26 and 27). This major change in the mix of fiscal and monetary policy was not a carefully articulated adjustment to reconcile internal and external policy objectives, as advocated by economists of the Keynesian school (above, page 199). On the contrary, the

Table 26   *US government finance: annual deficit*

Year ending 30 September	$ billion
1979	36
1980	76
1981	79
1982	126
1983	203
1984	178
1985	212
1986	221

Source: IMF International Financial Statistics, December 1986 and April 1987.

Table 27   *US Federal Funds interest rate 1975–87 (annual average)*

	%		%
1975	5.8	1982	12.3
1976	5.1	1983	9.1
1977	5.5	1984	10.2
1978	7.9	1985	8.1
1979	11.2	1986	6.8
1980	13.4		
1981	16.4		

Source: *IMF International Financial Statistics*, March 1982 and December 1987.

budgetary deficit was the unplanned outcome of ill-coordinated Presidential and Congressional initiatives, while the high interest rates were the Federal Reserve's reaction to a fiscal policy which it judged to be too expansionary in the circumstances of the time.

Moreover, it was quite apparent that neither fiscal policy nor monetary policy was being directed to an external objective: benign neglect was the order of the day, as we have already noted on page 223, and a combination of high US interest rates plus large new issues of US government securities, highly attractive to foreign investors, bid up the external value of the dollar to a level unsustainable in the longer run. Knowledgeable analysts explained the phenomenon in terms of 'over-shooting' and 'bandwaggon effects', and predicted that very soon the bubble would burst. Nevertheless the rise of the dollar continued right into 1985: its eventual decline did not begin until March of that year (see Table 28).

The appreciation of the dollar was far from welcome to the US authorities, since it made US manufacturing industry increasingly uncompetitive in world markets and led to demands for increased protection – which ran counter to President Reagan's objective of freer international trade. It also led to a massive deterioration in the US balance of payments on current account (see Table 29). Nevertheless, benign neglect of the exchange rate continued with only minor interruptions up to September 1985, by which time the effective exchange rate of the dollar was some 25 per cent higher than its average in 1981 (Table 28).

Table 28 *The US dollar's nominal exchange rate against 15 other industrial-country currencies, 1980–87; 1980–82 = 100*

	Annual Average	
1980	90.7	
1981	99.5	
1982	109.8	
1983	114.2	
1984	122.4	
1985	127.1	(136.9 in March and 125.2 in September)
1986	106.0	(109.0 in March)
1987	94.2	(96.9 in February and 95.8 in August)

Source: *World Financial Markets*, August 1983, April/May 1986 and December 1987.

Table 29 *Various countries' balance of payments on current account, 1978–86 ($ billion)*

	US	Japan	W. Germany	Developing Countries
1978	−15.4	+16.5	+9.0	−35.0
1979	−1.0	−8.8	−6.0	+6.4
1980	+1.9	−10.7	−15.7	+30.4
1981	+6.9	+4.8	−5.2	−48.5
1982	−8.7	+6.9	+4.1	−87.1
1983	−46.3	+20.8	+4.2	−64.0
1984	−107.0	+35.0	+8.4	−33.0
1985	−116.4	+49.3	+15.3	−23.9
1986	−141.4	+85.8	+35.4	−46.4

Source: *IMF Annual Report*, 1987, page 17.

International collaboration

From the beginning of the 1980s up to September 1985, the most obvious obstacle to international collaboration on exchange rates was the US commitment to benign neglect. The UK also initially favoured benign neglect, but UK participation in any collaboration was not essential, and anyway her espousal of benign neglect was short-lived. All the other major powers were from the start disappointed at the US reversion to benign neglect under the Reagan administration.

The first really significant evidence that the US was shifting her position away from benign neglect was the communiqué issued after a Group of Five meeting on 22 September 1985 in the Plaza Hotel, New York. Nevertheless, there had previously been several rather half-hearted attempts at concerted intervention in the foreign exchange markets, the first one in August 1983. In that month the central banks of the US, Germany, Switzerland and Japan sold nearly 3 billion dollars in the market, to counter the rise in the dollar. However in practice it seems to have made very little difference.[8] Thereafter, apart from a sally by the Federal Reserve and Bundesbank into the exchange market in September and October 1984,[9] little further concerted action seems to have been taken until the next year.

1985 began with a G-5 initiative in January. Following a meeting on 17 January, the G-5 members 'reaffirmed their commitment to undertaking co-ordinated intervention as necessary' but there followed 'little evidence of a broad co-ordinated intervention effort'.[10] In particular, there was little intervention by the US authorities: of official dollar sales by the G-5 members of some $10 billion between 17 January and 1st March, the US contributed less than $1 billion.

Then at the Plaza meeting of G-5 on 22 September 1985, Treasury Secretary James Baker launched a major initiative which led to an agreement by the G-5 countries, subsequently extended to all the G-10 countries, to take official action to depress the US dollar in the foreign exchange market. Such action was indeed taken in September and October 1985, after the Plaza meeting, and it was duly followed by a depreciation of the dollar, as may be seen from Table 28. The Plaza initiative was significant in four respects:

1   The decision-taking forum was G-5 and not the IMF, despite the fact that the Second Amendment to the Fund Agreement asserts the IMF's responsibility for the surveillance of exchange rates. The reason for the US preference for launching an exchange-rate initiative in a very small forum had been made clear by Mr. Volcker way back in November 1975, when he said: 'The central problem primarily concerns a small number of major countries – if their currencies are reasonably stable,

the rest can fall in place'.[11] On this view, a bigger forum than G-5 is both unnecessary and inefficient.

2 The Plaza initiative was the first occasion since the joint US/ German effort to support the dollar in November 1978 that the US had been prepared to engage in international collaboration on exchange rates on a substantial scale. (Admittedly, the US authorities had cooperated with other central banks to mitigate the dollar's rise in August 1983, September 1984 and January 1985, but the scale of dollar sales by the US was too small to make much impression.)

3 The apparent success of the Plaza initiative supports the opinion, advanced in June 1984 by the House of Commons Treasury and Civil Service Committee, that international monetary coordination should focus on trying to achieve a common view as to a viable pattern of exchange rates. As the Committee put it:

> focusing on exchange rates forces the representatives of different countries to face the fact that the national policies they adopt inevitably have an international impact. For example any policy change which shows up in a change in the £/DM rate clearly has a comparably serious impact on the British and German economies.[12]

4 Apart from a small and temporary raising of Japanese interest rates in October 1985, the action actually taken after the Plaza agreement to depress the dollar was simply sterilized intervention in the foreign exchange market. Moreover the intervention was on a comparatively small scale – some 13 billion dollars from the Plaza meeting to early November. The apparent success of the operation is therefore difficult to reconcile with the conclusions reached by the Jurgensen committee, whose report in March 1983 had been so sceptical as to the effect of sterilized intervention (above, page 199).

Does the apparent success of the Plaza initiative mean that sterilized intervention is after all a more efficacious instrument of policy than it seemed to the Jurgensen committee? It would seem that the circumstances of September and October 1985 were untypical in two respects. First, the official intervention was designed to drive the dollar in the direction it was already moving; i.e. it was a case of 'driving the rate', not of 'leaning against the wind'. Second, as mentioned above, the US authorities seemed committed for the first time since the late 1970s to taking decisive official action: some 3 billion of the 13 billion official dollar sales were by the US authorities.[12] This style of intervention may well have been interpreted by the market as a signal that the great powers, and in particular the US, were on that occasion unusually determined to act together to achieve a common objective.

By March 1986 the dollar had depreciated by 13 per cent as compared with September 1985 (see Table 28) and the attention of the G-5 countries turned to the need to reduce interest rates. Early in March 'a co-ordinated round of official interest rate reductions by the Deutsche Bundesbank, the Bank of Japan, the Federal Reserve and a number of other central banks'[14] was achieved. Then in the following month 'a second round of co-ordinated cuts in official interest rates was implemented by the US, Japanese and major European central banks except the Deutsche Bundesbank between the 14 and 25 April'.[15]

However, from then onwards international cooperation proved to be much more difficult, since the US on the one hand and Germany and Japan on the other had irreconcilably different remedies for the prevailing international disequilibrium (which was characterised by a large US deficit on current account and correspondingly large surpluses in the case of both Germany and Japan, as may be seen from Table 29). The US looked to Germany and Japan to assume a locomotive role in the world economy, with more expansionary fiscal policies and lower interest rates – failing which there would need to be a further depreciation of the dollar in terms of the DM and yen.[16] On the other hand Germany and Japan looked to the US to reduce her budget deficit and to cooperate in stabilising the dollar in the exchange markets.

The economic summit which took place in Tokyo early in May 'did not produce evidence of general official readiness to support the dollar at this stage':[17] moreover the communiqué issued after the meeting seemed to ignore two lessons implicit in the Plaza initiative. First, it emphasised the surveillance role of the IMF, rather than of the Group of Five. Second, far from enjoining policy makers to focus on exchange rates, it directed their attention to a list of no less than ten so-called 'indicators',[18] among which exchange rates were given no special emphasis. Not surprisingly, no coordinated action proceeded from the Tokyo meeting.

In September 1986 the finance ministers and central bank

governors of the EEC countries appeared to be lining up with Germany and Japan against the United States. They met at the Scottish golfing resort of Gleneagles and

agreed on a united front to persuade the US to stabilise the value of the dollar and end the current upheaval in the international currency markets.

They expressed anger and dismay at last week's remark by Mr. James Baker, the US Treasury Secretary, apparently seeking to 'talk down' the value of the dollar, in response to the refusal by the West German Bundesbank to sanction a further cut in its discount rate. . . . The finance ministers refused to put direct pressure on Bonn for an interest-rate cut, as the US wishes, [and were] adamant that the decision should be left to West Germany. . . .

A key concern emerging from Gleneagles is that the US Administration has got its economic analysis wrong. The ministers believe Washington is putting too much store by the need for faster growth in West Germany and Japan, or on a lower dollar, to correct its $180 billion annual trade deficit. They believe attention should be rather on the US budget deficit as the principal culprit.[19]

At the end of October 1986 the tension between the United States and her partners was somewhat relieved by an agreement between James Baker and the Japanese Finance Minister Miyazawa,

on cooperative action by their governments. As part of this agreement, Japan reduced its discount rate from 3.5 per cent to 3.0 per cent. A supplementary budget to support economic activity has also been submitted, and Japan has expressed its intention to implement a tax reform as soon as possible. For its part, the United States has just enacted a tax reform and has continued to resist protectionism. Secretary Baker and Minister Miyazawa expressed the understanding that exchange rate developments since the Plaza accord of September 1985 had resulted in a yen-dollar exchange rate that was broadly in line with the economic fundamentals, and they reaffirmed US-Japanese cooperation on exchange market issues.[20]

Despite this agreement, the dollar continued to depreciate in the foreign exchange markets, and the depreciation continued into 1987. In February 1987 the Japanese discount rate was cut again (to 2½ per cent compared with 5 per cent at the beginning of 1986) reflecting domestic concern over the impact of the appreciation of the yen on the economy. The German authorities, however, did not reduce official rates again in 1986 after the cut in the Spring;[21] the next cut, by ½ per cent to 3 per cent, occurred on 23 January 1987,[22] and a further ½ per cent cut followed in December 1987.[23]

The reduction in Japanese interest rates in February 1987 occurred on the eve of a meeting on 22 February at the Louvre in Paris of the finance ministers and central bank governors of G-5 plus Canada. The six nations concerned 'agreed to stabilise the currency market, but gave no details of how this was to be achieved'[24] – indeed the substance of the Louvre agreement was not revealed until early May, when the President of the Bundesbank (Mr. Poehl) delivered an address at Harvard University:

He said the so-called 'Louvre Accord' in February between the group of five countries and Canada did at least confirm the US shift away from 'benign neglect [over the dollar] to active concern'. But Mr. Poehl categorically denied that the February agreement was aiming to bring in any kind of 'target rates' for the dollar to replace the floating exchange rate system.[25]

The dollar exchange rate as from the Louvre meeting until the stock market crash in October 1987 did in fact display much more stability than in the preceding months (see Table 28), thanks *inter alia* to official purchases of dollars by a number of countries, especially the UK and Japan, but this stabilty seems to have owed little to improved international collaboration. The next relevant international meeting after the Louvre meeting was a meeting in Washington early in April 1987 of G-5 plus Canada and Italy. At this Washington meeting 'the US attitude to a further depreciation of the dollar remained equivocal',[26] which serves to

explain the qualified language of the Group of Seven's communiqué. 'Around current levels' exchange rates are 'broadly consistent' with economic fundamentals, it says.

And even then it makes clear that the judgement depends on everyone living up to their economic policy commitments. . . . But while both the Bonn and Tokyo governments have acknowledged that there is some scope for a further reduction in their market rates, they believe that it is relatively small.

Much more important, most officials believe, is the need to provide the markets with concrete evidence that the US administration is able to bring down its budget deficit and that the Japanese Government will meet its growth pledges.

That in turn will need a breakthrough in the political conflicts paralysing both the US Congress and the Japanese Diet. In the meantime, though central banks may make occasional successful raids, the markets seem set to rule.[27]

The *Review* of the Federal Reserve Bank of New York reported that after the Washington meeting,

many in the market continued to doubt that the authorities were sufficiently committed to exchange rate stability to make major adjustments to domestic economic policies. . . . In Japan, official comments suggested that there would be no further easing of credit policy, and there seemed to be little evidence of movement towards a more expansionary budget.[28]

The Venice summit in June 1987 left the market still without credible indications as to the action to be expected from the United States and Germany in support of the dollar. In the case of the US authorities, their attitude at the summit made it reasonably clear that henceforth they would not threaten Japan and Germany with the possibility of further dollar depreciation if they failed to accept US advice about reflating their economies. Even so, a seemingly accidental public remark by President Reagan after the summit meeting was interpreted as meaning that the US government had only a very limited commitment to support the dollar, if (as might well happen) it came under pressure sometime in the future.[29] With regard to the US budget deficit, President Reagan

disappointed European hopes that he might consider some modest tax increases if the Democrat-controlled Congress turns away from his planned reductions in the 1988 budget deficit. Higher taxes were simply not an option, he told his colleagues, although his Treasury Secretary, Mr. James Baker, did hint that they might have to be.[30]

(Later in 1987, the US Congress adopted tax increases and spending cuts designed to reduce the budget deficit by $30.2 billion in the fiscal year beginning 1 October 1987, and by $45.8 billion in the following fiscal year: this package was however not well received by the market, which judged it inadequate to afford effective support for the dollar). Germany's attitude at the Venice summit remained disobliging in not responding to suggestions that her fiscal stance should be less deflationary:

The seven's joint commitment to stable exchange rates has been reaffirmed, but the policies shakily underpinning the dollar remain unchanged. West Germany was still unmovable at the summit in its view that no new measures are needed to stimulate its economy ahead of the package of tax cuts planned for next January. West Germany as a locomotive? 'This will not occur', affirmed Chancellor Helmut Kohl at his closing Press conference.[31]

Only Japan seemed ready to face up to her international responsibilities:

Japan whose Y6,000bn package of public spending increases and tax cutting measures was generally well-received at the summit can claim more than most to live up to its commitments to stimulate its economy.[32]

As from the time of the stock market collapse in October 1987 until the last few days of the year, the market took the view that for the time being there would be no resumption of effective international cooperation to manage the dollar exchange rate, which thereafter depreciated steadily, despite the US fiscal package and the subsequent statement issued by the Group of Seven countries, which merely papered over their continuing differences about measures needed to stabilise the dollar. It was recognised that a number of countries were from time to time making large official purchases of dollars, but this did little to reassure the market, since such official action appeared to arise mainly from purely national preoccupations (in the UK's case, from the Chancellor's determination to keep the pound below three DM). By the end of 1987, the dollar, which on 22 October had been worth DM 1·82 and 144 yen, was down to about 1·60 and 123 respectively.

As from 28 December, 1987, there was some sign of a resumption of international co-operation, in the limited sense of co-ordinated official purchases of dollars by many of the major powers, including the United States, specifically to prevent the further depreciation of the US currency. There was also by this time a clear indication that Japan (unlike Germany) was taking steps to assume a locomotive role in the world economy. However, up to the time of writing (20 January 1988) there is still no solid ground for confidence that the halting steps already taken towards more international collaboration will progress much further in the immediate future.

So the Baker initiative at the Plaza meeting in September 1985, which initially seemed to promise coordinated international action to tackle the acute balance of payments disequilibrium between the United States on the one hand and Germany and Japan on the other, lost its impetus even before mid-1986, since when the course of events has served only to emphasise the seeming impossibility of sustained international monetary cooperation.

23 The international debt problem of the 1980s

A reason why recycling might be more difficult this time is that by contrast with 1974 banks are not starting out with relatively clean sheets but are already heavily burdened with third-world risks. They may therefore have less scope than before to expand their international risk exposure more rapidly than their balance-sheet totals. Conversely, the debt burdens of certain groups of countries *vis-à-vis* the international financial markets have increased substantially since 1974, which has certainly not helped their risk ratings.

BIS *Annual Report*, 1980

The two oil shocks

Chapter 19 recounted the story of two oil shocks – the dramatic increases in the price of oil at the end of 1973 and again in 1979. As we saw, the international monetary system survived the first shock remarkably successfully. The industrial countries (the main importers of oil) initially suffered a business recession, but the stance of their monetary and fiscal policies was in due course adjusted to offset this, at any rate to some extent. By the second half of 1975 a recovery was under way in the United States and recovery in other industrial countries followed. The oil-importing developing countries adopted policies which, taken as a whole, allowed their rate of economic growth to proceed unabated, even in the years immediately following the oil price rise.

Since prosperity was maintained more consistently in the oil-importing developing countries than in the industrial countries, the countries whose current account deficits were the counterpart to the OPEC surpluses were predominantly oil-importing developing countries, rather than industrial countries, and (as explained in Chapter 19) this disequilibrium proved to be intractable and persistent. However, it was financed much more successfully than anyone expected. Much of the financing comprised the recycling of 'petrodollars' by the big private-sector banks, but there was also a good supply of official finance, including in 1974, 1975 and 1976 the IMF's 'oil facilities' (drawn on by the UK and Italy as well as by developing countries) followed in 1979 by its supplementary financing facility (see Appendix A, pages 250 and 252). By the end of the decade, the outstanding debt of the developing countries had reached about $400 billion, of which bank loans (excluding export credits mostly guaranteed by the governments of the exporting countries) accounted for $130 billion.[1]

Then at the end of the 1970s came the second oil shock, which in 1980 (the last year treated in Chapter 19) was expected to have more or less the same aftermath as the earlier shock. However, it soon became apparent to discerning observers that history was not going to repeat itself:

1   In the first place, by contrast with 1974 the private sector banks were not starting with a clean sheet but were already heavily lent, if not over-lent, to the developing countries, as noted in the quotation at the head of this chapter.
2   The global economic environment turned out to be far more difficult for borrowing countries in the 1980s than in the 1970s. Governments and other economic policymakers in the major industrial countries increasingly became convinced that the upward ratcheting of inflation during successive business cycles had to be brought to an end by deflationary fiscal and monetary policies, with record-high nominal and real interest rates.
3   In contrast to initiatives after the first oil shock, no low-condition IMF oil facilities were established after the second.
4   In the early 1980s the main victims of these events were oil-importing developing countries. Their oil bills increased greatly, until the collapse of oil prices which began in the course of 1982. Due to the wide-spread business depression, they suffered in both 1981 and 1982 a serious fall in their export prices in relation not only to oil prices but also to the prices of their imported manufactures. They nevertheless sought – successfully up to about mid 1981, though not subsequently – to continue with their development programmes and to maintain the rate of output growth they achieved in the 1970s. In consequence their balance of trade deteriorated, and their current balance of payments deteriorated even more, since

their ever growing external debt had to be serviced at ever higher interest rates.

5   With the weakening of the oil market as from 1982, followed by its collapse in 1986, the difficulties faced by the oil-importing developing countries spread to the oil exporters, and especially to those which had developed a voracious appetite for imports in connection with ambitious development programmes.

The financing of developing countries' unfavourable current balances, as set out in Table 29 on page 228, was initially achieved mainly by their stepping up their public-sector borrowing, especially from the private-sector banks. In consequence there occurred an enormous increase in their outstanding foreign-currency debt, to no less than $626 billion at end 1982,[2] of which $210 billion was to banks (not including any of the $148 billion of export credit mostly guaranteed by the governments of the exporting countries). By 1985 the total had risen to nearly $1,000 billion, of which about half was owed by 15 countries classified by the IMF as 'heavily indebted' (see Table 30).

The countries that borrowed heavily to sustain 'debt-led growth' through the 1970s suffered in 1982 and 1983 a collapse in their credit standing; in consequence they now found themselves obliged to accept stringent austerity programmes in order to balance their international payments on the basis of the sharply reduced levels of capital flow available to them. This represented a major setback to their economic development. It also represented a setback for the lending banks.

The re-scheduling of debts

One of the first members of the banking fraternity to give public warning of the dangers of excessive international lending by banks was Rimmer de Vries, of Morgan Guaranty, who spoke to this effect in December 1979. But this warning was not taken very seriously until the spring of 1982, and was not widely acted upon until Mexico threatened to default in August 1982. As a consequence of that crisis the Mexican debt had to be re-scheduled, and soon afterwards similar action was needed in the case of other Latin American borrowers, including Brazil and Argentina. Unfortunately for the banks, their difficulties with their Latin American customers occurred at a time when they had already run into problems with their Eastern European customers, especially with Poland; the total bank

Table 30 *Total external liabilities of 15 'heavily indebted' develop-ing countries, end 1985*

	$ billion	% private source
Argentina	51	87
Bolivia	4	39
Brazil	107	84
Chile	21	87
Colombia	11	58
Equador	9	74
Ivory Coast	8	64
Mexico	99	89
Morocco	14	39
Nigeria	19	88
Peru	13	61
Philippines	25	68
Uruguay	4	82
Venezuela	34	100
Yugoslavia	20	64
	439	80

Source: World Bank, World Debt Tables, 1985–86.

debt of Eastern Europe is large ($52 billion in September 1982) and much of it has had to be re-scheduled.

The re-scheduling of international debts presented a problem of enormous complexity. A country like Mexico, and its residents, may be indebted to many hundreds of banks, as well as to governments and other lenders, and every debt is peculiar in its terms and conditions. Each of the lending banks, in its own immediate self-interest, had an incentive to 'cut and run', rather than re-schedule its outstanding debts, let alone continue with net lending. But banks *as a whole* cannot 'cut and run'; if a debtor country is unable to repay its debt in total, any one of the lending banks can obtain repayment only by getting other banks to take over the borrower's commitment, which of course they will not want to do. Individual banks may attempt to refuse further net lending to their doubtful customers, and many were indeed beginning to act in this way in the latter part of 1982, but the consequences for the lending banks as a whole would in due course be disastrous, since the borrower would then be forced into default. Clearly then, the best outcome for all the parties concerned called for a re-scheduling operation, tied in with an agreement by the borrowing country to pursue prudent economic policies and by the lending banks to continue net lending, albeit on a more modest scale than in the 1970s, to allow time for the borrower's prudent policies (usually involving measures of fiscal and monetary deflation) to take effect. But in such cases there are so many parties involved, and their respective interests so diverse and complicated, that in practice agreement would be virtually imposs-ible without the intervention of a public-sector agency as a mediator. Even then, the mediating agency cannot expect to carry sufficient weight in the negotiations except by making a financial contribution in its own name. In practice the role of mediator was assumed by the IMF, which took charge of the Mexican negotia-tions in 1982, holding out the promise of new Fund finance if all the other parties would co-operate on the lines put forward by the Managing Director, and the Mexican case served as a precedent for subsequent re-scheduling operations.

It will be apparent that all the IMF-backed re-schedulings had three essential ingredients:

1   The commercial banks agreed to re-schedule their outstanding debt, and to make a modest contribution of net new lending.
2   Their lending was supplemented by finance from the IMF.
3   The IMF's contribution was conditional on the borrower under-taking an austerity programme.

The re-scheduling operations of 1982 undoubtedly proved effective in staving off the immediate danger of widespread defaults and a banking crisis, but the basic problem – that the developing countries' interest payments have come to represent an unsustainably high proportion of their export earnings – remained unresolved. This was especially the case with the 15 middle-income countries identified by the IMF as 'heavily indebted', as may be seen from Table 31. In consequence, many of these countries suffered a collapse of their credit standing, such that they were unable to obtain new bank loans beyond those negotiated under re-scheduling agreements: see Table 32. Nor did the developing countries, particularly the 15 'heavily indebted' ones, obtain much finance from the IMF, other than as the result of the IMF's role in re-scheduling in 1983 and 1984: see Table 33.

Table 31 *Exports and interest payments of 15 'heavily indebted' developing countries, 1979–86*

	Exports (f.o.b.)	Interest Payments	
	$bn	$bn	As % of exports
1979	94.2	17.1	18
1980	127.1	25.1	20
1981	126.1	37.0	29
1982	111.5	45.5	41
1983	111.1	41.5	37
1984	123.4	46.0	37
1985	119.2	44.0	37
1986	98.6	38.2	39

Source: IMF World Economic Outlook, April 1987, page 163. The 15 'heavily indebted' countries are those listed in Table 30.

Table 32 *International syndicated bank loans to developing countries, 1981–86 ($ billion)*

	Spontaneous	Non-spontaneous[1]
1981	48.0	—
1982	42.3	11.2
1983	13.0	13.7
1984	10.6	6.5
1985	5.6	2.3
1986	8.4	8.0

[1] New lending in connection with the re-scheduling of outstanding debt.

Source: BIS Annual Report, No. 57 (1987), page 108.

In view of their predicament, the countries concerned had no choice but to implement the austerity programmes which the IMF prescribed as a condition for access to its financial facilities: in consequence their national growth rates were depressed and indeed in many cases became negative: see Table 34.

Table 33 *Use of IMF credit by the developing countries, 1979–86 ($ billion)*

	All developing countries	15 'heavily indebted' countries
1979	0.2	0.1
1980	1.4	0.5
1981	6.1	1.2
1982	6.7	2.2
1983	11.2	6.3
1984	4.9	3.3
1985	0.3	1.8
1986	−2.1	−0.1

Source: IMF World Economic Outlook, April 1987, page 179.

Table 34 *Developing countries: annual increase in real GDP, 1969–86 (annual changes, in per cent)*

	Total %	15 'heavily indebted' countries %
1969–78	6.1	6.1
1979	4.2	6.1
1980	3.5	5.0
1981	2.1	0.5
1982	1.6	−0.4
1983	1.4	−3.4
1984	4.1	2.2
1985	3.2	3.1
1986	3.5	3.5

Source: IMF World Economic Outlook, April 1987, page 122.

Mr. Baker's initiative at Seoul

In October 1985, at the annual meeting at Seoul of the IMF and World Bank, US Treasury Secretary James Baker put forward proposals based on the recognition of the need for renewal of growth and investment in the heavily indebted developing countries. His initiative had three elements:

1   implementation by the debtor countries of policies to promote adjustment, structural reform and freer markets,
2   continuing net lending to the indebted developing countries by the commercial banks,
3   an increase in the World Bank's annual disbursement to the indebted developing countries.

The IMF's role in the Baker plan was initially left rather unclear. From the time of the Venice Summit in 1980, the major powers had seen the IMF (rather than the World Bank) as the appropriate international agency for overseeing the developing countries' debt problem, so that Mr. Baker's emphasis in October 1985 on the World Bank's role may have implied some downgrading of the IMF's role. Mr. Baker's remarks at Seoul about the IMF were however not unfriendly, and in the event the IMF reacted to the Baker plan as an opportunity to be seized. This became apparent in the first round of negotiations conducted under Mr. Baker's guidelines – those with Mexico in 1986.

The package of measures agreed between Mexico and her numerous creditors began with a round of negotiations with the IMF in July 1986. The novel features in the terms agreed by the IMF were:

1   a clear understanding that the agreement was directed to the resumption of economic growth, as well as to the adjustment of a balance-of-payments disequilibrium;
2   a more realistic assessment of what size of fiscal deficit was acceptable, in the case of a country whose budget is burdened with nominal interest charges reflecting a high rate of inflation;
3   the new finance envisaged for Mexico was substantial, and its amount was made dependent on the rate of growth of the Mexican economy and the future course of the price of oil.

The package as a whole, as eventually agreed in April 1987 by the interested parties, provided that Mexico should get $12½ billion of external finance in 1986 and 1987, of which about one half to come from official sources (the IMF, the World Bank and the G-10 governments), the remaining half being in the form of new lending by the commercial banks. About $½ billion of the commercial bank lending would benefit from a World Bank guarantee. The banks would also undertake a further major rescheduling of their existing holdings of Mexican debt.

The Mexican agreement was followed in July 1987 by a somewhat similar debt package for Argentina, under which part of Agentina's outstanding debt was to be rescheduled and new money to the tune of $5.3 billion provided by commercial banks, the IMF and the World Bank. Agreements had already been reached with Chile, Venezuela and the Philippines.[3] However Brazil's suspension of interest payments to banks in February 1987 was a serious setback to Mr. Baker's initiative at Seoul. In May 1987 Citicorp, the big New York bank, put aside loan-loss provisions equal to 25 per cent of its exposure to developing countries, and other US and UK banks heavily exposed to the third world have followed suit. In December 1987 the Bank of Boston went beyond the mere addition to loan–loss provisions and wrote off completely $200 million of its $1 billion of loans to developing countries. Taking into account also its loan–loss provisions, this put the bank in the position of being able to forgive 20 per cent of its third world loans, without any further effect on its balance sheet and to forgive 63 per cent of such loans without eating into its profits in subsequent accounting periods.[4] The Bank of Boston's action may well set a precedent for a much more realistic approach to the obvious inability of some debtor countries to pay a commericial rate of interest on their outstanding debts, let alone repay these debts in the foreseeable future.*

---

* An ingenious arrangement was announced at the end of December 1987 for the restructuring of part of Mexico's $78 billion debt to banks. This arrangement would *inter alia* write down the principal of the restructured debt, without however reducing the annual interest payments in anything like the same proportion: hence it leaves the major problem largely still unresolved.

Appendix A*
How countries use IMF resources

Members of the Fund may draw on its financial resources to meet their balance of payments needs. They may use the reserve tranche, and, under tranche policies, the four credit tranches. In addition, there are three permanent facilities for specific purposes – the facility for compensatory financing of export fluctuations (established in 1963 and liberalized in 1975 and 1979), the buffer stock financing facility (established in 1969), and the extended facility (established in 1974).

Furthermore, members may make use of temporary facilities established by the Fund with borrowed resources. For 1974 and 1975, for example, following the sharp rise in oil prices, the Fund provided assistance under a temporary oil facility designed to help members meet the increased cost of imports of petroleum and petroleum products. In 1978, a supplementary financing facility was established with borrowed resources amounting to SDR 7.784 billion from 13 member countries or their institutions, and the Swiss National Bank.

This appendix (which should be read in conjunction with Tables 35 and 36) describes the policies and principles governing members' access to the Fund's general resources under the tranche policies and the permanent and temporary facilities. For any drawing, a member is required to represent to the Fund that the desired purchase is needed because of its balance of payments or reserve position or developments in its reserves.

Use of resources

When a member draws on the Fund, it uses its own currency to purchase the currencies of other member countries or special drawing rights (SDRs) held by the General Resources Account. Thus, a

---

* Taken mainly from *IMF Survey Supplement*, September 1984 and 1987, and the *Bank of England Quarterly Bulletin*, December 1983 and March 1984.

Table 35   *Maximum access to the Fund's resources in 1987 (per cent of quota)*

	Where regular access is through:	
	Stand-by arrangement (a)	Extended arrangement (a)
Regular facilities		
Reserve tranche	(b)	(b)
Credit tranches:		
First credit tranche	25	25
Upper credit tranches	75	—
Extended Fund Facility	—	140
Supplementary Financing Facility } over 3 year period	170/230 (c)	105/165 (c)
Enlarged Access Policy		
Total maximum access		
Over 3 year period	270/330	
Cumulative	400/440	
Special facilities		
Compensatory Financing Facility	105	
Buffer Stock Financing Facility	45	

(a) For clarity, access is shown as being entirely through one or the other of a stand-by or extended arrangement. In practice, a member can draw under one arrangement while still indebted to the Fund for purchases made under a previous arrangement (of the same or a different type), but only up to a limit, depending on the size of the balance of payments problems and the strength of the adjustment programme, of up to 270 per cent over three years and 400 per cent cumulatively (increased to 330 and 440 per cent respectively where a member is making strong adjustment efforts to deal with a severe balance of payments difficulty).

(b) Whatever percent of quota brings Fund holdings of the members' currency up to 100 per cent of quota.

(c) Maximum access to SFF and enlarged access resources under stand-by arrangements is limited, depending on the size of the balance of payments problems and the strength of the adjustment programme to 170 per cent of quota over three years: under extended arrangements, maximum access is limited, depending on circumstances, to 105 per cent of quota over three years (increased to 230 and 185 per cent respectively where a member is making strong adjustment efforts to deal with a severe balance of payments difficulty).

Table 36 *IMF annual disbursements,[1] 1973–86 (SDR billions)*

	Credit Tranche	Extended Facility	Compensatory Financing	Buffer Stock	Oil Facilities	Trust Fund	Total
1973	0.2		0.1				0.3
1974	1.3		0.1		1.7		3.1
1975	0.6		0.2		3.0		3.9
1976	1.5	0.1	2.3		2.1		6.0
1977	2.9	0.2	0.2			0.2	3.5
1978	0.4	0.2	0.6			0.7	1.9
1979	0.9	0.2	0.6			0.5	2.2
1980	1.8	0.6	1.0			1.3	4.7
1981	3.4	2.1	1.2			0.4	7.2
1982	2.5	2.1	2.6	0.1			7.4
1983	4.9	4.6	2.8	0.3			12.6
1984	3.1	3.3	0.8				7.3
1985	2.6	0.4	0.9				4.0
1986	3.0	0.3	0.6			0.1[2]	4.0

[1] Excludes purchases of reserve tranche positions in the Fund.
[2] Structural adjustment facility.

Source: IMF Survey, June 15, 1987 and earlier issues.

drawing results in an increase in the Fund's holdings of the purchasing member's currency and a corresponding decrease in the Fund's holdings of other currencies or SDRs that are sold.

A member incurs an eventual obligation to repurchase its currency from the Fund to the extent that the Fund's holdings of the member's currency are in excess of 100 per cent of the member's quota.

Usually, repurchases are required to be made within three and one-quarter to five years after the date of purchase; but under the extended facility, the period for repurchases is within four and one-half to ten years, under the oil facility within three to seven years, and under the supplementary financing facility and the enlarged access policy within three and one-half to seven years.

Tranche policies

If the Fund's holdings of a member's currency are less than 100 per cent of the member's quota, the difference is called the *reserve tranche*. Purchases in the reserve tranche are not subject to prior challenge, to economic policy conditions, or to repurchase requirements.

Further purchases are made in *four credit tranches* each of 25 per cent of the member's quota. The total of purchases under credit tranche policies is normally limited to 100 per cent of the member's quota.

When a member makes a purchase that is not a reserve tranche purchase, the member has an obligation to repurchase not later than a specified time. In addition, a member is expected normally to repurchase as its balance of payments and reserve position improves, and the Fund may convert this expectation into an obligation.

All requests for the use of the Fund's resources other than use of the reserve tranche are examined by the Fund to determine whether the proposed use would be consistent with the provisions of the Articles and with Fund policies. Under credit tranche policies, use must be in support of economic measures designed to overcome a member's balance of payments difficulties. Prior to submission to the Fund of a request to purchase, a member discusses with Fund staff its adjustment program, including fiscal, monetary, exchange rate, and trade and payments policies.

A credit tranche drawing may be made outright, under a stand-by arrangement with the Fund or (see below) under the extended facility. A stand-by arrangement, which typically is of 12–24 months' duration, gives the member an assurance that it will be able to make drawings on the Fund during a given period and up to a specified amount without review of its performance and policies, as long as it has observed the performance criteria and other terms included in the arrangement. The criteria used by the Fund in determining whether its assistance should be made available are more liberal when the request is in the first credit tranche than when it is in the higher credit tranches.

In the case of a request for a first credit tranche drawing, the member is expected to show that it is making reasonable efforts to overcome its difficulties. In practice, this criterion has often meant that, when differences of judgment arise, the member receives the benefit of the doubt.

Requests for purchases in the higher credit tranches require substantial justification. Such purchases are always made under stand-by arrangements. The stabilization program presented by a member requesting assistance in an upper tranche is comprehensive. The amount available under a stand-by arrangement in the upper credit tranches is phased to be available in portions at specified intervals during the stand-by period, and the member's right to draw is always subject to the observance of certain key policy indicators described in the program or to a further review of the situation. The indicators, also called performance criteria, cover credit policy and policy on trade and payments restrictions; they may also extend to the financing requirements of the government, contracting, or use of, short-term and medium-term foreign debt, and changes in external reserves. Performance criteria allow both the member and the Fund to assess progress in the implementation of policies during the stand-by arrangement. Failure to meet the criteria signals the need to examine whether further measures are necessary to achieve the objectives of the program. In this case, the member consults with the Fund in order to reach further understanding on needed changes in its program before requesting further purchases.

Extended facility

Under the extended facility, established in 1974, the Fund may provide assistance to members to meet their balance of payments deficits for longer periods and in amounts larger in relation to quotas than under the credit tranche policies. For example, a member might apply for assistance under the facility if it has serious payments imbalances relating to structural maladjustments in production, trade, and prices and if it intends to implement a comprehensive set of corrective policies for two or three years. Or, use of the facility might be indicated by an inherently weak balance of payments position that prevents the pursuit of an active development policy.

In requesting an extended arrangement, a member is expected to present a program setting forth the objectives and policies for the whole period of the extended arrangement, as well as a detailed statement of the policies and measures that it will follow in each 12-month period to meet the objectives of the program. Purchases are phased and made subject to performance clauses relating to implementation of key policy measures. Drawings under extended arrangements may take place over periods of up to three years. Purchases outstanding under the extended facility may not exceed 140 per cent of the member's quota, reduced by any tranche drawing beyond the first credit tranche. Repurchases under the extended facility must be made within four to ten years after each purchase in 12 equal instalments.

Supplementary financing facility

In January 1976, pending the implementation of the Sixth General Review quota increases (which eventually became effective in April 1978), the Fund temporarily enlarged the credit tranches by 45 per cent (i.e. each credit tranche was expanded from 25 per cent of quota to 36.25 per cent). It decided to further augment members' access to conditional resources through the so-called supplementary financing facility, for which the Fund undertook new borrowing. The SFF became operational in February 1979 and has been used to supplement ordinary resources provided both through the credit tranches and the extended facility. Purchases financed from the SFF have a maturity of three and one-half to seven years.

Enlarged access

The SFF was fully committed by February 1982. In view of the continued deterioration in general economic circumstances, the

Fund undertook to make further supplementary resources available to its members under a policy of enlarged access, which went into effect in May 1981. In 1984, access under the enlarged access policy was subject to three-year limits of 306 and 375 per cent, and cumulative limits of 408 and 500 per cent, the latter figures in each case applying only 'where a member's balance of payments difficulty was severe and where strong adjustment efforts were being made'. These limits are subject to an annual review; the three-year limits for 1987 were down from 306/375 to 270/330 per cent of quota, and the cumulative limits from 408/500 to 400/440 per cent.

For a member qualifying under a stand-by or an extended arrangement, the amounts available for enlarged access to Fund resources are apportioned between ordinary quota-based resources and resources the Fund has borrowed. Under a stand-by arrangement purchases are made with ordinary and borrowed resources supplied in the ratios of 2 to 1 in the first credit tranche and 1 to 2 in the next three credit tranches. Thereafter purchases are made with borrowed resources only.

Under an extended arrangement, purchases are made with ordinary and borrowed resources in the ratio of 1 to 2 until the outstanding use of the upper credit tranches and the extended Fund facility equals 140 per cent of quota. Thereafter, purchases are made with borrowed resources only.

Special facilities

Access to low-condition assistance was expanded beyond the first credit tranche by the establishment of special facilities designed to address particular balance of payments problems. The most important of these facilities is the Compensatory Financing Facility (CFF) introduced in 1963. This is mainly intended to deal with shortfalls in the export earnings of primary producers. Conditionality has been moderated because of the cyclical nature of the balance of payments problems being addressed. However, some conditions have been retained under the CFF because cyclical problems are often associated with more deep-seated difficulties; they have taken the form of the requirement that the member 'will co-operate' – and above a certain level of access 'has been co-operating' – with the Fund in an effort to find, where required, solutions to its balance of payments problems. In May 1981, the CFF was further broadened to include temporary excesses in cereal import costs (which are treated in effect as negative exports).

Related to the CFF, the Fund established the Buffer Stock Financing Facility (BSFF) in 1969 to finance members contributions to commodity buffer stocks intended to dampen cyclical export price fluctuations.

Towards the end of 1983 the Fund reviewed the limits on members' access to the Compensatory Financing Facility (CFF) and Buffer Stock Financing Facility (BSFF). It was decided to limit access to the CFF to 83 per cent of quota in respect of export shortfalls and the same in respect of cereal import cost excesses, subject to a combined limit of 105 per cent of quota. Access to the BSFF is limited to 45 per cent of quota.

Other forms of low-condition assistance offered by the Fund have been the temporary Oil Facilities of 1974 and 1975, and the Trust Fund, the latter financed by the auction of part of the IMF's gold stock (above, page 184). The last purchases under the Oil Facilities were made in February 1976. The last Trust Fund loans were disbursed in March 1981.

Structural adjustment facility

This facility was established in March 1986 to provide finance on concessional terms in support of the balance of payments adjustment efforts of low-income countries. The resources to implement the SAF are to be provided in the first instance by repayments of Trust Fund loans. In December 1987 the IMF announced a so-called Enhanced Structural Adjustment Facility, to be financed by a $8.4 billion fund, thereby bringing to about $11.4 billion the special concessional financing available from the IMF for the benefit of some 62 of its low-income member countries. These countries will be able to borrow up to 250 per cent of quota at a subsidised interest rate of 0.5 per cent, the cost of the subsidy being borne *inter alia* by contributions from developed member countries.

Appendix B*
The European Monetary System

The European Monetary System (EMS), which the EEC heads of government or state, meeting at Brussels in December 1978, agreed to establish, came into force on 13 March 1979. There is a widespread belief that the UK, alone among the then member countries, opted not to be a founder member of the EMS; such, however, is not strictly the case, though the UK has not participated in the exchange rate mechanism (ERM) which became operative for all other eight members as from 13 March.

We need to distinguish four separate aspects of the EMS scheme, the second of these being the one in respect of which the UK elected not to be a founder participant:

the European Currency Unit (ECU)
the exchange rate mechanism (ERM)
the credit facilities
the projected European Monetary Fund (EMF)

The European Currency Unit

The ECU is a basket of fixed amounts of EEC currencies. Its initial composition is the same as that of the European unit of account (EUA) previously in use within the Community; but the amounts of each currency in the basket may be changed by agreement of the council of Ministers.

The ECU performs two functions:

1   It is a denominator for expressing debts and claims as between central banks. An exchange rate risk is unavoidable whenever there is the possibility of an exchange rate adjustment, but by denominating debt and claims in ECUs, the EMS has introduced the concept of Community burden-sharing in respect of

* In this appendix I have drawn heavily on an article on the EMS in *Midland Bank Review*, Winter 1979.

the exchange rate risk, in that the risk is no longer borne wholly by the debtor nor wholly by the creditor.

2   It is an instrument of settlement between Community central banks. In this role the ECU is an *asset*, brought into existence by a procedure described on page 258, which EMS members acquire as reserves. ECUs thus acquired are to be used primarily as a means of settling debts arising from official market intervention in Community currencies, with the priviso (later discontinued) that a creditor central bank may not be obliged to accept ECUs over and above an amount equal to 50 per cent of its claim.

The exchange rate mechanism

The EMS exchange rate mechanism (ERM) incorporates most of the operational and institutional features of the old snake, which had had a continuous, if chequered, existence since April 1972. However, there were various new features introduced in the ERM, including a so-called 'divergence indicator'.

The UK joined the original snake at its inception but defected in June 1972 and never rejoined. The UK has not so far participated in the ERM, nor have yet Greece, Spain and Portugal.

Under the ERM arrangement, as with the old snake, 'pivot' or 'central' exchange rates are settled as between each pair of member currencies (and hence between each of these currencies and the ECU). On each side of each central rate, maximum margins of fluctuation have been established. Normally these are of plus or minus 2¼ per cent of the relevant central rate. However, member countries of the Community whose currencies were not in the old snake may temporarily establish fluctuation margins of up to plus or minus 6 per cent, but should gradually reduce these margins as soon as economic conditions permit. Italy decided to make use of this option.

Changes in central rates are to be made by 'mutual agreement' and in accordance with a 'common procedure'. In practice, this means that final decisions are taken by the ministers of the countries participating in the EMS. So far (up to January 1988) there have been eleven adjustments of exchange rates under the EMS.

The grid of bilateral central rates and the agreed margins of fluctuation (normally 2¼ per cent, but 6 per cent in the case of Italy) set the limits at which official exchange market intervention is obligatory. When official intervention takes place at the compulsory intervention limits, there is no limit as to its amount, and it has to be conducted in participating currencies; that is, *not* in US dollars. Intervention within the margins is however not excluded and may take place either in participating currencies or in third currencies. In practice a number of EMS central banks have adopted a strategy of keeping their exchange rates well within the band of the ERM and have carried out their intervention mainly in US dollars, rather than in the currencies of other members.

The divergence indicator

In addition to the grid of central rates, there is a 'divergence indicator', which serves as an early warning device to signal whether a currency diverges in its development from the average of the others. For this purpose, 'divergence' is measured by the divergence of a participating currency from its central rate in terms of the ECU, not in terms of any other participating currencies. The indicator flashes when the market value of a currency crosses its 'divergence threshold', expressed as a specified percentage divergence from its central value in terms of the ECU.

When a currency crosses its threshold of divergence, this was intended to create a presumption that the authorities concerned will correct this situation by suitable measures. In practice, however, the indicator has never been fully able, as its proponents had hoped, to assume the role of linking exchange rate developments to an increasing convergence of economic policy.

The credit facilities

The EMS incorporates and expands the three previously existing EEC credit mechanisms, namely: the very-short-term financing and the short-term monetary support (STMS), both of which are the responsibility of the central banks, and medium-term financial assistance (MTFA), which is granted by the Council.

Very-short-term financing

This formed part of the mechanism for operating the old snake, and with minor improvements fulfils the same role in the ERM. Very-short-term credit facilities are unlimited in amount, and are granted by the participating central banks to each other in order to permit official market intervention in Community currencies. The duration of such financing has under the EMS been extended to 45 days from the end of the month in which it is drawn, compared with 30 days previously. The repayment period may be automatically extended for three months, up to the limit of a prescribed ceiling. The medium of repayment is in practice either US dollars or ECUs.

Short-term monetary support

The STMS was originally established as an agreement among the central banks of Community members in February 1970. It was widened in January 1973 to cover the three countries then joining the Community (United Kingdom, Ireland and Denmark) and was substantially enlarged in 1974. Under the EMS it has been enlarged again although the UK's previous scale of participation will not be increased until such time as it decides to join the ERM. The STMS provides for credits to the central banks of Community members for the financing of temporary balance-of-payments deficits. Credits are granted without economic policy conditions, but they trigger subsequent consultations. The mechanism is based on a system of debtor and creditor quotas which determine each EEC central bank's borrowing entitlement and financing obligations. Originally the duration of STMS credits was three months, renewable for a similar period at the request of the beneficiary central bank. Under the EMS the possibility of a further three-month extension has been introduced.

Medium-term financial assistance

The MTFA facility was originally set up by a decision of the Council of Ministers of 22 March 1971. As with STMS, an enlargement took place in connection with the accession of new members to the Community in 1973. A doubling of the amounts was decided on in December 1977. Under the EMS there has been a further increase, in which the UK is participating. Credits may be granted to any member country in difficulties or seriously threatened with difficulties as regards its balance of payments: they are for two to five years and are subject to economic policy conditions to be laid down by the Council of Ministers. The MTFA has creditor ceilings but no debtor ceilings for individual countries, except that normally no member state may draw more than 50 per cent of the total credit ceilings.

The total of the short- and medium-term credit facilities just described amounts to about 25 billion ECU of effectively available credit, equivalent to about $35 billion at end-1980 exchange rates, so fixed to be equivalent to about 20 per cent of the official reserves of member states.

In addition to the credit facilities associated with the EMS, there exists a further Community medium-term balance of payments loan facility, whereby the Commission borrows from capital markets to on-lend to member states as noted above on pages 126–7.

At the time when the EMS was negotiated, it was agreed that to help less prosperous countries fully participating in the scheme, loans enjoying interest subsidies of 3 per cent per annum might be made to them by the European Investment Bank. Ireland and Italy were designated beneficiary countries, and by the end of 1983 they had together borrowed the equivalent of about $5 billion on this basis.

The use made of the EMS credit facilities

Of the four credit facilities available to EMS members, the very-short-term financing facility was until September 1987 available only for obligatory intervention at the margins in participating currencies and, with the widespread practice of intra-marginal intervention, had come to be only rarely used. In November 1987 it was used for the first time (by France) for intra-marginal intervention: it remains to be seen how often this precedent will be followed. The 'short-term monetary support' facility and the 'medium-term financial assistance' facility were each used once (by Italy) in the 1970s, but neither has been activated since the establishment of the EMS. Finally, the Community medium-term balance-of-payments loan facility has been used only twice: by France in 1983 and Greece in 1985, as noted above on page 127.

The European Monetary Fund

The European Monetary Fund (EMF) was not intended to come into existence until 1981, and in practice has not yet been established, but in the meantime the old European Monetary Co-operation Fund (EMCF) will continue to exist as a forerunner of the proposed new institution. The EMCF was created by the Council of Ministers in April 1973, without being given any very clear task. In the event, the EMCF took formal responsibility for snake operations between Community participants and for STMS credit operations. The decisions that implemented the EMS now empower the EMCF 'to receive monetary reserves from the monetary authorities of the member states of the Community and to issue ECUs against such assets'. The ECUs issued by the EMCF are used as one means of settlement between the monetary authorities of the member countries and for transactions between those authorities and the EMCF.

In practice, the EMS members, including the UK, have duly deposited 20 per cent of their reserves of gold and foreign exchange with the EMCF in return for ECUs. The deposits run for three months: the gold and foreign exchange are then repaid in their original amounts, revalued on a formula based on the recent market prices of gold and of reserve currencies, and then deposited once again in return for the appropriate amount of ECUs. The initial creation of ECUs was about 26 billion, equivalent at the time to about $29 billion.

The dollar exchange rate

In the light of experience of the working of the EMS in practice, it is clear that a shortcoming has been the lack of a common EMS attitude towards the value of the US dollar in relation to the currencies of EMS members. The Council resolution of December 1978 explicitly called for 'co-ordination of exchange rate policies *vis-à-vis* third countries and, as far as possible, a concertation with the monetary authorities of those countries' but in fact there has been no such coordination.

Instead, Germany's fellow members of the ERM have hitherto delegated to Germany the responsibility of executing a common dollar policy. The main reason for this is technical. As we have seen, the ERM rules, until they were modified in September 1987, did not put the Bundesbank under any obligation to assist in the support of parities as long as the market exchange rate lay within the relevant mandatory intervention limits. Hence German membership of the ERM did not impose any constraint on the Bundesbank's monetary policy whenever other ERM members followed their usual strategy of keeping their exchange rates well within the mandatory intervention limits by undertaking market transactions in dollars. Thus the discipline of the ERM rules has until recently applied to Germany's partners, but not to Germany herself, leaving Germany free to pursue an independent policy on the dollar/DM rate.

An example of how the Bundesbank has accorded higher priority to the dollar rate than to the maintenance of EMS parities is afforded by what happened following the shift in US monetary policy in October 1979, and the consequential higher dollar interest rate: the following is a quotation from an article on page 9 of the Swiss Bank Corporation's review *Prospects*, No. 183, 1982/3:

the resulting portfolio shifts into the dollar had a greater depreciation effect on the DM than on any other EMS currency. Over several months in 1980, the DM was consequently at the bottom of the EMS . . . [however] when the Bundesbank finally raised its Lombard rate in February 1981, this turned the DM back into one of the strongest currencies within the EMS but did little to help against the dollar's strength. . . . The Bundesbank chose to solve this predicament by selling dollars heavily and . . . by a revaluation within the EMS on 5 October 1981. In terms of intervention policy, the net deceleration of the central bank money growth in Germany seems to indicate that it solved the dilemma it was faced with by observing certain exchange rate margins *vis-à-vis* the dollar rather than the intervention rules *vis-à-vis* the EMS.

Notes and references

Chapter 1: The bilateral phase, 1945–9

1 BIS *Annual Report* no. 19 (1949), p. 118.

2 ibid., pp. 118–19.

3 Greece, however, was given transferable account status in 1951.

4 Quoted in BIS *Annual Report* no. 18 (1948), p. 146.

5 See OEEC, 'A decade of co-operation: achievements and perspectives', report no. 9 (April 1958).

6 The occasional members were Austria, Denmark, Greece, Norway, Portugal, Sweden, the United Kingdom and the French zone of Germany.

7 BIS *Annual Report* no. 18 (1948), pp. 148–9.

8 *Agreement for Intra-European Payments and Compensations*, Cmd 7546 (HMSO 1948).

9 Except for Switzerland and Portugal.

10 The Economic Co-operation Administration, the American agency administering the Marshall Plan.

11 Neither Switzerland nor Portugal participated in indirect aid under the first IEPA, but only Switzerland did not participate under the second IEPA.

12 See Ekker, 'Equilibrium of international trade and international monetary compensations', in *Weltwirtschaftliches Archiv*, vol. 64, no. 2 (1950). This authoritative article provides the basis for many of the arguments in the remainder of this chapter, and should be consulted by readers who want a more rigorous exposition.

13 Ekker. See also the figures quoted by the BIS, above, page 21.

14 See Ekker.

15 The label 'strongest' is purely for purposes of identification and does not imply that it is praiseworthy to be 'strong'.

16 The figures in Table 2a are actually taken from the first half of Table 88 of the ECE's *Economic Survey of Europe in 1949*, p. 167, except that closed circuits have been eliminated and the names of imaginary countries substituted for certain groups of countries. Thus Latinnia corresponds to the Latin American republics, Britannica to the outer sterling area, and so on.

17 It is not logically necessary that all countries with overall surpluses

should in all circumstances be stronger than countries with overall deficits. If, for example, in Table 2 Europa's bilateral deficit with the UK had been 1200 instead of 200, the appropriate order of the countries would be unchanged, but the UK would then have had an overall surplus, not an overall deficit.

18 In fact, the US authorities did not, in the early post-war years, accumulate the currencies of any other countries.

19 Since Latinnia has a deficit only with the USA, there could be no currency more acceptable to it than US dollars.

20 The label 'surplus' (or deficit) country refers of course to a country with an *overall* surplus or deficit.

Chapter 2: The binary phase, 1950–8

1 BIS, *Annual Report* no. 29 (1959), p. 186.
2 Oscar R. Hobson, 'The new commodity inflation', *Lloyds Bank Review*, April 1951.
3 IMF *Annual Report*, 1951, ch.1.
4 IMF *International Financial News Survey*, 6 October 1950. The Canadian float lasted until May 1962, when a new par value was fixed.
5 United Nations, *World Economic Report*, 1951–2, p. 89.
6 ibid., p. 89.
7 ibid., p. 35.
8 ibid., p. 37.
9 See R. A. Conan's article in the *Banker*, August 1954, p. 103.
10 See J. R. Sargent on 'Convertibility', *Oxford Economic Papers*, February 1954.
11 See the *Banker*, April 1954, p. 183.
12 London banks authorized by the Bank of England, under the British exchange control regulations, to deal in foreign exchange.
13 Some capital account transactions were conducted in 'security' sterling. See page 78.
14 Brian Tew, *International Monetary Cooperation 1945–70* (Hutchinson 1970), ch. 14.
15 IMF, *Sixth Annual Report on Exchange Restrictions* (1955), p. 3.
16 The agreement was published by HMSO. See *Documents relating to the EPU 1950* and *Agreement for the Establishment of an EPU 1950*, Cmd 8064.
17 For details see Tew, *International Monetary Cooperation*, p. 158.

Chapter 3: Convertibility, December 1958

1 BIS *Annual Report* no. 29 (1959), pp. 184, 188–9.
2 Broadly speaking the Commonwealth countries other than Canada, plus Eire.

3 As from 1966 there was deliberate diversification, especially into dollars, by the overseas sterling area. See Table 10, page 124.

4 USA, Canada, Japan, UK, France, Germany, Italy, Belgium, Holland and Sweden. Switzerland was also an honorary member, making eleven countries in all. See below, page 117.

5 See Chapter 15. The snake market transactions there described are an *optional* alternative to the dollar intervention which the snake countries have continued to practise on a large scale.

6 The market transactions of the 1960s which we are thereby ignoring were of three kinds:

   In gold. Such transactions appear to have added $1.3 billion to total reserves in the period from end-1958 to end-1969. See Table 5.

   In non-dollar currencies, other than Eurocurrency transactions. Their contribution to the increase of $14.5 in foreign exchange reserves in the period from end-1958 to end-1969 (Table 5) was small, probably about $1 billion.

   In the Eurocurrency markets. Monetary authorities not only buy and sell other countries' currencies in the foreign exchange market but have increasingly also borrowed and lent them in the credit markets, especially the Eurocurrency markets. Such transactions greatly affected all categories of foreign exchange reserves in the 1970s: in the 1960s they were much less important, but even so they gave rise to at least $5 billion Eurodollar reserves and smaller amounts of other Eurocurrencies (Table 5). See below, Chapter 13.

7 If the German mark were in excess demand, this does not of course mean that more marks were bought in the foreign exchange markets than were sold – which would be nonsensical. It means that purchases were matched by sales, but that some of the latter were made (against dollars) by the Bundesbank. The dollars thereby obtained by the Bundesbank measure Germany's surplus, as we are here using the term.

8 The figures come from the US *Survey of Current Business*, June 1975. See also Table 6, page 104.

Chapter 4: Adjustment in theory

1 The rise in the prices of imported goods, and particularly of necessities for which no suitable locally produced substitute is available, may induce workers to press for higher wage rates. If workers do exact higher wage rates, producers are likely to pass on their extra costs to their customers in the form of higher prices, and those higher prices may be held to justify a second round of wage increases. This process could continue through many rounds.

2 If export prices in terms of Nottspounds remained unchanged, they

would fall in terms of sterling to the same proportionate extent as the devaluation of the Nottspound in relation to sterling.

3   I do not make any explicit assumptions as to the conditions governing the supply of Nottinghamshire's imports, because the conditions to be found in practice would almost never be unfavourable to the success of devaluation as a cure for an external deficit. In so far as Nottinghamshire's demand for imports fell off as the result of devaluation, this would tend, if anything, to reduce the sterling prices of imports, never (in any likely circumstances) to increase them.

4   If prices change in the ratio of 100:90 and quantity bought in the ratio of 100:112, total value will change in the ratio of 100×100 to 90×112 or 100 to 100.8.

5   *Strengthening the World Monetary System.* The annex (p. 84) is a memorandum by Franklin A. Lindsay. See also the view of the US Council of Economic Advisers, below, page 73.

Chapter 5: Adjustment in practice

1   Working Party No. 3, *The Balance of Payments Adjustment Process* (OECD, August 1966), para. 10. The role of the WP3 is described in Ch. 12.

2   Quotations are from the WP3 report, paragraph 21.

3   A footnote at this point in the report defines 'surplus' in this context as the balance of foreign transactions (receipts minus payments) of private sector transactors; this will usually correspond fairly closely to our usage of the term 'surplus' in Chapter 3. See above, page 54.

4   This was the view of the eminent economist, Jacques Rueff. Michel Debré, when France's minister of economics, complained in an interview in 1967 that the monetary system 'allows the reserve currency countries to finance their balance of payments deficit, thanks to the accumulation of holdings in their currencies by the foreign central banks. This possibility defers the play of corrective mechanisms on international deficits in the case of the reserve currency countries and undermines the discipline that each country should impose on itself to maintain the necessary equilibrium in world payments'. *Banker*, February 1967, p. 102.

5   Jeremy Morse thought that, since sterling was the intervention and reserve currency of the sterling area, the UK as well as the US were under less pressure than other countries to correct a balance of payments deficit. He said that the system of the 1960s 'allowed reserve centres like the US and UK to run persistent deficits and did not put enough pressure on countries like Germany and Japan to correct their surpluses': *The Financial Times*, 25 September 1974.

6   Address to the European-Atlantic Group, London, 19 February 1976.

7   R. C. Marston and R. J. Herring, *National Monetary Policies and International Financial Markets* (North–Holland 1977), p. 157.
8   Or 'central values' as they were then relabelled.
9   See the quotation at the beginning of Chapter 8, page 91.
10   The Per Jacobsson Foundation, *Steps to International Monetary Order* (Washington, DC 1974).
11   *Economic Report of the President and Annual Report of the Council of Economic Advisers* (US Government Printing Office 1973), pp. 115–16.
12   Canada was the exception. The Canadian dollar was unpegged during the period October 1950 to May 1962.
13   Pieter Lieftinck, 'Recent trends in international monetary policies'. Princeton University *Essays in International Finance*, no. 39 (September 1962), p. 9.
14   WP3 report, para. 19.

Chapter 6: Adjustment: long-term capital

1   John H. Makin, 'Capital flows and exchange rate flexibility in the post-Bretton Woods era', Princeton University *Essays in International Finance*, no. 103 (February 1974), p. 1.
2   'Strengthening the world monetary system', a statement published by the Committee for Economic Development, July 1973, p. 46.
3   *The Role of Exchange Rates in the Adjustment of International Payments. A Report by the Executive Directors* (IMF 1970), pp. 24 and 25.
4   Sir Alec Cairncross, *Control of Long-term International Capital Movements* (Brookings Institution 1973).

Chapter 7: Adjustment: short-term capital

1   Per Jacobsson Foundation Lecture, 31 August 1975. Mr Hayes had then recently retired as president of the Federal Reserve Bank of New York.
2   *The Role of Exchange Rates in the Adjustment of International Payments* (IMF 1970), p. 25.
3   From *Le Monde* of 18 August 1976: 'Il n'est pas douteux que le poids de la spéculation privée, par apposition à la spéculation institutionnelle (firmes, sociétés multinationales, etc.), a été marginal dans la baisse récente du franc. Certes, les achats de titres étrangers ou de biens immobiliers hors de France, les sorties de capitaux illégales vers la Suisse, ont pesé. Mais ces opérations ne représentent qu'une très faible partie des ventes de francs, qui sont pour l'essentiel alimentés par le commerce international.'
4   Wealth owners wishing to switch out of dollars into sterling are offered a wide variety of public-sector sterling debt which is in effect created

specially for them, in exchange for their dollars. If they are ready to hold such public-sector debt, in whatever form, they do not then deposit with the UK banking system, nor do they bid for existing securities in the secondary markets. The insulating mechanism breaks down however if the preferred sterling asset is a deposit at a bank or other private-sector institution, or corporate stocks or shares.

5   Hayes, Per Jacobsson Foundation Lecture. A good survey of this problem is Eric Chalmers, *International Interest Rate War* (Macmillan 1972). The earliest publicized attempt by multilateral co-operation to co-ordinate interest rates was the meeting at Chequers on 21 January 1967, of the finance ministers of the USA, the UK, Germany, France and Italy to 'agree to co-operate on lower interest rates': see *The Financial Times*, 23 January 1967. However, the consequences of this co-operation were short-lived, and the competitive spiral of interest rates resumed its course later in 1967. Nor were later initiatives any more successful.

. 6   Bank of England *Quarterly Bulletin*, March 1970, p. 39.

7   On this see Arthur L. Bloomfield, 'Official intervention in the forward exchange market: some recent experiences', Banca Nazionale del Lavoro *Quarterly Review*, March 1964, p. 3.

8   Otto Emminger (then deputy governor of the Bundesbank), address to the European-Atlantic Group, London, 19 February 1976.

9   Rodney H. Mills Jr, 'The regulation of short-term capital movements in major industrial countries,' *Staff Economic Studies* (Federal Reserve System 1972), pp. 1–5.

10   ibid., p. 4.

11   ibid., p. 7.

Chapter 8: The Bretton Woods charter

1   *Economic Report of the President and Annual Report of the Council of Economic Advisers* (US Government Printing Office 1973), pp. 121–2.

2   *United Nations Monetary and Financial Conference, Bretton Woods, New Hampshire, USA*, Cmd 6545 (1944).

3   *Proposals for an International Clearing Union*, Cmd 6437 (1943).

4   *United States Proposal for a United and Associated Nations Stabilisation Fund* (reprinted by HMSO 1943).

5   The corresponding account in the Jamaica charter is the 'General Resources Account'.

6   The corresponding tranche in the Jamaica charter is called the 'reserve tranche'.

7   A member country's 'reserve position' in the General Account, as shown above in Table 5, page 52, comprises the amount by which the

Fund's holding of the member's currency falls short of 100 per cent of the member's quota.

8   The Fund's holding of the currency of the drawing member, A, would fall short of 75 per cent of A's quota if at some earlier time another member, B, had drawn A's currency from the Fund.

9   R. F. Harrod, *The Life of John Maynard Keynes* (Macmillan 1951), p. 544.

Chapter 9: The dollar in the 1960s

1   Fred H. Klopstock, 'The international status of the dollar', Princeton University *Essays in International Finance*, no. 28 (May 1957), p. 7.

2   ibid., p. 20.

3   ibid., p. 21.

4   Sir Donald MacDougall, *The World Dollar Problem: A Study in International Economics* (London 1957).

5   'The dollar problem: a reappraisal', Princeton University *Essays in International Finance*, no. 35 (November 1960).

6   The US authorities could alternatively use the swap network to obtain foreign currencies for the purchase of dollars in the market, thereby relieving other countries' central banks of some of the market support required for the dollar in order to prevent an undue appreciation of dollar value of their own currencies. However, this alternative was little used during the pegged-rate regime, though it was utilized under the floating regime; that is from July 1973 onwards.

7   *1967 Guidelines for Bank and Nonbank Financial Institutions*, circular no. 5916 (13 December 1966).

8   *Federal Reserve Bulletin*, January 1970, p. 11 (which gives full details).

9   ibid., p. 11.

10 That is, company investment in branches or subsidiaries overseas.

11 In addition to the measures directed towards private capital outflows, the President requested a series of other programmes to improve the US surplus on *current* account. In particular, the President appealed to Americans to defer non-essential travel outside the Western hemisphere, and requested the Congress to earmark $500 million of Export–Import Bank funds to provide improved export insurance, and generally broaden the scope of government financing of US exports, as part of a more comprehensive export-promotion programme. At the same time, it was announced that negotiations would be initiated with NATO allies to offset the foreign exchange costs of US military spending in Europe – a goal that could be achieved either by increasing their defence purchases in the US or through investments in special US Treasury securities.

12 Not only had the demand for gold on the free markets declined, but the

supply of new gold to them had increased: South Africa and other gold producers had to an increasing extent permitted the sale of their output in the free markets, instead of selling the whole of their output to central banks.

13 Bank of England *Quarterly Bulletin*, December 1960, p. 10.
14 IMF *Annual Report*, 1963, pp. 176–7.
15 At that time Belgium, Italy, the Netherlands, Switzerland, the United Kingdom, the United States and Western Germany. It was disclosed in November that France had ceased to take an active part in the gold pool in July 1967.
16 Bank of England *Report* for the year to 29 February 1968, p. 3.
17 Charles A. Coombs, *The Arena of International Finance* (John Wiley 1976), p. 160.
18 Federal Reserve Bank of New York *Annual Report*, 1961, p. 32.
19 *Midland Bank Review*, August 1962, p. 7.
20 Article on Federal Reserve swaps, in the Federal Reserve Bank of Cleveland, *Economic Commentary*, 9 February 1976.
21 *Federal Reserve Bulletin*, March 1963, p. 312.

Chapter 10: The IMF General Account in the 1960s

1 The first public mention of such a scheme was in the address by the IMF managing director, Per Jacobsson, to ECOSOC in April 1961.
2 A big increase at the end of 1983 brought the total to some $16½ billion (including Switzerland).
3 See Horsefield, 'Drawings, repurchases and currencies', IMF *Finance and Development*, no. 4 (1968), p. 20.
4 Horsefield, pp. 22, 23. There are various additional complications to which I have not referred: for these see Horsefield's article.

Chapter 11: Basle and Brussels

1 Per Jacobsson Foundation Lecture, 31 August 1975.
2 On the role of the BIS in providing facilities for discussions and negotiations between central banks, see the interview with its general manager, M. Gabriel Ferras, in the *Banker*, September 1966.
3 From the Bank of England *Quarterly Bulletin*, September 1961, p. 10.
4 Bank of England *Report* for the year to February 1962, p. 4.
5 Bank of England *Quarterly Bulletin*, September 1966, p. 209.
6 Austria, Belgium, Canada, Denmark, Germany, Italy, Japan, the Netherlands, Norway, Sweden, Switzerland and the United States.
7 Bank of England *Report* for the year to February 1969, pp. 13 and 14.
8 Bank of England *Quarterly Bulletin* September 1969, p. 280.
9 *The Financial Times*, 16 March 1976.

Chapter 12: Reform in the 1960s

1   Address on 17 March 1967, published in the *Banker*, April 1967, p. 339.

2   The Organization for Economic Co-operation and Development, set up in 1961 to replace the OEEC. The membership was the European countries previously members of the OEEC, plus the USA and Canada. Finland joined in 1963, Japan in 1964, Australia in 1971 and New Zealand in 1973.

3   'The Working Party was instituted in 1961. [Its] purpose is "the promotion of better international payments equilibrium"; and its terms of reference state that it "will analyse the effect on international payments of monetary, fiscal and other policy measures, and will consult together on policy measures, both national and international, as they relate to international payments equilbrium". . . . The countries directly represented on Working Party No. 3 are: Canada, France, Germany, Italy, Japan, the Netherlands, Sweden, Switzerland, the United Kingdom and the United States [i.e. the "Ten" minus Belgium plus Switzerland]. The Working Party consists of senior officials from Ministries of Finance and other key government agencies and Central Banks concerned with balance of payments questions within their own administrations; and has established the practice of holding its meeting at six- to eight-week intervals' (from WP3's report, *The Balance of Payments Adjustment Process*, August 1966, p.8 n).

4   A Link proposal is briefly considered in the Ossola Report (May 1965), p. 69.

5   Bundesbank *Report* for the year 1965, pp. 39, 40.

6   Ossola Report, para. 10.

7   Bundesbank *Report*, 1965, pp. 40–1.

8   ibid., p. 42.

9   Back in 1965, when de Gaulle was extolling the advantages of gold, the French had temporarily favoured a variant of the reserve unit scheme, in which reserves would be held, and transferred, in 'baskets' of gold and national currencies, in fixed proportions. This proposal was tacitly withdrawn when it was seen not to be negotiable. See page 181.

10   J. J. Polak, in article on Special Drawing Rights, in *Finance and Development*, December 1967, p. 277.

11   See Emminger Report, paras. 37 and 98(4).

12   By the end of 1969 it was known that 104 countries would participate in the initial distribution. The eleven non-participants were China, Ethiopia, Iraq, Kuwait, Lebanon, Libya, Nepal, Portugal, Saudi Arabia, Singapore and Thailand.

13   Much of this section is quoted verbatim from an article by Martin

Barrett and Margaret L. Greene, 'Special Drawing Rights: a major step in the evolution of the world's monetary system', Federal Reserve Bank of New York *Monthly Review*, January 1968. The text of the new IMF Articles, with a detailed commentary, was published as a White Paper in June 1968 (Cmnd 3662).

14 Participant A may ask the Fund to designate other participants to buy A's SDRs only if A needs the transaction 'because of its balance of payments or its reserve position or developments in its reserves, and not for the sole purpose of changing the composition of its reserves'.

Chapter 13: The Eurodollar market

1 Norris O. Johnson, *Eurodollars in the New International Money Market* (First National City Bank 1964), pp. 6, 7. I have in this chapter drawn heavily on Mr Johnson's pamphlet.

2 'Euro' is a misleading label, in that it refers to deposits *anywhere* outside the US.

3 Official Eurocurrency holdings reported in this chapter are taken from the IMF *Annual Report*, 1978, p. 53, but expressed in dollars instead of SDRs.

4 As Norris Johnson explains in the quotation at the beginning of this chapter, Eurobanks worthy of the name follow the practice of on-lending any dollars they take in. However, in certain cases, for example Japan, a central bank, for reasons of domestic monetary policy, may by a deposit or a swap put native dollars from its reserves temporarily into the hands of commercial banks, on specially favourable terms but specifically on condition that they are *not* on-lent. In such a case the native dollars temporarily held by the commercial banks effectively remain (for purposes of the argument of this book) in the central bank's official reserves, even though they may not be so recorded in official statistics.

5 If the bank itself switches into marks before on-lending to the customer, the outcome will be just the same.

Chapter 14: The collapse of Bretton Woods convertibility

1 *Economic Report of the President and Annual Report of the Council of Economic Advisors* (US Government Printing Office 1973), p. 122.

2 See F. H. Klopstock, 'Eurodollars in the liquidity and reserve management of US banks', Federal Reserve Bank of New York, *Monthly Review*, July 1968, p. 130.

3 In addition US banks were as from 16 October 1969 required under Regulation M to maintain for the first time reserves against deposits received from their foreign branches.

4　In 1971 US authorities temporarily offset part of the contraction in lending by foreign branches to head office by offering them a succession of special issues of high-yielding three-month dollar securities. See Table 11, page 147. This temporarily mitigated the tendency for such branches to on-lend their dollars in a way which would add to the dollar reserves of other countries' central banks. No issues were made after Mr Nixon's speech on 15 August 1971.

5　Smaller, since a part of the US official reserve transactions balance was settled in each year by the US authorities drawing down their own reserve assets.

6　IMF *Annual Report*, 1975, table 14, p. 38.

7　C. A. Coombs, 'Treasury and federal reserve foreign exchange operations', Federal Reserve Bank of New York, *Monthly Review*, October 1971, pp. 214–15.

Chapter 15: The dollar standard, December 1971–March 1973

1　Board of Governors of the Federal Reserve System, *Annual Report*, 1971, p. 52.

2　C. A. Coombs, 'Treasury and federal reserve foreign exchange operations', Federal Reserve Bank of New York, *Monthly Review*, October 1971, p. 214.

3　Rodney H. Mills, 'The regulation of short-term capital movements in major industrial countries', Federal Reserve *Staff Economic Studies* (Federal Reserve System 1972), p. 5.

4　ibid., p. 6.

5　As we shall see below, the Smithsonian precedent was followed in February 1973.

6　See his speech on 28 May 1971 at the International Banking Conference of the American Bankers Association at Munich: Federal Reserve Bank of New York *Monthly Review*, July 1971, p. 146.

7　Many central banks encounter legal and political difficulties if they make book losses on the local-currency value of their holdings of reserve assets. See below, page 160.

8　This is a different use of the labels 'strongest' and 'weakest' from that in Chapter 1, where strength or weakness was based on the criterion of bilateral surpluses and deficits. The criterion now being used instead is simply exchange rates.

9　Most countries' central banks are in this position. The UK, where all reserves have since 1932 been held in a Treasury account, the Exchange Equalization Account, is the exception.

10　The increase in the foreign exchange reserves of the industrial countries in the 1970s, up to the end of March 1973, was $54 billion (Table 14) and this increase corresponded to the increase in US liabilities to foreign official agencies (see footnote to Table 15 on page 162).

(Non-industrial countries increased their foreign exchange reserves by $32 billion, but this was mainly in Eurodollars or in non-dollar currencies.)

11 Mills, pp. 6 and 7.

Chapter 16: The Grand Design, 1971–3

1 Address to the IMF annual meeting, September 1971.
2 Changed in 1981 to five.
3 Annex 2 to C–20's *Outline of Reform* dated 14 July 1974, in *International Monetary Reform Documents of the Committee of Twenty*, published in 1974 by the IMF.
4 J. Marcus Fleming, 'Reflections on the international monetary reform', Princeton University *Essays in International Finance*, no. 107, December 1974, p. 11.
5 ibid., p. 9.
6 Address on 7 June 1974, published in IMF, *Finance and Development*, September 1974.
7 Published by the IMF in *International Monetary Reform: Documents of the Committee of Twenty.*
8 'Après l'enterrement de la réforme monétaire: M. Jeremy Morse et sa momie', *Le Monde*, 18 June 1974.
9 The USA would have incurred in their place a new liability to the IMF the terms of which would have needed to be negotiated.
10 Mr John Connally, then Secretary of the US Treasury, was bitter about the 'indecision' displayed by the EEC representatives in October and November 1971 and looked for an alternative forum in which the EEC would have a smaller proportional representation: *Le Monde*, 16 February 1972.
11 'Le groupe des Dix, qui a été ressuscité et qui tiendra sa prochaine réunion à Paris en novembre. . .': Paul Fabra in *Le Monde*, 6 and 7 October 1974.
12 Jean Denizet, quoted in *Le Monde*, 15 December 1973.
13 'Les affaires monétaires de ce monde sont plus que jamais réglées – quand elles le sont – par un petit groupe de nations qui, au sein du groupe des Vingt, se sont détachées et commencent même à se réunir au vu et au su de tous. Il s'agit du groupe des Cinq. . .': Paul Fabra in *Le Monde*, 17 January 1974.
14 Federal Reserve Bank of New York, *Monthly Review*, January 1976, p. 8.

Chapter 17: The dollar recovers, 1973–5

1 Paul Volcker, then president of the Federal Reserve Bank of New York, speech on 17 November 1975; published in Federal Reserve Bank of New York, *Monthly Review*, January 1976, p. 3.

2   IMF *Annual Report*, 1975, p. 26.
3   Quoted in *Le Monde*, 4 and 5 November 1973.
4   IMF *Annual Report*, 1975, p. 27. See also Table 18, page 177.
5   Paul Volcker in Federal Reserve Bank of New York, *Monthly Review*, January 1976, p. 5.
6   ibid., p. 6.
7   Paul Lewis in *The Financial Times*, 21 December 1973.

Chapter 18: From Bretton Woods to Jamaica

1   Otmar Emminger of the Bundesbank, 'The quest for stability', address to the European-Atlantic Group, London, 19 February 1976.
2   'On ne voit pas qu'il puisse y avoir de critère, d'étalon autre que l'or. Eh! oui, l'or, qui ne change pas de nature, qui se met indifféremment en barres, en lingots ou en pièces, qui n'a pas de nationalité, qui est tenu éternellement et universellement comme la valeur inaltérable et fiduciaire par excellence.' General de Gaulle, press conference, 4 February 1965.
3   Susan Strange, *International Monetary Relations*, vol. 2 of *International Economic Relations of the Western World, 1959–1971* (Oxford University Press 1976), p. 239.
4   IMF, *International Financial Statistics*, January 1972, p. 23. The figures do not include Eurodollars.
5   See Gilbert Mathieu in *Le Monde*, 7 September 1965. The French proposal was set out in the Ossola Report of May 1965, p. 26, as the 'Collective reserve unit scheme'. Also see note 9, Chapter 12.
6   See interview of M. Michel Debré, then French minister of economics and finance, in the *Banker*, February 1967, where M. Debré said, 'But it is clear that under the gold standard system which France prefers, reserves would be principally constituted in gold and the deficits and surpluses in the balance of payments would involve movements of the precious metal' (p. 106).
7   As we saw above, page 160, some central banks have legal and political reasons for being concerned about the book value of their reserve assets.
8   The 'official price of gold' was simply the gold parity of the dollar as settled under Article IV of the Bretton Woods charter and embodied in the Bretton Woods Act passed by the US Congress.
9   In fact it was terminated after two years.
10   See article by Paul Fabra in *Le Monde*, 2 September 1975.
11   Federal Reserve Bank of New York *Annual Report*, 1975, p. 20.
12   'Les "franco-européens" sont partisans de changes "fixes mais ajustables", expression qui implique la définition de parités fixes pour d'assez longues périodes': Paul Fabra, reporting Giscard d'Estaing's lecture to the Law Faculty, rue d'Assas, *Le Monde*, 15 December 1973.

13   Anthony Thomas, *The Times*, 29 October 1973. He quotes as follows from a speech by Representative Henry Reuss, chairman of the Joint Economic Committee's Subcommittee on International Exchange and Payments: 'And Congress, unless I am very much mistaken, will simply not approve a so-called "reform" which puts the United States in the box of fixed but adjustable rates, with floating only permitted "in particular situations". The rest of the world should be aware of this now.

     'The United States should speedily extricate itself from the maelstrom into which it is descending. We should withdraw our (implicit) endorsement of the Nairobi meeting of the International Monetary Fund recommending fixed but adjustable rates reform.

     'We should make it clear that the United States – and anyone else so minded – should have the option of floating their currencies.'

14   *Le Monde*, 14 August 1975.
15   Paul Fabra in *Le Monde*, 1 November 1975.
16   Federal Reserve Board *Annual Report*, 1975, p. 77.

Chapter 19: Oil prices and adjustment, 1973–80

1   Paper on 'The allocation of oil deficits', by Robert Solomon, of the Board of Governors of the Federal Reserve System.
2   ibid.
3   ibid.
4   Princeton University *Essays in International Finance*, no. 116 (May 1976), p. 6.
5   IMF, *World Economic Outlook* (June 1981), table 22, p. 129.

Chapter 20: The principles and practice of floating

1   Sweden left the snake in 1977, and instead pegged on a currency basket.
2   See Dr Emminger, as quoted above, on page 71.
3   *Report of the Working Group on Exchange Market Intervention* (the Jurgensen report) January 1983.
4   Bank of England *Quarterly Bulletin*, September 1979, p. 292.
5   *76e rapport de la Banque Nationale Suisse*, pp. 10 and 13.
6   Minutes of Evidence (question 820) to Treasury and Civil Service Committee of the House of Commons, on *International Monetary Arrangements*. HMSO, March 1983.
7   John Williamson, *The Exchange Rate System*, Institute for International Economics (Washington 1983).
8   C. W. McMahon, addressing the *International Herald Tribune*'s 9th Annual Conference on 15 November 1983.

Chapter 21: The floating pound

1 The Chancellor of the Exchequer's evidence on 20 November 1986, to the House of Commons Committee on the Treasury and Civil Service.
2 Address by the Governor of the Bank of England, published in the Bank of England *Quarterly Bulletin*, Vol. 13, December 1973, p. 476.
3 *Midland Bank Review*, May 1977, p. 13.
4 ibid., Spring 1981, p. 13.
5 ibid., Summer 1982, p. 10.
6 *Financial Times*, 11 May 1984.
7 Treasury and Civil Service Committee of the House of Commons, *Report on Exchange Rate Policy*, February 1985; paragraph 9.
8 BBC Radio Woman's Hour, 16 January 1985. Reported in *The Times*, 17 January 1985.
9 TV Eye, 24 January 1985.
10 Short-term sterling interest rates were cut by 2 per cent in March–April–May 1987, but increased by 1 per cent in August. There was a cut of ½ per cent in October, following the stock market collapse, and two further cuts of ½ per cent each in November and December.

Chapter 22: The floating dollar

1 Per Jacobsson Foundation Lecture, 31 August 1975.
2 Paul Volcker, Fred Hirsch Memorial Address, Warwick University, November 1978.
3 Charles Coombs, of the Federal Reserve Bank of New York, in the *Banker*, December 1975, p. 1483. In fact the agreement was concluded on 1 February 1975.
4 Weir M. Brown, 'World afloat: national policies ruling the waves'. Princeton University *Essays in International Finance*, no. 116 (May 1976), p. 24.
5 Although the initial agreement was bilateral, all six countries represented at Rambouillet blessed it in principle, and later it received the support of the G–10.
6 The repeal of the Swiss restrictions imposed earlier in the 1970s was also completed in August 1980.
7 Paul Volcker, Fred Hirsch Memorial Address, Warwick University, 9 November 1978.
8 See article by Wolf in *Le Mois* (published by Société de Banque Suisse), November 1983, page 23. Also BIS *Annual Report*, no. 54, (1984), p. 133.
9 Federal Reserve Bank of New York *Quarterly Review*, Winter 1984–85, p. 47.
10 BIS *Annual Report*, no. 56 (1986), p. 142.

11 Above, p. 173.
12 Treasury and Civil Service Committee of the House of Commons, *Report on International Monetary Arrangements*, paragraph 4.18, HMSO, June 1984.
13 BIS *Annual Report*, no. 56 (1986), p. 145.
14 BIS *Annual Report*, no. 56 (1986), p. 147.
15 ibid.
16 'During the fifteen-month period of dollar depreciation up to mid-May 1986 the yen, the Swiss franc and the Deutsche Mark all appreciated by over 60 per cent against the dollar.' BIS *Annual Report*, no. 56 (1986), p. 147.
17 ibid.
18 Growth of GNP, inflation, interest rates, unemployment, the fiscal deficit, current account and trade balances, monetary growth, reserves and the exchange rate.
19 *Financial Times*, 22 September 1986.
20 *IMF Survey*, 17 November 1986, p. 353.
21 Bank of England *Quarterly Bulletin*, May 1987, p. 174.
22 *Financial Times*, 2 April 1987.
23 *Financial Times*, 2 December 1987.
24 *Financial Times*, 2 March 1987. The communiqué issued after the Louvre meeting is reproduced in IMF *Survey*, 9 March 1987, p. 73.
25 *Financial Times*, 11 May 1987.
26 *Financial Times*, 13 April 1987.
27 ibid. The 'occasional successful raids' by central banks included official intervention by the US in support of the dollar to the tune of some $4 billion in February, March and April 1987 (Federal Reserve Bank of New York *Quarterly Review*, Spring 1987, p. 62).
28 Federal Reserve Bank of New York, *Quarterly Review*, Spring 1987, pp. 61, 62.
29 *Financial Times*, 12 June 1987.
30 *Financial Times*, 11 June 1987.
31 ibid. The package of tax cuts would amount to DM 14 bn. in 1988.
32 ibid.

Chapter 23: The sovereign debt problem of the 1980s

1 OECD, *External Debt of Developing Countries, 1982 Survey*, Table 1. The figures exclude debts of a maturity of one year or less.
2 OECD, *op. cit.*
3 *Financial Times*, 1 July 1987.
4 *Financial Times*, 16 December 1987.

Reading list

Recent literature on the international monetary system includes Robert Solomon's *The International Monetary System 1945–1981: an Insider's View* (Harper & Row 1982); Charles A. Coombs's *The Arena of International Finance* (John Wiley 1976); Susan Strange's *International Monetary Relations*, vol. 2 of *International Economic Relations of the Western World, 1959–1971* (Oxford University Press 1976); and a long article by Tom de Vries on 'Jamaica, or the non-reform of the international monetary system', in *Foreign Affairs*, April 1976, p. 577.

There is an enormous flow of official literature, mainly periodical, commenting on the course of events in the field of international monetary affairs. Here is a selection:

The IMF's *Staff Papers*, fortnightly *Survey*, monthly *International Financial Statistics*, *Annual Report*, and annual *World Economic Outlook*
The BIS *Annual Report*
The US Department of Commerce's monthly *Survey of Current Business*
The US *Federal Reserve Bulletin* (monthly)
The *Annual Report* of the Federal Reserve Board
The *Annual Report* and quarterly, formerly monthly, *Review* of the Federal Reserve Bank of New York
The OECD's *Economic Outlook* (twice yearly)
The annual *Report* of the German Bundesbank
The Bank of England's annual *Report* and *Quarterly Bulletin*

The best continuous non-official commentary on monetary developments is provided by the *Midland Bank Review*, the *Banker* and the Morgan Guaranty Trust Company's monthly *World Financial Markets*. Other useful literature includes:

Chalmers, Eric B., *International Interest Rate War* (Macmillan 1972)
Chalmers, Eric B., *et al.*, *Forward Exchange Intervention: the British Experience, 1964–67* (Hutchinson 1971).
Gardner, R. N., *Sterling–Dollar Diplomacy* (McGraw-Hill 1969)
Hansen, A. H., *The Dollar and the International Monetary System* (McGraw-Hill 1965)
Horsefield, J. Keith, *et al.*, *The International Monetary Fund 1945–1965*, (IMF 1969)
Triffin, R., *Europe and the Money Muddle* (Yale University Press 1957)

Triffin R., *Gold and the Dollar Crisis* (Yale University Press 1961)
de Vries, Margaret G., *The International Monetary Fund 1966–71: the System under Stress* (IMF 1977) and *Balance of Payments Adjustment, 1945 to 1986* (IMF 1987).

Williams, J. H., *Post-War Monetary Plans* (Blackwell 1949)

I also recommend Princeton University's International Finance Section's *Essays in International Finance* and *Studies in International Finance*, Princeton University Press, and the series, *Policy Analyses in International Economics* published by the Institute for International Economics, Washington.

Index